Turning the Pages

*Conversations through Time
with Rabbi Isador Signer*

Compiled and Edited by Aliza Arzt

Ben Yehuda Press
Teaneck, New Jersey

Turning the Pages: Conversations through Time with Rabbi Isador Signer ©2024 Aliza Arzt. All rights reserved. No part of this book may be used or reproduced in any manner whatsoever without written permission except in the case of brief quotations embodied in critical articles and reviews.

Published by Ben Yehuda Press
122 Ayers Court #1B
Teaneck, NJ 07666
http://www.BenYehudaPress.com

To subscribe to our monthly book club and support independent Jewish publishing, visit https://www.patreon.com/BenYehudaPress

Ben Yehuda Press books may be purchased at a discount by synagogues, book clubs, and other institutions buying in bulk.
For information, please email markets@BenYehudaPress.com

ISBN13 978-1-953829-63-4

24 25 26 / 10 9 8 7 6 5 4 3 2 1 20240816

Dedication

This book is dedicated to

My parents and grandparents
who preceded me,
nurtured and taught me,
and are no more

My husband, Meredith Porter,
always by my side,
who started me on the journey
that has become this book

My children,
who carry within them
our future

Contents

Introduction ... ix

Rabbis and Institutions

Turning the Pages ... 2
   response from David Kronfeld ... 8

First Things First ... 13
   response from Debra Cash ... 18

Life's Pollyanna, Fear to Face Realities ... 20
   response from Jacob Bloom ... 27

Why I am a Rabbi ... 30
   response from Tamar Kamionkowski ... 36

Laws, Ethics and Politics

Self Determination ... 40
   response from Hillel Gray ... 47

Ethical Judaism ... 51
   response from Barry Schwartz ... 54

When Are Laws Just? ... 56
   response from Ray Arzt ... 59

What's in a Name? (The Meaning of Your Name) ... 62
   response from Ronnie Levin ... 69

Prophets of Peace: Woodrow Wilson ... 72
   response from Jonathan Sarna ... 77

Jews, History and Return to Israel

Science And Faith: What Effect Has Science Upon a Belief in God?   82
    response from Betsy Forester   86

When Evil Hastens Good   89
    response from Debora Gordon   93

Seeing Judaism Whole   98
    response from William Kavesh   105

And He Lived   111
    response from Mitchell Chefitz   119

Birth and Parenting

How to Be Born   126
    response from Noam Arzt   131

Are Parents People?   134
    response from Claudia Kreiman   140

The Role of Parenthood in the 20th Century   143
    response from Helen Levy-Myers   150

Value of Literature

Poetry in Religion   154
    response from Lawrence Rosenwald   157

Truth Will Be Crowned   160
    response from Chaya Rowen-Baker   165

A Virtuous Vice: Creative Expectations   168
    response from Shalom Flank   175

Solomon Ibn Gabirol   179
    response from Debby Arzt-Mor   185

Joy, Goodness and Caring

Happiness 190
   response from Aliza Arzt 193

Don't Lose Your Nerve 195
   response from Adam Arzt 201

Double Talk Or Saying It Two Ways 203
   response from Ezra Porter 207

The Song in the Night 209
   response from Leora Zeitlin 214

The Sermons of Rabbi Isador Signer
   A Reflection by Lionel Moses 220

Acknowledgments 223

INTRODUCTION

Truth is timeless; truth is bound by time. A young rabbi in his 20s tries to convey his fundamental truths of "modern life" to his congregation in the America of the 1920s. The Holocaust, the Depression and global communication are still beyond his horizon. Some of his teaching is tragic because of what he can't know, and some is astonishingly prescient. If only we could reach out to him to share what history has shown us and what we're learning from him.

For decades he was only a picture to me. "Grandfather's Picture" sat on our living room table and remained my primary association with him. His death was likely a catalyst for my parents' marriage and ultimately for my birth. I am named after him.

I was provided with a way into Isador Signer the man when I received a collection of his typed sermons after my mother's death. Over the course of six months, I read and summarized 66 of his sermons and developed an awareness of the topics and themes that moved and motivated him. The alchemy of what he put into his sermons, what I know about my grandmother, my mother, and the surviving relatives of his birth family, as well as the history of the times in which he lived has taken me well beyond "Grandfather's Picture."

Isador Signer was born in January 1900 near Piatra Neamț, Romania, the youngest of eight—three boys and five girls. He was more than 20 years younger than his oldest sibling. The family emigrated to Montreal, Quebec, Canada in 1900 when he was an infant. He grew up in that city speaking English and, most likely, Yiddish in his home. According to the family, his father, Abraham Joseph Signer, had trained as a rabbi but never received *Smicha* (rabbinic ordination) since the relative funding his studies passed away in his final year of study. One of his sisters reported that Abraham Joseph, on his deathbed, told her that the family was descended from Italian Jews who traced their ancestry to Spain and the 12th-century Jewish and secular scholar Maimonides. There is no way to corroborate this information. Signer's father provided many ritual services to his Jewish community in Montreal as a scribe, *shochet* (ritual slaughterer) and *mohel* (circumciser). He wrote a copy of the book of Esther in Hebrew for each of his daughters; the handwritten letters of the scroll are not much more than

1 millimeter high. His wife, Malca, owned a brass shop. Many of her descendants own brass Sabbath candlesticks from that shop.

Isador left Montreal for New York in 1917 to enroll in City College of New York and the Jewish Theological Seminary. He received a BA from City College and rabbinic ordination from the Jewish Theological Seminary in 1924. He most likely became an American citizen and he referred to himself as an American in his sermons. He spent his entire rabbinical career as a pulpit rabbi, primarily at Temple Beth El in Manhattan Beach, New York (1927-1953). Before coming to Beth El, he served at Temple B'nai Brith in Somerville, Massachusetts (1924-26) and B'rith Shalom Community Center in Bethlehem, Pennsylvania (1926-27). While at B'rith Shalom, he benefited from a close connection with rabbinic colleagues Max Arzt, who was Rabbi of Temple Israel in Scranton, Pennsylvania, and Louis Levitsky, Rabbi of Temple Israel in Wilkes-Barre, Pennsylvania. They occasionally preached in each other's synagogues. After Signer's death, his daughter married one of Rabbi Arzt's sons.

In addition to his congregational duties, Signer also authored the Conservative Movement's Rabbi's Manual and served on the committee that produced the Silverman Machzor. He spent several summers during World War II serving as a chaplain at military bases in the United States. He died suddenly and unexpectedly of a heart attack a few weeks before his 53rd birthday, in 1953.

In his sermons, Signer rarely, if ever, provides details about his personal life. He preached a sermon called "How to be Born" two days after the birth of his first child and never mentioned this experience despite beginning the sermon with a poem by Margaret Tod Ritter about the agonies of birth. Family stories about him suggest that he was a somewhat remote man who was not particularly comfortable in social situations. A close reading of his sermons sheds light on other aspects of his inclinations: he was passionate about literature and drama, often devoting entire sermons to an analysis of a current play or book. He was equally passionate about the land of Palestine, as it was called then, feeling strongly that the development of a Jewish homeland as a political entity was crucial to the survival and fulfillment of the Jewish people. At the same time, he embraced life in America. He respected the traditions that American Jews had brought with them from Europe but encouraged his congregants to immerse themselves in lives that were both American and Jewish. He also had a strong respect for Jewish institutions, especially the synagogue and the rabbinate. He was quite critical of congregants who didn't do their part to support both.

Who was he preaching to? The members of his congregations were most likely reasonably well-off. They were in the process of reinventing themselves as American Jews and figuring out what an "American Jew" should be. Most of them had likely been born in Europe but may have spent most of their childhoods in the United States. They were comfortable speaking English, were aware of the political climate of their times and enjoyed contemporary books, plays and films. Most of the sermons presented in this book were written in the 1920s, a time of relative prosperity and optimism. Signer's sermons contain many of the themes prevalent in sermons today: the importance of ethical behavior, the dangers of becoming too caught up in work and mindless entertainment, coping with a world that seemed to be increasingly complicated and busy. Yet, the specter of the Holocaust and the decimation of European Jewish life does not haunt the background of his sermons as it so often does for us.

The 24 individuals who have responded to Rabbi Signer's sermons[1] in this book come from all walks of Jewish life. They include some of his family members, prominent Jewish thinkers of our time and regular Jewish people who may be much like Rabbi Signer's congregants of 100 years ago. Their responses make it clear that there are many aspects of the sermons that resonate with them and just as many that disturb them. Read the sermons carefully. They do contain language and ideas that we are glad to have left behind, including, for example, the exclusive use of the masculine when referring to people. They also contain the seeds of viewpoints that are crucial to us today: the complexity of modern life (in "First Things First"), social justice ("When Are Laws Just?"), critical race theory ("Prophets of Peace"), egalitarian marriage ("Happiness"), a bi-national State of Israel ("Seeing Judaism Whole").

Rabbis preach every week and seldom get feedback about their sermons from their congregants. The responses they do get usually come when someone takes exception to some detail that the rabbi has conveyed. In that respect, preaching is a lonely occupation. The sermons "spring up at daybreak, they wither and fade with the coming of the evening" (to paraphrase Psalm 90). While we can't engage Rabbi Signer in conversation, we can still "speak" to him by thinking seriously about the messages he tried to impart to his congregation, reflecting on the content that feels universal through time and space as well as on the information that reflects a different era. As we consider the realities of political, literary and daily life 100 years ago, and Signer's age at the time that most of these sermons were written, we can imagine the man who attempted to convey his sense of what was most

---

[1] Rabbi Signer wrote these sermons as personal notes to use when preaching, not for publication. Consequently, while Rabbi Signer's sermons have been transcribed verbatim, they have been lightly edited with occasional spelling, punctuation, and grammatical adjustment for the benefit of the reader.

important and true in his world over and over, week after week. By beginning their responses to these sermons "Dear Rabbi Signer," the respondents acknowledge their connection to this man through time. We would like to think that in some way a mutually enriching bond has been forged.

—Aliza Arzt

```
2   One of the great sentences in Moses' farewell address reads:
    See I set before you this day life and death, good and evil; choose life
    and live.
    Its counterpart can be found in Ezekiel: The soul that sinneth,it shal
    die.
    Here life and death have altogether a moral significance, and he most
    lives who is most worthy. There is a popular phrase known as seeing
    life. It means often embarking upon a round of debasing pleasures;
    enjoying its dazzle and its dissipation. The moralist would call that
    death. How the same word can have opposite meanings when used by diff
    erent men!    Here in these surroundings we would teach life in
    terms of morals. We are concerned with its quality and not with its
    quantity. The world has ever produced men and women who lived more
    than the average allotted span of life only to beget sons and daughter
                                                  n                    s
    The world has ever produced Methuselahs, complete nonentities who deser
                                                                       ve
    well only because they fathered worthy children. That is their sole

3   excuse for living. To one who has had to officiate at burial ceremoni
                                                                       es
    the most difficult thing is to avoid giving voice to that dreadful
    epitaph which alone could characterize the life of so many individuals
    who have passed away, the awful truth that: it would have made no diff
    erence had they never lived at all. Yet there were generations of such
    in the Stone Ages, who as far as we know now, just marked time. They
    lived, they hunted to sustain life, and they ultimately passed away.
        Yet there is a class far worse than this one. Those who made the
    world worse for some by living, than had they never lived at all. I
                    the out-and-out           their own
    have not so much in mind wicked men from whom the        shrunk in hor-
    ror; the evil they did has long been forgotten. I have in mind some
    individuals who, tho long dead, their influence still mars the lives
    of some and whose example has been unfortunate for many. I think of
    those whose pernicious standard has become a precedent and model.There
```

This is a page from an original typed sermon, in this case from "And He Lived", which is included in the book on page 111. Note the handwritten English corrections and Hebrew insertions.

Rabbis and Institutions

Turning the Pages

Delivered in Somerville, Massachusetts at Temple B'nai Brith,
January 1, 1926, for *Parshat Vaychi*, Silver Anniversary

As we turn the pages of time back to early beginnings we see that when man first emerged from the oblivion of prehistoric times and faint glimmerings of a supernal and supernatural Being assailed his senses, man incorporated his fears and localized them in some concrete object. This he worshipped either in veneration because of supposed power for good it possessed; or this object he feared because of some malign power for possible evil which in his estimation was vested within it. The measures taken to propitiate spirits dwelling in a *Pesel* or מצבה, in an idol or a *Masseba*, a post, constituted the first rites of religious practice. Man's first attempts at organized worship were brought about by his fears of happenings and events he could find no explanation for.

Coincident with this, man's objects of worship and veneration were phenomena of nature—as they are now recognized—but for which no adequate explanation could be given in olden days. A roaring waterfall, an overflowing river, a shaft of lightning, the sun moon and stars were to early man veritable gods of power and greatness. These, man worshipped for and in themselves. They were the direct causes affecting his life and conduct and health for good or ill.

Soon we come to another page and we see man as having centralized his thoughts and beliefs. Man is no more the plaything of the gods, the instrument upon which the gods in their unholy glee practice their little jokes; he is no more the vessel into which they pour their humors. He feels within him strange stirrings of the divine. He conceives of himself as being created in God's own image. More than that, he becomes aware of the existence of one power transcending everything and yet immanent in himself. The new man is emerging from his chrysalis. He is Abraham, an אב המון גוים, an ancestor of a multitude of peoples, the physical father of an Isaac, the spiritual father of the world.

Yet another page reveals its story. Mankind is being given a definite belief. But mankind as a whole will not accept it. The God of Abraham and *the gods* are still warring for supremacy in the human breast. But the belief of an Abraham is accepted by his physical descendants and spiritual successors. He becomes ה' אלהינו the Lord who is our own God. The one we worship in contradistinction to other peoples, say Jacob's sons.

Then comes a page writ large with letters of fire. Jacob's sons have become a people—Israel—and Israel is elected to the service of the god of their ancestors.

The formula is now added to and we hear a Moses thundering forth in no uncertain terms שמע ישראל ה' אלהינו—Hear O Israel the Lord He is our own God. All Israel is to live a different life from now on—a unified bond of brotherhood of tribes. The God of Abraham is become the God of Israel. And the sign of the election is the contract which Israel and God are to observe towards each other: a contract never matched in the history of the world for conciseness and pithiness for justice to man and love for God. Upon Israel fell the mantle of glory to live up to the letter and spirit of this contract. But God, loving Israel, still loves His constitution and doesn't want to be parted from it. He is like a king who has an only daughter, a princeling comes along and marries her. The prince wishes to take his wife away but the king says to him, "This daughter I gave you is an only one. I cannot part from her; to forbid your taking her I can't because she is wedded to you. Therefore I ask of you this favor. Wherever you build your dwelling provide me with a room also so that I may be near you both." And so the Holy One Blessed Be He says ועשו לי מקדש ושכנתי בתוכם—Make me a sanctuary that I may dwell among you (Ex. 25:8).

Israel lives with this constitution and finds it good. Then come inspired teachers who tell her that if man is created in God's own image, and if all men are alike physically and follow similar processes of thought and are governed by the same feelings, instincts, desires and longings, are they not verily brothers?

Then is not the God of Israel also the God of the world?

And so the formula becomes שמע...אחד—Hear O Israel the Lord who is our God He is also the One God in that He is the God of the whole world as well.

Then is Israel sent out among the nations of the world to develop this doctrine and what is more, live this doctrine in their own lives. Page upon page of history is covered with blood and tears. Generation after generation has been crucified for this ideal. The world talks of brotherhood but will have none of it. The world professes a belief in the God of Abraham who is also the God of Israel who is the One God but it will have none of Him in actual life. The heart of the world has not yet been refined of its pagan dross. Israel therefore still suffers in bringing the ideal of justice, freedom and brotherhood to the world. But throughout these latter pages we see that Israel the prince has ever hearkened to God the King. Israel has always remembered the request ושכנתי בתוכם [that I may dwell among you] for Israel realized and never more so than when its citadel was stormed and its integrity well-nigh shattered, that its one hope of eternity, its one means of salvation, its one consolation in times of sorrow and stress lay in being close to its king and God, deriving from Him comfort and confidence, serenity and strength, with which to turn a calm and steadfast face toward persecution and calumny, towards unmerited shame and disgrace.

This, my friends, the pages of yesterday reveal as the heritage bequeathed to us. We are both the physical heirs of the people of Israel and the spiritual heirs of their ideals and their beliefs.

They who have come before as well as those who are here with us today have felt this to be so and in their own way and manner they longed to have a home where they might take their heritage, a מקדש מעט a "sanctuary in miniature" where their God and King might dwell in their midst to inspire them, to give them a consciousness of self, to develop themselves and teach their tradition to their children coming after them.

As to how well they builded [*sic*] we can see for ourselves. And yet sitting here we can but faintly feel the struggles they went through to make this Temple possible. Years ago the community living here were but few in number; they could but dream of a home, a building. They were further embarrassed by the lack of funds to put into effect the dream and the picture slowly taking shape in their minds. With the years more people settled here. But with their coming came an added difficulty, that of having almost as many opinions of what this Temple should be like as there were members enrolled in the cause. But even this greater hindrance was finally overcome. Plans were drawn—approved and work finally begun.

At last the fateful day arrived. How happy must that hundred people have been when standing knee-deep in snow, braving the cold blasts that came sweeping up the street as they finally placed their cornerstone—physical proof of conquest. Then was the building erected and used. For the first time Jews could point with pride and say:

בנה בניתי בית זבול לך מכון לשבתך עולמים

"We have surely built Thee a house of habitation, a place for Thee to dwell in forever" [1 Kings 8:13].

For the first time in 30 years and more was the reproach wiped off the lips of those who mocked at our Jewry with the taunt: "Where is your Church, Jew? The Jew had but to point to confound criticism and cynicism. No more would Jews and Jewesses go seeking their God in a hall or a house or a converted store for the occasion. No more would their children be without spiritual guidance and instruction, help and encouragement. No more would they worship at strange shrines. We had finally come into our own.

When we are together as now rejoicing in our twenty-fifth birthday we must remember the struggles of the years just passed; we must realize how courageous our older friends and our parents must have been to keep alive a spark of self-consciousness under bitter disappointments and heavy trials. Credit must be given to those gentlemen sitting here on this Pulpit this evening as well as to those not here. It was upon them that most of the responsibility rested as lay leaders of our movement. While in office they too frequently received more than their share of blame for failures beyond their control. We now give them the credit which is their due for all their earnest and unstinting application to work. As we thank the good God for achieving all this, we further feel grateful to that body of coworkers who have made themselves indispensable—without whose cooperation all this would not have been possible—our Sisterhood. These have together built so well that we are now stronger than ever before, presenting at last a united front, established firmly upon a solid basis.

As Congregations go in America, we are not as young as most. Others may have made more progress in a given time and greater advances than we—yet we, knowing the difficulties we faced, feel that our labor has not been in vain. We have unquestionably attained some measure of success. For this are we thankful, for this do we rejoice on our birthday. Before another quarter of a century rolls by we who are gathered here tonight will look back with pride to the fact that we are the successors of those who gave so much of themselves to this work, whose spirit lives in the air we breathe here.

But our main justification for rejoicing is the future which we are determined to carve out for ourselves. We, like the great majority of our sister congregations, are the pioneers in our communities, cities and states. It is we who are developing and molding the Judaism of tomorrow. What form it will finally take depends upon our decisions and actions. As I turn the blank page of the morrow, figures and visions appear there presenting the picture of the future American Israel. I perceive a community great in numbers, mighty in power, enjoying life, liberty and the pursuit of happiness; true life, not mere breathing space; full liberty, not mere elbow room; real happiness, not that of pasture beasts; actively participating in the civic, social and economic progress of the country, fully sharing and increasing its spiritual possessions and acquisitions; doubling its joys, halving its sorrows; yet deeply rooted in the soil of Judaism, clinging to its past, working for its future, true to its traditions, faithful to its aspirations; one in sentiment with their brethren wherever they are, attached to the land of their fathers as the cradle and resting place of the Jewish spirit; men with straight backs and raised heads, with big hearts and strong minds, with no conviction crippled, with no emotion stifled, with souls harmoniously developed, self-centered and self-reliant; receiving and resisting, not yielding like wax to every impress from the outside, but blending the best they possess with the best they encounter; not a horde of individuals but a set of individualities, adding a new note to the richness of American life; leading a new current into the stream of American civilization; not a formless crowd of taxpayers and voters, but a sharply marked community distinct and distinguished, trusted for its loyalty, respected for its dignity, esteemed for its traditions, valued for its aspirations, a community such as the prophet saw it in his vision:

ונודע בגוים זרעם וצעצאיהם בעמים כל רואיהם יכירום כי הם זרע ברך ה'[2]

> "And marked will be their seed among the nations, and their offspring among the peoples. Everyone that will see them will point to them as a community blessed by the Lord." [Isaiah 61:9]

In this picture of the Israel of tomorrow what shall Temple B'nai Brith stand for? What place will this Congregation take? It is for us who stand at the threshold of the years to come to determine what our program shall be. As the world grows, and changes take place, ideas and ideals must keep pace with the changes. The poet well says:

The old order changeth yielding place to new and God fulfills Himself in many ways lest one good custom should corrupt the world.[3]

When the world was much younger thou shalts and thou shalt nots were given to it to provide it with a working plan so that man could live with his neighbor and his God. In the Middle Ages when belief and faith were the questions agitating men's minds and troubling their conscience Maimonides gave us a credo to live by. The world today has developed its plan of conduct. The world today is no more so vitally interested in belief that everything shall hang upon it. Due to the strides which Science has made, the world realizes that the basic natural law which applies to an individual applies to a nation and a people as well. We know

---

[2] Signer has misspelled the Hebrew word for "descendants:" וצעצאיהם instead of וצאצאיהם. He also omitted the word בתוך from the quote.
[3] From *Morte d'Arthur* by Alfred Lord Tennyson (1809-1892).

that what a man wants he can get, if he wants it badly enough. The same applies to nations and groups. This idea we should apply to ourselves as well. We should express our longings and our ideals in terms of WANTS and if we want these things realized, we *will* have them.

WE WANT Judaism to help us overcome temptation and discouragement.

WE WANT the Jew to be so trusted that his yea will be taken as yea and his nay as nay.

WE WANT to make Jewish home life beautiful and spiritual.

WE WANT our children to accept with joy their responsibility as Jews.

WE WANT to be able to worship God in sincerity and truth.

WE WANT Jewish association to make for spiritual purpose and ethical endeavor.

WE WANT to cultivate the art of using our leisure to best advantage physically, intellectually and spiritually.

WE WANT to help in the upbuilding of Erets Yisroel.

WE WANT Judaism to be to us a living civilization, embodied in language, Literature, history, customs and social institutions.

WE WANT Judaism to find rich, manifold and ever new expression in philosophy in letters in the arts.

WE WANT our religious traditions to be made understandable in terms of human experience.

WE WANT the unity of Israel throughout the world to be based not upon visitations of calamity and distress, but upon constructive effort with a view to the future of Judaism.

WE WANT Judaism to function as a potent influence for justice, freedom and peace in the life of men and nations.

With such wants clamoring to be satisfied is there any doubt but that every dream of ours will become a reality? Can we then be anything but one of the choicest fruits in the Vineyard of Israel? This is our program. By that do we stand with no equivocation or mental reservation whatsoever.

response from
David Kronfeld

Dear Rabbi Signer,

What a jumble of thoughts and emotions rises within me upon reading your sermon!

Delivered almost a hundred years ago, and entitled "Turning the Pages," your homily seems so hopeful and forward-looking, as it marks a proud moment of achievement for your Somerville Jewish community.

And yet, in retrospect (dare I say it, although I intend it with no judgment or criticism) it also seems ironically naïve, for you cannot help but be blindly unaware of the many unexpected, unpredictable pages of Jewish history that will turn between then and now.

Your theology, Rabbi Signer, appears so direct, positive and rational. You seem so confident in human progress, as you outline a steady evolution of man's understanding of the divine, from its pagan origins to a more sophisticated monotheistic universality, imbued with moral precepts founded on the commonality of all people and the spark of divinity within each of us.

Oh, certainly, you acknowledge that this evolution has not been without setbacks, and that [the people of] "Israel . . . still suffers in bringing the ideal of justice, freedom and brotherhood to the world."

Nevertheless, you seem so assured that our people's "one hope of eternity, its one means of salvation, its one consolation in times of sorrow and stress lay in being close to its king and God, deriving from Him comfort and confidence, serenity and strength with which to turn a calm and steadfast face toward persecution and calumny, towards unmerited shame and disgrace."

Surely, this confidence mirrors the steady upward mobility and cohesion of your community, as you grow increasingly comfortable in your new American home, moving up from being anxious immigrants toiling in sweatshops to becoming prosperous tradesmen and professionals.

But unknowingly, you stand upon a precipice. So, to use your words, let us "turn the page . . . ."

In just a few years, your community, together with the American society around it, will face a long and crushing economic depression, robbing many of their growing confidence and comfort.

But in Europe, things will be much, much darker.

Of course, you are unaware of the coming Holocaust. You don't even know what I mean by the word—to you, it must still be a somewhat obscure, archaic term denoting a priestly burnt sacrifice. I am afraid even to tell you what its meaning is to become—a massive slaughter of our people, of those still left behind in Europe—a slaughter so savage, hate-filled, thorough, and demonically planned that your insides would quake and shatter if it were too suddenly revealed to your eyes. You would not even believe it could be true.

As horrific as they were, this devastation will make the pogroms and massacres which propelled your generation and that of your parents to uproot themselves and make the perilous and hopeful journey to new worlds, to seem merely an afterthought, or just a foretaste of bitterness to come.

You will not be able to comprehend it. All simple concepts of a just, all-knowing God will go out the window, or, rather, up the chimney, along with the millions of Jewish souls who will perish. The God of Israel, with whom you, along with so many of our people, had a respectful and yet easy, almost familiar, everyday relationship, will seem to have gone into hiding, eclipsed, to have failed us in our darkest hour. By some among our people, this God will even be considered to have died—if, in fact, He/She ever existed in the first place.

After this, all simple faith will be smashed to pieces. At best, we will pick up some of the broken bits and hold onto them as melancholy souvenirs.

Yet here, too, we turn the page.

For, even as our European communities were annihilated, that still-small community you refer to, almost in passing, in Eretz Yisroel, will achieve at last that Jewish dream of two thousand years—to again be a sovereign people in its historic homeland. It will seem a miraculous rebirth, a prophecy come true. Though facing a sea of troubles, the State of Israel will come into existence, and will be a shelter for our beleaguered brethren from all around the world.

Through sheer determination and brainpower, this new state will achieve stunning victories and technological advances. It will enable Jews to stand tall and strong in ways unavailable to us for two millennia.

But peace will escape it, even after decades of existence. Again, in almost Biblical fashion, it will contend endlessly with its neighbors; with some, sometimes in an uneasy truce, with others in a bitter, never-ending conflict. This will even pit Jew against Jew, arguing about who is wrong and who is right, under impossibly complicated circumstances.

And, like onlookers at a cockfight, other nations will noisily gather round, placing their bets and egging on one side against the other, at times allowing themselves to vent still-smoldering antisemitism with their wagers.

Thus, instead of becoming a nation where Jews can stand equally among the nations of the world, the world's one Jewish state will become the Jew among nations.

Our brothers and sisters in Eretz Yisroel, despite their achievements, will continue to need our support, as you point out back in 1926.

But let us again turn the page—and turn it back to America. Let us see how this American Jewish community fares, and compare it to your bold and hopeful vision, in which you state:

> As I turn the blank page of the morrow... I perceive a community great in numbers, mighty in power, enjoying life, liberty and the pursuit of happiness: true life, not mere breathing space; full liberty, not mere elbow room; real happiness, not that of pasture beasts; actively participating in the civic, social and economic progress of the country, fully sharing and increasing its spiritual possessions and acquisitions; doubling its joys, halving its sorrows; yet deeply rooted in the soil of Judaism...
>
> ...A sharply marked community and distinguished, trusted for its loyalty, respected for its dignity, esteemed for its traditions, valued for its aspirations, a community such as the prophet saw it in his vision... "Everyone that will see them will point to them as a community blessed by the Lord."

After the Holocaust in Europe, the Jews in America will indeed enjoy a period of unparalleled prosperity. America, revulsed by what it had seen and mightily fought against in Europe, will slowly let its social fences fall. Quotas and barriers, even to the most elite universities and powerful businesses, will be dismantled, and Jews will find themselves gaining entry into the mainstream of society, free to employ their intelligence and drive, and go on to be doctors and lawyers, scientists, artists and businessmen.

The Jewish community will grow wealthy, too, and build its own strong institutions. Its spirit and ideas will enhance all of American culture, and in government, Jews will scale previously unimaginable heights. In my own time, Jews will fill the very highest positions in the president's administration, they will become leaders of the Senate, and not one but three Jews, including two Jewish women, will simultaneously serve on the Supreme Court. Even the daughters of the 35th, 42nd, 45th and 46th presidents of the United States will marry Jewish men. The president will hold seders in the White House.

David Kronfeld

What would you think of that, Rabbi Signer? Even in your boldest, most ambitious vision, did you ever think that would come true?

And yet—despite the community's wealth and prestige, and the flowering of Jewish institutions, American Judaism will also undergo a tremendous falling away. By my time, a quarter of America's Jews will say they have no religion, and more than half of all marriages will be intermarriages. Some of our best and brightest will turn to Buddhism, atheism, agnosticism, or cynicism.

And the specter of *sinas hinam*—irrational hatred—will rear up in new ways. Hate-filled tortured souls will burst into synagogues and other Jewish venues to randomly shoot and murder. Previously unthinkable, synagogues will now place guards at their doors to protect peaceful worshippers on a Shabbat morning. Never before could we even imagine such things in America!

By my day, Rabbi Signer, we will be living in a world of so many contradictions that we simply cannot reconcile them. We absorb the body blows and move forward. Those with faith, however tentative or ambivalent, will persist not because of our confidence but despite our doubts. We will balance our wariness with hope, our pessimism with a wry humor.

I am sorry that all has not come to fruition quite as you imagined. But there is yet time.

So, I will leave you with a personal story. When I was a young man, I lived in Somerville, at Havurat Shalom, a small and unorthodox Jewish community across town from Temple Bnai Brith. Despite our proximity, I had never been to your synagogue, but one day our community decided to visit. We called ahead to let them know we would soon be coming.

A small, elderly group of congregants greeted us. By now, the congregation had dwindled to a precious few, who kept the synagogue barely afloat, hanging on by its fingernails. I would not be surprised if a few of them had been there fifty years earlier, when you were still their rabbi.

Services were being held not in the beautiful sanctuary, but in a small, dingy room downstairs. Holding services upstairs seemed unnecessary.

Still, they greeted us warmly and with excitement. As our numbers that day significantly increased the size of their minyan, if only proportionally, the rabbi decided to move the services back upstairs. We all made our way up to the large and stately, but empty and echoing, sanctuary, which all too often went unused.

It felt bittersweet to be there; although the congregants eagerly hoped we would return, we knew we were only tourists that day. We had our own little community to maintain. I had seen so many lovely, noble synagogues torn down over the years, as their congregations moved away or simply petered out. Such was common in America. I feared that Temple Bnai Brith would meet that same unhappy fate.

But turn the page again, to a time nearly fifty years after my visit. Temple Bnai Brith has undergone a remarkable revival. Jewish families have moved into Somerville, joined the synagogue and brought it back to life. The synagogue's website (a concept of which you are doubtless entirely unaware) boasts 180 families and a variety of educational and social activities.

Who could have known? Who would have expected it?

In many ways their Jewish lives and practices are very different from the ones you knew. So much has changed. The congregation is egalitarian (a term which perhaps baffles you), and the rabbi is a woman. Their service may contain elements that seem unusual to you. Some of the families may be differently composed than the ones to which you are accustomed. Many of their concerns may be about issues that you never conceived of.

And yet, you yourself state, "As the world grows, and changes take place, ideas and ideals must keep pace with the changes."

I wonder if you would feel comfortable in their midst. I hope so, but perhaps not. Still, I am confident that you would be welcome there.

David Kronfeld grew up in New York City and moved to the Boston area for college and graduate school. During the 1970s, while working toward a doctorate in comparative literature, he was also a member of Havurat Shalom, an alternative Jewish community in Somerville, Massachusetts. After completing his degree, he returned to New York and pursued a career in financial and corporate communications. He retired in 2019; today, he is engaged in a variety of volunteer activities.

He also wrote works of fiction, including Tales of the Havurah, *which is about life in the Jewish counterculture in post-1960s Boston. He lives with his wife, Sarah Jacobs, an artist who creates Jewish ritual objects in fabric. They have three grown children.*

First Things First

Delivered in Somerville, Massachusetts at Temple B'nai Brith,
April 9, 1926, for *Parshat Shmini*; in Bethlehem, Pennsylvania
at Brith Shalom Community Center, May 27, 1927, for
Parshat B'har; and in Manhattan Beach, New York at
Temple Beth El, May 30, 1930, for *Parshat Emor*

Rid[ing] on [the] 5th Ave. bus, [I heard the] talk of two women whose conversation was too loud for me to avoid hearing. They were evidently bosom friends and in a half-hour's conversation they gave a comprehensive outline of their characters. They loved to play bridge, etc. They loved the theatre, especially musical comedies. They loved to dance, and evidently when they were not playing bridge, dancing was their chief diversion. They loved their automobile trips. And as for dress how shall a mere man report their conversation? One listened in vain to see whether any other interest in life would be revealed, but this was all. Their talk had struck bottom.

These women are by no means an extreme example of the people we see all about us, men and women who are living in one of the most needy and critical generations of history, when a shaking civilization is striving desperately to get on its feet again, when there are great enterprises to serve, great books to read, great thoughts to think, and yet their lives like a child's doll, are stuffed with sawdust. They represent the great tragedy of our life; they are accountable for our failures. They are crowding out the things that really matter by doing things that do not matter so much. They are absorbingly busy with trivialities. They have missed the primary duty and privilege of life . . . that of putting first things first.

After careful thought, this seems to be the reason for the difficulties in American communities. Judaism could be maintained in America in one of two ways or in both. One factor which could go towards making us a vital community, possessed of life, would be a thorough knowledge of what it means to be called an עַם סְגוּלָה, a chosen people, or עַם הַסֵפֶר, people of the book. Not a superficial but a thorough knowledge would breed a love and understanding of Judaism, so that there would be no Jewish problem in America. To gain such a knowledge requires time, effort, energy and means. And these conditions are difficult to find. It is an ideal which we can only project into the future hoping that perhaps such a time will come. There is a זכות, merit, to be found; there are extenuating circumstances why this condition does not exist. The bulk of Jewry in America is made up of people who have come from Eastern Europe. They have brought with them a distrust of their environment bred in the bone through centuries of persecution. That cannot soon be eradicated. It will take many generations before that fear and distrust can disappear. Together with this fear of the environment, Jewry has brought a paramount urge for לֶחֶם לֶאֱכוֹל וּבֶגֶד לִלְבּוֹשׁ, bread to eat and clothes to wear, and every atom of their energy is being expended in making possible if not a life of ease, at least one of tolerable comfort. The first thing in their life is to own real estate and property. Food, appearance, clothes, reading, thinking, nothing matters when compared with the vital urge for possession. Some of our parents unfortunately have never had the opportunity to study for themselves. Life with its restrictions and demands has hemmed them in on all sides. The result we see before our eyes. If the perpetuation of Judaism in this country depended only on a love for Judaism brought about by a knowledge of *Torah* [scripture] Judaism would be a dead issue in a community where people know so little of their history, where Hebrew must be read '*mit pintalach*' [with diacritical vocalization] and then is not understood, where *Talmud* [Rabbinic writings] is merely a name and the Songs of Songs means to them only a melody without notes.

But thank God there is another way in which Judaism can be kept alive. Judaism can be made to flourish if not through knowledge then through action, when all Jews work together for some cause. When a Jewish community by a united effort builds a בֵּית יְתוֹמִים [orphanage], it is strengthening Jewish life; when a unified group erects a hospital it is furthering the cause of Judaism; when men and women are building a *Talmud Torah* [House of Study] or a Synagogue they are driving another beam as a foundation upon which Jewish life shall be established. When Jews come together in worship and service they are strengthening their national and religious bonds. It is then they feel that they are a part of a group with a glorious tradition and a past. It is then they feel that they are members of a people with a common ancestry and a common aim. It is then that they can present a united front against the multitude of forces that are seeking their disintegration.

If our Jews cannot have the love of Judaism developed through knowledge the only alternative is to have that love developed through action.

What prevents us from a united action? It is our inability to put the first things first. We forget that our life's time and our life's energy is limited. We are like street cars; we can hold our quota and no more; when all the seats are taken the standing room is absorbed and the CAR FULL sign is put up in front; whoever hails us next though he be the most promising man in our community, must be passed by.

It never was so easy to fail in this particular way as it is today. There have been times when life was sluggish and folk could move slowly. The Bible tells us that Methuselah lived for more than 900 years but so far as the record shows, he never did anything or thought anything to make his long life worthwhile. Life today cannot be dragged through with such dullness.

Today the currents of life are swift and stimulating and the demands of life are absorbing. There are more things to be done than we ever shall get done; there are more books to read than we can ever look at; there are more avenues of enjoyment than we ever shall find time to travel. Life appeals to us from every direction crying: attend to me here and look at me there. And so we are ready to let first come be first served. We let the loudest voices fill our ears forgetting that asses bray but that gentlemen speak low. There are temptations by the thousands to have us fritter away our time in vain trivialities, in meaningless gestures. We must therefore be on our guard more than ever to put first things first. We must avoid the crowding out of those things that partake of the essence of life when it is removed from the trappings of wealth and when the prospect of the Great Beyond stares us in the face.

Whereas there may be an excuse found for neglecting knowledge, and putting the desire for food, clothing and shelter first, no excuse can be found for allowing any half-heartedness or personal considerations to prevent action—for it is only in this second way that we Jews may be true to ourselves and our heritage, for if we do neglect our own culture and deny the call of community and keep aloof or stifle the inner urge to be ourselves, then what hope can we hold out for the Judaism of which we and others like us are the trustees?

The one burning message I have for you at this time is to allow first things to be first in your minds and thoughts—to make the effort which is asked of you at this time, viz, to strengthen the bonds which tie us to our people and our faith in the only possible way—by such action as will make certain the erection of that building which will mean for us the insurance through a physical form of all that we hold spiritually dear, not only of education but also of those social contacts which will make for our growth and the growth of our children.

Let us put first things first. Let us not give the logwood of our life to secondary matters and leave the chips for the highest interests we have. Let us not be so preoccupied with our own selves as to say some other time when conditions are better, when we'll have more leisure to think about such action, when money is freer, then we'll attend to the deeper and the finer relationships of life. For that time will never come—לכשאפנה אפנה שמא לא תפנה [when I have the time I will turn my attention to it, for it is likely that you will never turn your attention to it, Pirke Avot 2:4]. What we need to learn most is that the days which we are living through are not as a baseball field to be run over, but as gardens to be tilled, and that, if they are tilled well, they can grow those things of which heaven is made. For we must ever remember that Judaism is not on trial—it is we who are constantly on trial, and our actions and conduct must answer for us before the throne on High, for in the words of Rabbi Elieser ben Jacob:[4] העושה לו מצוה אחת קונה לו פרקליט אחד והעובר עבירה אחת קונה לו קטגור אחד he who does one *mitsvah* [commandment] has gotten himself one advocate and he who commits one transgression has gotten himself one accuser.

One of the first things which [we] as children have been taught is:

ראשית חכמה יראת ה׳, שכל טוב לכל עושיהם. ׳ללומדיהם׳ לא נאמר אלא ׳לעושיהם׳, תהילתו עומדת לעד.

"The fear of the Lord is the beginning of wisdom, a good understanding have they that practice it. His praise endureth forever."[5]

Therefore let us follow the advice of R[abbi] Nehorai who exhorts us: "Betake thyself to a home of the Torah; and say not that the Torah will come after thee; for there thy associates will establish thee in possession of it." הוי גולה למקום תורה ואל תאמר שהיא תבוא אחריך שחבריך יקימוה בידך[6]

Closing Prayer:

God give us unclouded eyes and freedom
from haste. God give us a quiet and
relentless anger against all pretense
and all pretentiousness and against all
work left slack and unfinished. God give
us a restlessness whereby we may neither
sleep, nor rest content, nor accept praise
till the results of our efforts equal our
calculations and approach our hopes. God
give us the clearness of mind to put first

---

[4] *Pirkei Avot* (Ethics of the Fathers) 4:11.
[5] Signer hasn't included the entire translation in his sermon in which he quotes *Tosefot* on *Sotah* 22b:5:1. In its entirety the translation is as follows: "The fear of the Lord is the beginning of wisdom, a good understanding have they that practice it, His praise endureth forever." (Psalms 111:10). The verse doesn't say "they that learn it," rather "they that practice it." This he interprets to mean that wisdom is obtained through acting on "the fear of the Lord," not simply learning about it.
[6] *Pirkei Avot* (Ethics of the Fathers) 4:14.

things first in our minds and hearts so that thereby our lives may be filled with color and content. God prosper us in our going out and in our coming in, O our God establish Thou the work of our hands, now and forever, Amen.[7]

---

[7] Adapted from the novel *Arrowsmith* (1925) by Sinclair Lewis.

response from
Debra Cash

Dear Rabbi Signer,

I wish I had met the "bosom friends" you overheard talking on the Fifth Avenue bus, the women who love musical comedies, dancing, and playing bridge, who talked loudly and uninhibitedly and were perhaps on a shopping trip together, two women completely comfortable with each other sharing their time and their lives. I know women like this: effervescent, trusting, engaged.

Since they loved musicals, maybe they bought tickets to see *Showboat*, whose plot turns on nonsensical laws against miscegenation and the notion that even one drop of blood can constrain your destiny. Or gone to a "movie palace" to watch *The Jazz Singer*, illustrating the tension between a pious tradition that does not fit anymore and a grotesque transformation. In the twenty-first century, we find both of these works offensive, but both hint at an awareness of the omnipresent undertow of American racism and choices that are no choices at all. Maybe these chatting friends were responding, if only subliminally, to those emerging ideas in shows not at all coincidentally written by Jews.

You call these women dolls "stuffed with sawdust," but you have no idea about the facts of their lives. What would happen if you took the time to imagine their stories? Perhaps one works in a settlement house while her friend tends to a disabled grandmother. One was sexually abused by a shop owner, the other fled an abusive marriage and endured a humiliating divorce; public dancing is the way they get close to men without putting themselves in danger. One had an aunt who died on the pavement outside the Triangle Shirtwaist Factory in Greenwich Village and ever since, has refused to cross a picket line and donates her "pin money" to a strike fund. The other listened at the doorway while her brother was being taught to chant his bar mitzvah *parshah* [biblical text]—a skill and a ceremony denied to her, so that she does not know how to read Hebrew with *or* without the vowels. Both set a beautiful *Pesach* [Passover] table and remember to invite in the stranger. When the first one dies, her bereft friend will be inconsolable.

You are young and doctrinaire. And you are a man and a rabbi in a world where that gives you the authority—no, the incentive—to condescend and judge what is the "first thing" that should be put first.

While the shadow haunting your "shaking civilization" was the First World War—which, despite its billing, was not the "war to end all wars"—my era contends with its own instability. You experienced the violent clash between nation states. We are at the verge of climate catastrophe which, like a Sisyphean rock, threatens to crush us permanently. Both of us are threatened by members of a society eager to embrace autocratic leadership that professes it can scrub the world of troubling nuance and frightening complexity.

Rabbi Signer, you paint a utopian vision of a future where the virtue and sobriety of the Jewish community is so compelling that American antisemitism disappears in a cloud of admiration. But sadly, this has not come to be. No matter how much Torah scholarship we master, how many beautiful synagogues demonstrate our aesthetic sophistication, or how many hospitals we build with Jewish money, we are not safe. In 1926, you could not know this, but after Jewish people were locked in burning synagogues in Riga and shot in the pews of a shul in Pittsburgh, we do. As an *am segulah* (chosen people), we were not and are not protected.

You end your sermon quoting R. Noharai who asserts that having "associates" (*chaverim*, or friends) in a house of Torah will help a person gain possession of the Torah's wisdom by proximity. Call it peer pressure for the sake of heaven.

With all due respect, I read this passage differently.

It is friends—indeed "bosom friends"—who lead us not to Torah exactly, but to whatever matters most. Friendship and shared experience bind us together. Making time for your friends, for culture, and yes, for pleasure, is not trivial. On the contrary, it is a treasure that we must not squander. That is what the women you overheard on the bus were doing: enjoying each other's company. They were experiencing the joy of simply being alive.

Torah study can coexist with Broadway musicals. Civic activism can coexist with comfort. Both build communities and give us the strength to persevere in hard times. As another Jewish woman said in 1912, "what the woman who labors wants is the right to live, not simply exist [...] the right to life, and the sun and music and art [...] The worker must have bread, but she must have roses, too."[8]

And that too, Rabbi Signer, is Torah.

Debra Cash is Chief Development Officer for the Jewish Women's Archive. She was an arts critic for The Boston Globe *for 17 years and is a founding Contributing Writer and Board Member of The Arts Fuse. Her poetry has appeared in Hanging Loose, AJS Perspectives, Persimmon Tree, the Open Siddur Project and elsewhere, and has been anthologized in Anita Diamant's books on the Jewish lifecycle and in the Reform and Reconstructionist prayer books. Her first book of poetry,* Who Knows One, *was published by Hand Over Hand Press in 2010. A new collection,* The Bumblebee's Diwan, *is in development. She is a longtime member of the extended havurah community.*

---

[8] From a speech delivered in 1912 by Rose Schneiderman of the Women's Trade Union League of New York. This quote was likely inspired by a statement first made by American suffragist and worker's rights activist Helen Todd.

Life's Pollyanna, Fear to Face Realities

Delivered in Somerville, Massachusetts at Temple B'nai Brith, February 13, 1925, for *Parshat Yitro*

Attitude exists that all's well with the world.⁹ Good to have bright hopeful outlook but carried to the extreme it is ridiculous. This attitude current because people don't like to face real facts squarely and boldly; but they willingly and consciously blind their eyes.

This attitude has given rise to a character in fiction, the name of which is going down in our vocabulary to stay. We speak of an excessive optimist who colors everything in life and makes it into a rosy hue or who looks at life continually through rose colored glasses as a Pollyanna and we sneer at such a person and belittle him. There is some justice in such action on our part, because there is no denying that life is a mixture of the bitter and the sweet; the sad and the gay, and one cannot live a complete life by ignoring the one at the expense of the other.

This fear of facing realities, this Pollyanna-like attitude is noticeable:

a) in business where stock-taking is so often delayed because of the unpleasant truths it may reveal.

b) authors are compelled to change endings of books and plays.

c) growth of the realistic school in opposition to the romantic.

d) the Jews fall victim to this fear too—דבר אתה עמנו [You speak with us].¹⁰

e) prophet Jeremiah cries out against this tendency on the part of the wealthy class who willingly and with malice and the hope of gain blinded the eyes of their fellow-Jews. He prophesies that nothing but evil will result from such conduct.

This attitude makes lasting progress impossible because we don't know what to correct.

a) Christian Science looked at from this angle is harmful if only because it ignores the realities of life and its sadnesses; because it teaches and practices the mollycoddling of the self.

---

⁹ Signer's manuscript begins in a telegraphic style as if he were typing notes for his sermon, but soon reverts to full sentences.

¹⁰ Exodus 20:16—the Israelites are overwhelmed hearing the Ten Commandments spoken at Sinai and say to Moses: "You speak to us . . . and we will obey but let not God speak to us lest we die."

b) France would discuss anything at the Peace Parley[11] except the things that were the most vital to her, that affected her, because she was afraid of what the result would be. This attitude has kept Europe an armed camp, six years after the Armistice was declared.

Indeed because of such unfortunate occurrences that crop up time after time people have begun to ask themselves, is progress a fact? And they doubt the existence of marked progress in life's functions because of the prevailing tendency to get all out of life and put nothing in, in return.

And there is justice in the contention of these people as we look about us in life. Our institutions, if not an actual failure, are far from improving us and being the benefit to us that they could be if we faced realities. Nor have they made lasting progress among many; nor can they make for lasting progress as long as we fear to face realities.

We must distinguish between progress and improvements in the institutions affecting human beings. Matthew Arnold says: Human progress consists of a continual increase in the number of those who, ceasing to live by the animal life alone and to feel the pleasures of the sense only, come to participate in the intellectual life also.[12] The latter certainly is true, the former is often not.

We have made improvements and advances in the institutions of

a) Marriage—we no longer buy our wives, ceremonies not barbarous treatment of our other halves.

b) Religious practices—beautiful buildings, organs, choirs, superstitious element has been in some measure removed.

c) Economic life—improvements constantly day by day.

d) War—improvements guns gas submarines aeroplanes.

e) Life in general—luxurious life we live today has no parallel.

Yes, we have made advances and improvements, but have we made progress? Have we faced or are we facing its realities with a view to improving them so that they may improve us? To this quest our answer must be in the negative. Our institutions so often have failed.

Our marriage institution has proved a failure when such a phrase as "the first 50 years" is used so commonly by people in referring to it. They take it tacitly for granted that marriage must have difficulties which it takes a lifetime to iron out. Our marriage institution is a failure when two people are allowed to enter into it blindly without understanding its responsibilities. I am not exaggerating matters.

---

[11] Paris Peace Conference following World War I, 1919-1920.
[12] Quote from the essay "A French Critic on Milton" by the British poet and scholar Matthew Arnold (1822-1888).

Look at any newspaper in any city any day any year and see whether the divorce courts are not the busiest. Read the scandals caused by the people faithless to their marriage vows. These people have failed to make a go of it because they refused or feared or were not taught to face its realities. The only motive controlling the contracting parties seems to be to get as much as possible for as little as possible. How I pity the people who come before me to get married and see how they look upon their marriage vows. Suppose these same people had entered a business venture together. Would they have done so without coming to definite understanding of the rights and privileges of the other? Would they have done so without being willing and ready to put in each his share of effort and industry to make it a success? We have far to go yet before we shall have achieved lasting progress because we fear to face realities of the responsibilities which marriage imposes upon us.

Economic life is a failure. We have made improvements in machinery, systems of distribution, division of labor, but we have also enslaved the workman in a deadening routine, we have robbed him of initiative and made of him *too* a machine, nor does he get proper reward for his labor. Our economic society is governed largely by the acquisitive instinct and the idea that you should get all you can out of the other fellow. Shall you be content with a reasonable profit? No! Get all the market can hold, charge all the traffic will bear. Our economic society is governed even today by the idea of unfair monopolies in restraint of trade. [The] Teapot Dome Scandal[13] is indicative of the price a country like ours pays for its democracy and the right of self-government; in other words, the right of the few to gouge their neighbours, for self-aggrandisement.

Our economic life is a failure nor do we give people a chance to work out a plan to bring about an industrial democracy within the present scheme of things. We are afraid to face the realities of life because they will affect our own interests and rather than do that let justice suffer. The prophet's denunciation may well be applied to the state of our economic life today: הוי מגיעי בית בבית . . . עד אפס מקום [Those who add house to house . . . till there is room for none but you . . . Isaiah 5:8]. We have made improvements—we build houses today better than ever before but have we made progress in our ideas? People never before have had such difficulty in getting decent quarters to live in for the money they can pay. Economic life you say is a failure but have we given it a chance? Have we squarely faced the realities [of] the issues at stake?

---

[13] Major scandal in 1921-23 when President Harding's Secretary of the Interior, Albert Fall, leased several oil fields, including the Teapot Dome field in Wyoming, to oil companies in return for substantial bribes.

In war we also have made improvements but where is our progress? Has the world-idea grown any from the belief that war is necessary? Has America? We entered into it with a beautiful resolve to make the world safe for democracy. How the ad writers must have labored to get this slogan across! That was our battle-cry. And we sent the flower of our youth to be mowed down by ruthless, inhuman measures. Yet after the bloody carnage was over, even after the God of War was wholly satiated and appeased, when we could have helped untangle the mess which we only helped Europe get into where were we? Where was our slogan? Where were our beautiful resolves and determinations not to come back till it was over, over there? We were afraid to face the realities, to admit that we the allies were at all in the wrong. We have made little progress in the war to end war when we could have done so much.

Our whole lives are often such tremendous failures and disappointments because we are afraid to face its realities. We shirk our responsibilities to our families, our people, our society, to our God. We are afraid of discomfort and we close our eyes to the call of conscience and the right. We are Pollyannas of the most despicable kind. In our communal life we want to get the benefits and let others do the work; and what adds insult to injury is the fact that each one of the slackers takes to himself the right of criticizing what his neighbor has labored so much to accomplish. The activities fostered by this Temple are meant for the community at large. For the grown-ups and the children of all the Jews in this vicinity. Yet how disgusting it is to see the excuses that people give for not doing their share. When nobody was here to [see to] the needs of the community they howled for a leader—תנה לנו מלך ["Give us a King"—First Samuel 8:6] and now that their desire is granted they fall back on the lame excuse that they HAVE helped 5 years ago or 20 years ago. They close their eyes to the realities of today to the vital needs of today. Our people fear to face realities because their pocket-books will suffer and so they take refuge in personal animosities, fancied dislikes of the leader and philosophic ideas which they haven't digested and haven't the ability or the training to understand.

Our life is a failure because we fear to face realities. DEATH is the greatest, and most awe-inspiring and terror-provoking reality we have in life. Yet we do not make ready to face it when it comes. The only thing we can store up for ourselves is a good name and good deeds, good works. It is our only legacy that can be transmitted that prevents our name being blotted out from the mind of man.

Yet how many of us face this reality? How many of you face this reality? הכון לקראת אלהיך ישראל [Prepare to meet your God O Israel—Amos 4:12]. You never know when your hour of accounting will come. Are you prepared to give an accounting now? No. Will you remain passive until it is too late?

Our religious institution is a failure because we fear to face realities. Our churches and Synagogues are empty all over the world. People have no use for these buildings. It doesn't satisfy their needs nor does it meet their moral and aesthetic demands. But have we given it a chance to develop? It is true that religion must be conservative and cannot, if it is to be stable, accept all new doctrines on their face value; but haven't the leaders closed their eyes and shut the door in the face of all progress in modern thought and modern needs?

Have we given the leader—the Rabbi—a chance to develop and progress? That the Rabbi today is different from the Rabbi of old is not readily recognised by the average run of people. A change certainly has taken place in the function of the Rabbi. I have told you before and you know, that in olden times the state and religion were united in Judaism. Thus a Moses, a R[abbi] Akiba[14] was the Prophet, leader and judge. You will remember that the chief function of the Rabbi in olden times was that of דין—judge, and arbitrator. He decided judgements between individuals. Indeed, so fond of the judgements of the Rabbis were the Christians in the Middle Ages that in coming to the Rabbis to have their differences straightened out they neglected their own judges with the result that laws had to be passed forbidding Christians to go to the Rabbis with their cases on pain of excommunication by the Church. And we want to keep in mind the fact that the Rabbis of this time had absolutely no means of enforcing their decisions. Yet they were implicitly obeyed and their decisions were unfailingly carried out. Today however, that important function has been taken away from the Rabbi to a greater and greater degree. Jews go to the civil courts. Jewish courts of arbitration have been established in the larger centers where Jews are found. So that now that the function of the Rabbi as the *DAYON* [Judge] has ceased, something else may take its place, viz., caring for the צרכי צבור [needs of the community], caring actually for that which is necessary for the welfare of the community—material things as well as spiritual. The emphasis of the world today—the great thing that the world has learnt is that man is a *social being*. We cannot find a man who lives among other men who is not social in some degree. The very contact he has with his next door neighbor makes him a social being—he cannot live by himself alone and so the crying need for today is for social justice, to see that that is established in the world. In that way can the Rabbi become the שותף [partner] of הקב'ה [the Holy One of Blessing, i.e., God]. But is the Rabbi given a chance to bring social justice about and thereby assure progress in the world? Listen to what a wealthy parishioner told his Rabbi not so long ago. The Rabbi had preached a sermon on

---

[14] An important Rabbi of the Mishnaic period, famous, among other things, for not beginning his education until the age of 40.

the labor situation in his community and had shown that wherein the employers were wrong at that particular time. At the conclusion of the service the layman went up to him and told him not to preach about such things as labor and social justice—that wasn't religion he said. What is religion or godliness if not the every-day actions and the conduct of the individual as related to himself and his fellow-man?

If religion has failed it is because the minister, the leader, is hampered and hindered in his work; because the people who ought to direct the everyday activity of the community, the people who ought to care for the material as well as the spiritual needs of the community are not looked up to; because his people won't let him face the realities of life when he is inclined to do so.

Because of the shortcomings of our institutions today many people have begun to be skeptical about the idea of progress in the world. Some are even ready to deny such a thing. But if we are to give ourselves over to pessimism then indeed life wouldn't be worth living.

As a matter of fact, when the realities are faced with courage, progress results. When Ezra returned from Babylonia he saw the sad condition in which Judaism found itself in Palestine. It required courage of the highest order to straighten out matters if Judaism were to live. Yet neither he nor the Jews flinched despite the heartache and the discomforts and the pain. The order was given: Put away your strange wives! Intermarriage means ruin! And he was obeyed. And Judaism could live again.

It is to the credit of the Puritans that they were not afraid to face the realities of life when restrictions were not pleasant ones. And so they could make progress.

When we Jews stressed education then we made progress because we faced the reality that an ignorance of Judaism would mean a dead Judaism. They are cowards who say, "Once a Jew always a Jew." Facts prove the lie to this statement. I have just learnt of two families not 100 miles from the Temple who are a living proof of this. Both families come from Orthodox homes. The father of one was recently seen decorating a Christmas tree for his grandson whose mother was a *Shikseh* [i.e., not Jewish]—the other refuses to be known as a Jew. It may hurt his practice. Both have changed their names so that the casual person wouldn't recognise them as Jewish.

If the whole of life and all our institutions are to be worthwhile and to function properly we must be ready to face realities. A Pollyanna-like attitude is equally as destructive as is the dyed-in-the-wool pessimist. Life certainly has much to offer if we don't come to it empty-handed. We ought to ask ourselves: Is it right to take everything life has to offer without giving anything in return? Shall we make it a policy of grabbing at everything we can merely for the sake of having it? Shall we lose our beautiful ideals in the process of this insatiable hunger? In a recent play the minister who insisted on giving part of his salary and his patrimony to the establishment of a house of shelter and refuge in the slums was rebuked for throwing away his money by a wealthy friend of his. [There was a] single room the minister occupied with the large estate he and his friends possessed. "But," answered the minister, "do you live in more than one room at a time?" Ought we to measure progress in such a materialistic fashion? Surely not. This is merely improvement. It adds nothing to our spiritual treasures. Shall we not rather content ourselves with a little less of the material things in life in order to cultivate some of the spiritual things life has to offer us?

The Bible presents us with a picture of the pessimist and the cynic—Job. But his pessimism vanishes when he sees God. "I have heard of Thee by the hearing of ear. But now mine eye seeth Thee! Wherefore I abhor my words thereput, Seeing I am dust and ashes"—לְשֵׁמַע אֹזֶן שְׁמַעְתִּיךָ וְעַתָּה עֵינִי רָאָתְךָ עַל כֵּן אֶמְאַס וְנִחַמְתִּי עַל אָפָר וָאֵפֶר—Job 42:5-6.

And now he is content for he has that precious quality of faith and belief in the moral order and a moral purpose governing the world.

The painter who struggles all his life in the midst of dire poverty for the recognition that comes to him after he is gone is the symbol of humanity. Despite all the trials he has to go through, he still continues his work and why; because he has faith; because he believes in himself. So too with us. Let us emulate the warrior that the poet Cowper talks about in The Christian Warrior:

> Where duty bids, he confidently steers,
> Faces a thousand dangers at her call,
> And, trusting in his God, surmounts them all.[15]

---

[15] William Cowper (1731-1800), a British poet and writer of hymns. He translated a work of the lyric Roman poet Horace's writing about the Golden Mean (Ode II, Book 10) and then wrote his own reflection from which Signer quotes.

response from
Jacob Bloom

Dear Rabbi Signer,

    I have a few comments concerning your sermon of February 13, 1925, about people fearing to face realities. You give many examples, and a number of these examples are powerful, but to me, they seem to deal with realities which are unrelated to each other. These seem to me to be examples of different points, and going from one point to an unrelated point causes the previous point to be forgotten. I think that you have material for more than one sermon here.

    You started off by directing your sermon toward those who are overoptimistic, who refuse to face the reality that changes are needed in the world, who say that everything is fine as it is right now, who don't want to hear about necessary change because they are doing well, and any change would be likely to cost them money. You say, "People never before have had such difficulty in getting decent quarters to live in for the money they can pay." That's one subject—and a statement that rings as true now as when you wrote it. It could be elaborated. You could make the point that ignoring this problem is a bad idea for our society as a whole, and make clear the realities which need to be faced in our economic life.

    By the way, since I read your sermon long after you wrote it, I don't know if the year in which you wrote it was a particularly optimistic time, or if perhaps you were trying to get through to a particular clique of well-off people in your congregation who had complained that they didn't want to hear about the needs of the poor. My own perspective is colored by my era. I don't hear people claiming that we are in the best of all possible worlds, and no changes are necessary, but I have heard some people—only some, but they talk loudly—claiming that greed is good, that the world will work well if everyone takes all that they can. On the other hand, there are also people around who are discouraged, who have been trying to dig themselves out of a hole for years, and have only seen the hole get deeper. I know that you know of such people, since you refer to people who "have begun to ask themselves, 'Is progress a fact?'" I see a need to address the people who are hopeless, as well as the people who are too smug.

    So the subject of the realities which need to be faced about economic life in our society is one point which could be made in a sermon. Or, you can take that point and narrow it down, specifically to the Jewish community. You refer to the prophet Jeremiah protesting about wealthy Jews who deliberately misled their fellow Jews for that purpose. Narrowing down your subject to Judaism would lead naturally into narrowing it down still further to what you have seen in your own congregation: those members of the congregation who refuse to face the reality that the community has needs now, who criticize the members of the community who are currently working to help the community, and who excuse themselves from helping now by saying that they helped out years ago. That might take some delicate wording, but it would be a call to action. Tell them: "We need your help here now!"

You speak briefly of marriage, and say, "Our marriage institution is a failure when two people are allowed to enter into it blindly without understanding its responsibilities." This is a separate subject, and one about which much more should be said. The issue here is not people deliberately denying realities out of self-interest, but of them being completely unaware of what those realities are. What are those responsibilities of marriage? How can young people be made aware of them?

You speak briefly of war, and of how we have developed weapons that are much more effective at killing people than older weapons were, but that at the end of our wars we give no thought to establishing a world order which is fair enough that no nation will find it necessary to start another war in a few years. This is another subject about which too little has been said. What realities need to be faced about war? Do we actually have a reason to believe that following a certain path at the end of a war would help prevent the next war? Mentioning how many people died in the last war brings up some powerful emotions, but it doesn't really support any of your other points.

You give Death as an example of a reality that we all fear to face. This has to be considered as a special case, since there is no way that anyone can possibly avoid death. The reality which you would have us face is that the good memories that people will have of us can only be created by our good deeds, and that those good deeds need to be performed while we have the chance, before it is too late. This is not a new point, but we all need to be reminded of this point regularly. It could easily be a sermon of its own.

Finally, as an example of the necessary work of humanity, you cite a "painter who struggles all his life ... for the recognition that comes to him after he is gone." I'll grant you that your painter is a good symbol of all of humanity, but not for the reason you give. A painter who spends his life imagining what people will think after he is dead seems to me like a very sad figure, whether or not he actually receives any recognition after he is dead. On the other hand, if a painter spends his life making the paintings that he feels compelled to paint, following his own vision, if, as you put it, "he believes in himself," then I would say that painter has led a successful and admirable life, whether or not there is public recognition of those paintings after the painter is gone. That's what makes your painter a symbol of humanity that can inspire us. The people who see reality, who see what they believe needs to be done to make the world a better place, and who proceed to do those things, are the people that we can aspire to be.

So while there is power in your sermon, with all of its points, I think that separate sermons on each of those points would be more likely to inspire your congregation to action.

Jacob Bloom is a former member of Havurat Shalom in Somerville, Massachusetts. He currently belongs to two shuls, and has been married for thirty-five years. He has sold hardware, designed software, and told old Yiddish stories, and for forty years has been finding ways to help people enjoy dancing.

Why I am a Rabbi

Delivered in Manhattan Beach, New York at Temple Beth El, December 16, 1927, for *Parshat Vayeshev*

I have been led to take myself as the subject of tonight's discussion because of two things. Firstly, because of the question which has been asked of me as to why I am a Rabbi; Secondly, because of the desire to counteract, if possible, the feeling which today characterizes most people in their attitude towards Rabbis and the Rabbinate. Although all the arts and professions are overcrowded, the Jewish youth, when faced with the problem of choosing his life's calling, reflects the attitude of his elders by the distrust he has of the Rabbi and the dislike for the Rabbinate. So that in the language of the Prophet, congregations thirst for the waters of the spirit and there are but too few Rabbis to quench it.

In order better to understand the role which the Jewish minister plays, let us review the objections which people have to ministers in general. People today still maintain primitive beliefs as to the minister's function and his work. Chassidic Jews still look on the Rabbi as the medicine man as do the Catholics upon many priests and the shrines within their keeping. To some people the priest is the representative or agent of God on earth and he therefore assumes the qualities of a miniature deity. He can loosen the spiritual bonds and bind the free. He can impose penances and control the keys to paradise; to others, the minister is to be hired like a lawyer to intercede for poor sinful and sinning man before the heavenly throne. To still others he is the intermediary—the agency through whom people may appeal to the Deity and to find communion with the Divine. And lastly, to an overwhelming majority of people of all faiths the minister, priest, Rabbi or *hakim*[16] is expected to practice the tenets of his particular faith so that the true believers of that faith may be considered as worshipping vicariously. He is to pray for his people, lead their virtuous lives for them, and bear the brunt of any spiritual punishment for them should such be visited on his people or the race.

Looked at dispassionately and objectively, it is surprising that so many people should retain a mediaeval, primitive, almost savage and uncivilized attitude towards the man of religion. With the elimination however, of the grosser superstitions which make the individual a slave to religion rather than have religion serve man, the minister who has lived his life in conformity with the prevailing idea his parishioners have held, has been left high and dry. The so-called emancipated man looking upon the minister as a relic of a bygone age sees no benefit to himself in

---

[16] A learned or wise Muslim.

maintaining a curio and a museum-piece. So that there is bred in him a dislike for the minister and all he represents; at best it takes the form of passive indifference which not even a Christmas, Easter, *Rosh Hashana* [the Jewish New Year] or *Yom Kippur* [the Day of Atonement] can dispel. The layman of our age, therefore, not having found himself religiously, will not think of entering a profession like the ministry or the Rabbinate.

Has the minister a place in the world? Has he any function to perform? Decidedly yes. All religions have developed or are evolving a greater understanding of what godliness is, and it is the minister's task to discover, analyze, and explain these longings prompting men in their life's work the spiritual urge to find communion with one's God, whether through prayer which is the expression of the social longing of men, or whether through some other form of expression. It may well be that the world has outgrown its one-time ancient terminology and forms of expression but the needs which gave rise to them—these wants are still with us.

The minister who has realized this value is coming forward as a factor in the remaking of our civilized life and as a guide in the new relationships which the ease of international communication is ever presenting us with. For example, the work of The Interchurch Movement,[17] John Haynes Holmes and his Community Church.[18] The attempt enlightened ministers are making to explain religion in the terms of the new morality. This is no different than creating a new commentary to reinterpret the demands of religion to cope with our present-day problems. Jews have always felt the need of commentaries to understand the new truths which they could find in the Torah. Upon these commentaries the machinery of Jewish life was based. We today need our modern commentaries and the machinery for living that goes with them, just as did our ancestors. The men who are doing this vital work are not radicals. They sound very conservative; they are even considered reactionary by some. Yet they probe and experiment and each of them is giving

---

[17] A confederation of Protestant Churches, generally called the Interchurch World Movement, operating between 1918-1920 with the aim of consolidating some of the functions of Protestant churches to reduce duplication of effort.

[18] A Unitarian minister, (1879-1964) pacifist and activist who left the American Unitarian Association due to that organization's insistence on requiring support of World War I. Between 1918 and 1949, when he retired as minister of his church, he changed its name to the "Community Church of New York" and it functioned as a non-denominational church. Holmes was also involved in interfaith activities, worked with Rabbi Stephen Samuel Wise of New York and was co-founder of the ACLU and the NAACP.

their co-religionists a philosophy of life. Such men are typified by a Grant,[19] a Fosdick[20] and in Jewish life especially by a Mordecai Kaplan.[21]

The trouble, of course, is that so many ministers are not ready to tackle the things they feel should be tackled and prefer to talk about theology, to mouth pious phrases and sonorous, high-sounding, ear-filling bombast and to address lengthy prayers to the Deity commanding Him to shower man with blessings from on High. That is easier you know, than making an honest conscious attempt to cope with the problems which the modern world presents for solution.

As for the Jewish minister. Why should any man go into the Rabbinate? Time was when every mother crooned her child to slumber, when every father blessed his child by wishing for him the career of Rabbi when the dearest wish of every family was to have a man of God and a Godly man in their midst. Why is there a definite reaction against it today, even among pious Jews? There is the feeling that they wouldn't like it, that they're sacrificing something for Judaism and their people. They don't consider it as a profession for proud self-sustaining men to enter, but for the weak, the humble and useless. What is the cause?

A comparison with the priest will help us understand the situation.

The Rabbi at his best was never looked upon as a magic worker. He acted as any *Beth Din* [Jewish Court] could. What he could do any 3 or 10 laymen could do.

He was primarily a scholar, a depository of knowledge, a walking encyclopaedia of Jewish lore, custom and practice. He was not even a preacher.

He was a consulting lawyer, an authority on Jewish law. He decided not the direction of Jewish activities but what was legal.

He acted further as a Judge who interprets, applies and propounds the law but doesn't make it or help in its development. Few exceptions were there of Rabbis who had a world outlook because the status of the Jew and his economic and social condition made it unnecessary to change his mode of life from that of his grandfathers 500 years removed.

Then came EMANCIPATION together with a flood of forces tending to break up the unity and harmony of Jewish life and the Rabbi found himself unable to cope with the situation. In Western European countries the Rabbis soon adjusted themselves and assimilated Western culture and education and attempted to hold as much of the old and gain as much of the new as they could and there especially

---

[19] Referent unknown.
[20] Harry Emerson Fosdick (1878-1969) a liberal minister who preached against Christian Fundamentalism and served as pastor to a variety of churches during his career, including Riverside Church in Morningside Heights, New York.
[21] Mordecai Kaplan (1881-1983) was the founder of Reconstructionist Judaism and may have been one of Signer's professors at the Jewish Theological Seminary.

in Germany the Rabbi very soon became important, recognized and valued for his contribution to Jewish life. Yet he hadn't strayed from the other Rabbis only in training.

In America the vast bulk of Jews are Eastern European. Jewish manners and ways have been affected mostly by Jews from these countries and the Jewish conception of the Rabbi is identical with that current in the old country. The synagogue Jew seeing his own hopelessness of assimilating himself to American life divorces himself entirely from the outside world and so demands the same from his Rabbi.

RESULT: American Jewry has retained more as relics and as monuments of past glories these men here and there of supposedly great learning not that they actually were able to command the obedience of American Jewry but that they satisfied the preconceived notion of what the Rabbi should be.

EFFECT ON THE RABBI. The Rabbi therefore has assumed the attitude of complete detachment from this world. Therefore the Rabbi has become other-worldly. The average young man looking on that type and not understanding his place in the evolution of Jewish leadership or not having sympathy with them is ready to mock and deride these men. It is for that reason too that the average American father objects rather definitely and positively to any relative of his entering the ministry. It is not a necessary thing he argues to maintain a memory, to propagate not a man of action but a curio as to what Judaism was [at] one time. Is this *our* notion of Judaism and <u>our</u> concept of what leadership should be?

We of the modern age of Jewish thought, the younger generation, and by that I mean all those who—

1. Hope for a future for themselves or their people.
2. Believe Judaism has a future and can be rejuvenated.
3. Long for culture and education.
4. Realize their debt to society.

All of us would deny that the only thing Judaism can do today is to maintain the old without creating anything new and going farther afield and it is as the spokesman of that forward-looking, hopeful, youthful group of men and women that the modern Rabbi as we conceive him *is* to be:

1. Not a curio; rather out to break curios.
2. Not a model of what has been; probing and seeking as to what should be.
3. Seeks to interpret not so much our memories but our HOPES. We've been living in hopes and on hope these last 200 years. How can they be translated into action?

4. Not the stoop-shouldered, head-bowed, humble, cloistered individual but rather militantly working for what he considers to be the right.

5. Has nothing of which to be ashamed or apologetic.

6. Is ready to carry Jewishness and Jewish ideals everywhere.

7. His is not a Judaism of one kind on *Rosh Hashana* and an altogether different kind the rest of the year.

8. Hasn't one standard of conduct and morality in the home and another in the marketplace.

9. His Judaism must harmonize with life.

10. Complements religion with life and supplements life with religion.

I have been asked for my CREDO; I would write it down something like this:

I am a Rabbi because:

1. I believe the true and complete faith of Judaism and the Jewish people.

2. I believe with perfect faith that the Jewish people have not lost their spiritual or mental energies—that they can offer to a waiting world spiritual, moral and aesthetic truths.

3. I believe in Zion and that it is the duty of the Rabbi not only to pray but to work actively for the realization of the dream, hope and longing of our people through weary centuries.

4. I believe in the dignity and nobility of the soul which God has implanted within me—.נשמה שנתת בי טהורה היא[22] I believe in myself.

5. Even as I believe in myself I believe in my fellowmen for they are like unto me in gifts and capacities.

6. I believe in saving my soul from wealth and from poverty and from all the physical circumstances of life. They must not touch my soul.

7. I believe that I owe a debt to my God and to my fellowmen for the soul which God has given me and for the education which society has afforded me.

8. I believe in service first as a payment of a just debt and secondly, as the only avenue by which men and women can ever find or ever have found real soul-contentment and happiness.

9. I do not believe in being ordinary and average and commonplace. The one ambition of my mortal days would be to break through all the confining circumstances of my world; to rise above the dead level of mediocrity and to raise others, to teach others, even as I am willing to be taught; to give them something of myself even as I want what they can offer; to lead, even as I am first content to follow; to be a pathfinder; to blaze a trail through life.

---

[22] Quote from the first line of a prayer at the beginning of the weekday morning service.

With such a faith, consuming and all-powerful, the modern Rabbi is not an object of pity. He seeks no charity. He seeks no sympathy. He is ready to fight his way for the things he holds dear and to give his all if need be for their recognition.

With confidence, a sense of dignity, a sense of obligation and a desire for service the Rabbi has no fear of the community he happens to find himself in. He is ready to speak boldly and bluntly for what he considers right and just. He is ready to come among the scoffers of religion, the mockers of Judaism and maintain even among such the magnificence and sanctity of Judaism.

If the Jewish parents would be permeated with such faith in Judaism, if the Jewish father would but realize the magnificent possibilities for service to oneself for leadership, the great possibilities and to one's fellow-men that old blessing: יזכו לגדלו לתורה ולמעשים טובים—May they acquire the merit of raising their son with scholarship and good deeds—no more will it be an empty phrase mumbled by a Reader.

The Jewish mother would again croon her child to slumber closing each stanza with "תורה איז די בעסטע סחורה" [Yiddish for "[the study of] Torah is the best reward"].

The Rabbi would again become not merely a mausoleum, a sort of antiquity that is prized and must be kept indoors not to be destroyed, but would again become the leader of his people.

And so my prayer for the Rabbinate is that of the poet:
God give us men, tall men, sun-crowned,
Men who live above the fog,
Men with a will to live, men with a will to die.[23]
Amen.

---

[23] Loosely based on the poem *God Give us Men* by Josiah Gilbert Holland (1819-1881).

response from
Tamar Kamionkowski

Dear Rabbi Signer,

I was delighted to read your sermon, "Why I am a Rabbi" and to reflect on how relevant your observations are to those of us living in the 21st century. I appreciate your frustration regarding the perceived role of the rabbi among our communities. Let me begin by summarizing your points: You feel frustrated by antiquarian views of the rabbi and by old-fashioned superstitious thinking. You believe that the role of religion in the modern era is treated as a relic of the past, so all the benefits of religious living are overlooked. Most importantly, you provide us with your personal "credo" regarding the role of the rabbi in early to mid-20th century Judaism.

As I read your words regarding early modern views of the rabbi, I was struck by how relevant these assumptions are for us today. I do believe that most American Jews still hold on to some sense of the rabbi as an intermediary between people and God, or as a lawyer who intercedes on behalf of sinners. And while I believe that many Jews would deny this, I think that many people still view the rabbi as an ideal Jew who worships vicariously on behalf of followers. I admit that when I was studying in divinity school, I was shocked to learn that Christians studying for the ministry let loose, acted irreverently and had their vices. And I liked to think of myself as an enlightened young adult!

Your comments about the role of the rabbi in history still need to be heard and understood by contemporary Jews. Most Jews do not really understand that for centuries rabbis were primarily scholars and authorities on Jewish law. It was only with the emancipation and the emergence of the modern era that rabbis needed to adjust their roles for a changing world and to become more involved in various arenas of Jewish life.

I must admit that I hadn't given much thought to the inner dispositions of rabbis in your era. You refer to rabbis as apologetic about their Jewish living or even ashamed, as focused on memories of what was rather than on hopes of what could be. I'm happy to report that many rabbis today do not focus on Jewish survival but on Jewish thriving. There are a growing number of rabbis who serve not to preserve the past, but to rejuvenate Jewish living by bringing the past into the present.

You long for a time when young Jewish men would choose to be rabbis out of a sense of the dignity of service, when Jewish leaders would be action-oriented and willing both "to lead and to follow and to blaze a trail through life," and when rabbis would believe that the "Jewish people can offer a waiting world spiritual, moral and aesthetic truths." That time has come!

Since the time you articulated these words, the rabbinate and rabbinic roles have become more diverse and more in tune with modernity.

The modern rabbinate looks more and more like the Jews whom they serve and there is less of a divide between clergy and lay people. For example, women now serve as rabbis in non-Orthodox communities and within Orthodoxy, programs for women's ordination are emerging. In more recent years, openly gay and lesbian Jews have joined the rabbinic ranks. And we are currently witnessing the admission of trans-Jews and Jews of Color into rabbinic leadership roles. As I said, rabbis now reflect the Jews whom they serve. In fact, Jews with non-Jewish partners now have a home for rabbinic studies!

Your vision of a more service-oriented rabbinate has also come to fruition. Many Jews are now drawn into the rabbinate by a longing to make positive contributions to the world in general. They indeed seek to bring insights from spiritual and moral truths into a world beyond the synagogue. I have been working with rabbinical students for 25 years and every one of them is a star, neither "ordinary (n)or mediocre." They are passionate and dedicated, book-smart and savvy, eager to serve and humble.

Of course, today's rabbinate is also fraught with challenges. Rabbinic salaries have declined significantly, in part due to the influx of women into the field and in part due to the diminishing status of the rabbi as a person of God. Also, in your time, every Jew belonged to a synagogue and rabbis served those synagogues. In our time, synagogue membership is in significant decline and synagogues are merging or closing. As Jews become more enmeshed in mainstream American life, it is more challenging to create and sustain traditional Jewish communities. Today's rabbis work on college campuses, in educational institutions, as hospital chaplains, as CEOs of non-profit organizations, and as entrepreneurs. In many of these settings, they serve both Jews and non-Jews. With rising tuition costs for rabbinic education and lower compensation packages after schooling, rabbis have a more difficult time supporting themselves.

As I read over your words again, I wonder how far we have come in getting the average Jew to understand the role of the rabbi in Jewish life. I believe that most rabbis today can do what you so hoped for in your time: articulate a powerful vision of "why I am a Rabbi." Now I believe that the next step is for our communities to understand more deeply everything that rabbis do, apart from officiating at funerals and leading services. Our rabbis are teachers and scholars, activists and prayer leaders, social workers and spiritual guides. They mourn with us and celebrate with us. Thank you for your service!

Dr. Tamar Kamionkowski is professor of Biblical Studies at the Reconstructionist Rabbinical College, where she has taught for about 25 years. Her most recent publication, Leviticus: A Wisdom Commentary *(Liturgical Press, 2018), is the first book-length feminist commentary on Leviticus. Kamionkowski is also the founder of the Kamionkowski Beit Midrash, an online center that provides courses, webinars and resources for classical Hebrew learning, Tanakh study and Torah chanting.*

Laws, Ethics and Politics

Self Determination

Delivered in Manhattan Beach, New York at Temple Beth El, February 28, 1930, for *Parshat Mishpatim*

[Preceding the actual sermon are notes about various Hebrew legal terms. It appears from the content that Signer was organizing his thoughts in anticipation of delivering this rather complex sermon.]

State difference between terms*

1 מצוות [*mitzvot*] all-inclusive. Positive and negative, depending on various factors as element of time

2 חוקים [*chukim*] ceremonies the meaning of which have been lost

3 עדות [*edot*] symbolic commands. Testifying to the Power of God

4 משפטים [*mishpatim*] civil and ethical laws regulating human life.

2 & 3 regarded as means of conciliating God and winning Him over to do our will. The great contribution of Judaism is in saying that 4 is also the commandment of God. The prophets had great difficulty in getting the people to realize and recognize that ethics and civil law were more important and the will of God made manifest in them more than in other things.

*We must learn to identify as religion all the efforts to improve human life

The function of Judaism is to get Jews to recognize that 4 represents the more important expression of God's will. As we practise it so do we realize His will in human relationships. We're still untutored as to what this implies.

Ahad HaAm[24] whose influence predominates the thinking of a large number of Jews the world over, wrote somewhere that what motivated him most in his writing was his desire to make people feel what the Golus[25] means in actual fact, and what they really were missing by being in Golus. His ardent desire was to prevent the Jews in the civilized countries of the Continent as well as the Jews in America, from sinking into a slough of contentment with themselves. They were rapidly suffering as he calls it from fatness of the mind brought about by the comparative peace they had gained as citizens of liberal countries. With this dominant motive he filled essay after essay, monograph upon monograph with warning of the dangers to which Jews were susceptible due to the amenities and

---

[24] Asher Zvi Hersh Ginsberg (1856-1927), known by the nickname "Achad Ha'am," "One of the People," an essayist and Zionist who believed that Israel should be established as a spiritual, rather than a political center and that Jews should feel it to be their spiritual home, not necessarily their physical home.

[25] The Hebrew term for "Diaspora."

agreeableness of our modern environment. In drawing ourselves after 1900 long years at last up to our full height in order to breathe deeply of the air of tolerance and freedom we were at the same time shaking off that which God gave us: our distinctiveness. His warning has borne fruit with regard to Zionism and Palestine.

What Ahad HaAm has done so nobly with Jewry at large I would like to imitate to some extent. Fully aware of my own inadequacies, well-realizing the fact that this Sermon will have little value in bringing about what it will advocate, it will nonetheless justify itself if it succeeds in pointing out the greatest danger which confronts our Jewry in America in the large and even our community in the small; if it makes us aware of what we lack; if it will in some few minds create a want. The purpose of this Sermon, therefore, is to point out that phase of Torah, viz, *mishpatim*,[26] which for one reason or another has fallen into disuse and to miss its absence, by realizing what this absence involves.

Due to the prevailing conception of religion, Judaism has suffered woefully. Our modern attitude is that religion is THAT ethical conduct which man is enjoined to practise towards his God like the עדות and חקים [laws and statutes] of Judaism. But for the behavior of man toward man, the law of the land is invoked.

That is to say: ethics and religion are abstract terms. As a matter of fact, search through the Scriptures and nowhere will you find the Hebrew for either ethics or religion. Ethics and religion are aspects or phases of the teachings of the Torah which the modern mind has taken away from LAW. By law we mean that which regulates human relationships, jurisprudence. Viewing religion, therefore, as ethical conduct to be practised towards God we have fallen into the same line of reasoning which accuses Judaism of being legalistic and impractical and outworn and conflicting with the civilization of the countries in which we live. In other words what we have done is this. We have weakened our Judaism by subtracting its ethics from its laws, by practising it as a religion instead of as a civilization. And by so doing we have at one stroke cut the knot which ties us to our past and which alone can make for our future. Therefore, in our saner moments we ask ourselves what will become of Jews and of Judaism? And in all seriousness the prospect as I can see it is nothing short of gradual disintegration leading to ultimate annihilation. Because following the inevitable, unchanging law of physics, the momentum of the past, which is carrying us along now, MUST in time be slowed down until it ceases completely.

Let us examine what we have said in the light of clear reasoning. What is the difference between LAW or jurisprudence and ethics? Considering the difficulty

---

[26] *mishpatim*, a reference to civil law, and also the name of the biblical portion of the week in which this sermon was preached.

mathematically, we may say that LAW = ethics + social efficacy. Or we may say that LAW = ethics + social approval and disapproval; or again LAW = ethics + the machinery, the institutions which society has developed as, e.g., courts, police, jails and the like which, acting in concert with the approval of society, serves to act as a preventative to people acting in such a manner which may be detrimental to the ethical standards of a certain society.[27] This LAW represents the civilization of a people, and serves as an index of the stage of its development or civilization.

Ethics by itself is an abstraction. It is merely pious wishing. But Ethics added to social efficacy becomes LAW—the norm or standard by which men act. The law is therefore merely the enforcement of the ethical standard. And the law's function is not to punish but to act as a prophylactic, as another preventative to the would-be wrongdoer to prevent him from being antisocial. To illustrate with American history: Slavery, a century ago, was within the law. People believed that slavery was commanded by God, even as many people today believe that prohibition has its sanction in the Bible. That was the ethical standard. And so 97 years ago there began a trial which lasted for over 2½ decades as to whether a slave by the name of Dred Scott[28] could have his freedom. And the Supreme Court finally decided, according to the prevailing ethics, that he could not have his freedom since he was a chattel or property. Again in 1890 the ethical attitude of people incorporating their fears of combines in restraint of trade agitated for the passing of the Sherman Anti-Trust Act.[29] Similarly, the ethics of the day looked upon unions of laborers as agents of the devil. And yet, in these three isolated cases, as in so many others, as we all know, there took place a change in the ethical attitude which resulted in the 14th Amendment,[30] and in new laws circumventing the Sherman Act and in laws insuring the inviolability of unions. This explains what we mean when we say that law is the result of coupling ethics to social efficacy. The law serves both as a crystallization of ethics and as a stepping stone to the creation of a higher standard of ethics. And AS LONG AS YOU HAVE LAW YOU HAVE A CIVILIZATION! The prerogative of making your own laws is the indicator showing whether you are a living people.

---

[27] Signer did not include the mathematical signs "=" and "+" in his sermon; they were added by the editor based on his description of the formulas he was proposing.
[28] Dred Scott (1799-1858) brought a case to the Supreme Court in 1857, arguing that due to his having lived in slave-free territories, he should not be enslaved. The Supreme Court ruling was 7-2 against him.
[29] A law passed in 1890 setting limits on the ability of corporations to become monopolies.
[30] Adopted in 1868, the 14th amendment addressed citizen rights and equal protection under the law. In the context of this sermon, the amendment nullified the Dred Scott decision which stated that Dred Scott could not be granted U.S. citizenship.

Society or social life didn't start with abstract ethics or religion and yet we find clans and tribes living with one another. Why? Because they had certain standards—*mishpatim*—and anyone violating them suffered social disapproval in the form of fine, bodily-punishment, exile or death.

Jewish law also developed in this way, by the accumulation of *mishpatim* by their gradual change, modification or adaptation to meet with the ethics of the day. And that which gave primacy to Judaism throughout the ages was the fact that it was ALWAYS much more than a religious philosophy. What made of Judaism a civilization, besides the attributes of national life, such as their own country, is the fact that it gave first place in its system to *mishpatim*—to LAW rather than to ethics: אין לך בן חורין אלא מי שעוסק בתלמוד תורה ["none can be considered free except those who occupy themselves with the study of Torah—Ethics of the Fathers 6:2].

TORAH has a variety of meanings and the connotation of LAW is most conspicuous. In early Bible days the Prophets all without exception stressed this fact. Micah voiced the thoughts of them all when he urged: הגיד לך אדם מה טוב ומה ד' דורש ממך כי אם עשות משפט ["He has told you O man, what is good and what the Lord requires of you: only to do justice..." Micah 6:8]. When Elijah came to Ahab telling him of God's displeasure, it was the crime of his against Naboth[31] that he castigated Ahab for and called him a TROUBLER in Israel. When the prophet cries out: מלכם תדכאו עמי ופני עניים תטחנו ["How dare you crush my people and grind the faces of the poor?" Isaiah 3:15], he emphasizes the ethical standard as it should be crystallized in the law: דרשו משפט אשרו חמוץ שפטו יתום ריבו אלמנה Seek justice, relieve the oppressed, Judge the Fatherless, plead for the widow [Isaiah 1:17].

Throughout our history it was recognized that as a civilization Judaism could never content itself with being an advisory community, an ethical culture society, that if it were to function it must be primarily an executive community, a legislating community. Indeed it was in direct recognition of this principle that even in the darkest and dread days immediately following the Destruction,[32] when to practise Judaism meant death, the Rabbis held on to the rights of Jewish courts to formulate laws. They proceeded along the theory that the Jewish state was intact—and the Talmud and *Poskim*[33] are the result. Even during the bitter Mid-

---

[31] First Kings 21:1-16. Ahab desired the vineyard belonging to Naboth. Ahab's wife, Jezebel, acquired it for him by falsely accusing Naboth of cursing God and the King, for which he was stoned to death.

[32] i.e., of the Second Temple in 70 CE.

[33] The *Talmud* is the collection of legal documents composed of the *Mishneh* (200 BCE-200 CE) and the *Gemarah* (200-500 CE), an expansion of the *Mishneh*. The rabbis who adjudicated the laws were known as *Poskim*.

dle Ages the right to autonomy was never relinquished by Jews and the פנקסאות [notebooks], ש"ע [*Shulchan Aruch*—16th-century legal code], they alone made for Jewish survival. And even now the Jews in many European countries have minority rights, which means that they have self-determination with regard to their own schools and the application of their own laws to a large extent. Now given language and courts, a civilization need never be weakened nor suffer extinction.

In America the Jews have a different story to tell. Although Reform Judaism has been of tremendous service to the development of Judaism in America, they have nevertheless succeeded in undermining and destroying Judaism, by officially repudiating and renouncing the binding power of Jewish law when they willfully misinterpreted the principle first formulated by [Talmudic Rabbi] Samuel that דינא דמלכותא דינא [the law of the land is the law] which applies only to laws affecting Jews in their business relations with non-Jews, and making that principle apply to all the departments of Jewish life, including הלכות אישות, domestic relations. To them Judaism has lost its aspect of a civilization and they are Jews only as a religious sect. Orthodoxy in America, on the other hand, has quietly abandoned Jewish law and where Jewish law conflicts with their desires, as, e.g., in domestic law, they become reformers. The result is chaos. The basic difficulty in American religious life today is therefore the fact that few Jews unless they are Rabbis have a chance to apply their lives to Judaism.

It is this FACT that I would want you to be aware of—even if you do nothing about it. I would be unfaithful to my calling if I didn't make you uncomfortable in one way or another mentally and socially and ethically. And I want you to be uncomfortable about the prospect of what faces us when we relinquish our right to some degree of self-determination, of being to some extent self-governing and self-sustaining. If you could only read behind what is happening in Jewish communities at this moment and see what is implied therein, you would shed grievous tears at the חורבן [destruction] of Jewish life. Cleveland—בשר כשר [Kosher meat]. חלול השם [profaning the name of God], but more than that—giving up our own prerogatives.[34] Tintner suing his Congregation for $40,000. Torts and breaches of contract between Jews. See how even civil marriage and civil divorce have slipped out of our hands and realize the tragedy in which you have perhaps also participated.

You may perhaps point to Palestine as the source of hope. There will be developing a body of law. True, Palestine ultimately will help us, but it may take two

---

[34] These two sentences were handwritten in the sermon and appear to be notes relating to an example Signer provided. There was no information available about the specific situation to which he was referring.

centuries. Their problems for the next century will engross all their attention and absorb all their energies. We can help them financially and morally to establish themselves on a firm foundation but we must look to ourselves to solve the problems which confront us.

But having pointed out our problem and our danger you may say to me: "Well, what can be done about it? How can we maintain our Jewish civilization and yet not have it come into conflict with our Americanism?" I can suggest the remedy, but of course it will mean nothing unless congregations and communities will demand that it be put into effect.

Now don't misunderstand me. I'm not advocating a return to orthodoxy nor even a return to the *Shulhan Oruh* [see above]. I don't want that because the laws which were the result of a different ethical point of view are no longer applicable today. Furthermore, adherence to a *Shulhan Oruh* will not make us ethically creative. What WILL help us, however, will be the insistence that we do not give up our prerogative of our right of self-determination, which means the prerogative of having our own courts where the Jewish genius for ethical living will go a step ahead of the Law of the land, where we will be the stepping-stone for higher ethical living in America and thereby render our contribution to American life. Like the Catholic Church with their adherents we MUST NOT give up the prerogative of the control of marriage and divorce. To do that spells death. We must refuse to recognize any but a Jewish *Get* [divorce document] and set our face against the sanctity and binding power of a civil marriage. We must avoid the crowding of the civil courts with cases of torts, breaches of contract and agreements, between Jews, which create a חלול השם [profaning the name of God].

Jews must be the arbiters of conflicts arising between Jews and Jews. The American law recognizes as binding any decision reached impartially by a group of people who act as arbitrators. The Jewish Courts of Arbitration are a decided step in the right direction—faulty as they are. But given the ethical efficacy which in this case means the stamp of approval of the entire Jewish community and much may be done to correct the faults and make it function. Each community should have a court of its own to administer the law of the state—you see I don't mean that each Jewish court shall formulate its own laws, as is done in minority countries in Europe, but merely have the right, because of Jewish opinion, to administer our laws state and federal and interpret them in the light of the Jewish ethical standard which in every case will be higher than the existing law. For, by the time ethics becomes law it has already become hardened, crystallized and static, and at best should serve as a stepping stone to a higher ethical outlook.

Where shall these Courts get their views? FIRST by acting as the Circuit Court used to do in England.³⁵ There the judges found the law raw—they didn't accept Roman law and so they had few precedents to follow. Therefore, they just listened to cases and relied on their own judgment and common sense. This became in time the Court of Equity.³⁶ And thus did common law arise. So must our courts act in the beginning. These early decisions will be the basis for later Jewish law—for the ש״ע [*Shulchan Aruch*—16th-century legal code] of tomorrow. AND SECONDLY, by demanding as head of each court, in addition to laymen and lawyers, as the present Courts of Arbitration have them, by demanding as head of the court a new kind of Rabbi.

This is an age of specialization. We need the kind of Rabbi who is primarily a pastor, or a preacher, or a teacher or a social executive, and as a result of wanting them and needing them we have them. Similarly do we need the kind of men who will study LAW—Jewish law, modern law, Roman law, English law. Call them *Dayanim* [judges], if you will, or Rabbis or lawyers or Rablaws, Rabjurists. Historically, the lawyer of today, provided he is Jewish, is much more of a Rabbi than is the Rabbi of today. And so if Jewish communal life will develop this need, it must demand men who will give themselves by these studies to their people and who will act as authorities to regulate and legislate our ethics and point the way to a higher standard of living.

Thus besides our own educational system, which we haven't touched on this evening, by insisting on the prerogative of Jewish courts, not only will we avoid the חלול השם [profaning the name of God] which is going on but we will be able to be creative in America, i.e., to say, to maintain our own civilization and add thereto.

---

³⁵ Travelling judges holding court throughout England, with established routes (i.e., "circuits") first established in the 13th or 14th century.
³⁶ A Court of Equity was allowed to adjudicate certain types of situations on a case-by-case basis and to apply "conscience" and a sense of "equity" in its judgements that may contradict the strict interpretation of the laws as written.

response from
Hillel Gray

Dear Rabbi Signer,

I was touched and intellectually engaged by your sermon on *Mishpatim*, one of my favorite *parshiyot* [biblical weekly portions], in which your reverence for the law shines through.

Your *derashah* [sermon] addresses the malaise of a thriving American Jewish diaspora that you see "sinking into a slough of contentment."[37] You locate this concern in the writings of Ahad Ha'am, the pioneer of cultural Zionism, who was more concerned about the vitality of Jewish life than political self-determination.

Incidentally, I taught about Ahad Ha'am this past semester. Your take on him is salient. Writing in 1930, you were concerned that "his warning [about secularizing tendencies?] has borne fruit with regard to Zionism and Palestine."

You caution against a "fatness of the mind" as "the greatest danger" to American Jews. It's the danger of modernity, as you see it, insofar as our conception of religion is divorced from other aspects of culture and does not include, notably, the practicalities of law. By the same token, you're concerned that contemporary law reflects only the "prevailing ethics" and lacks the teachings of Torah.

Your solution is to ensure that law serves "as a stepping stone to the creation of a higher standard of ethics." To do so, you propose a vigorous Jewish dive into the *mishpatim* type of law, i.e., civil law. This dive would not update rabbinic laws, but rather involve a Jewish administration of secular law. It would require a new class of rabbis steeped in Judaism, Roman law, American law, and common law. These hybrid rabbis (or "rabjurists") would reinvigorate Jewish communities— who, to fulfill your vision, would demand the prerogative to enforce American statutes through Jewish courts. For conflicts between Jews, you believe that a Jewish court's interpretation of American law would be beneficial because "the Jewish ethical standard ... in every case will be higher than the existing law." I'm not convinced that our Jewish ethics are so superior, though I sense that Talmudic discourse shares much with Anglo-American law (cf. *An Introduction to Legal Reasoning* by rabbinic scion E. Levi).

I was struck by your approach to legislation. As a general principle, you say that "The prerogative of making your own laws is the indicator showing whether you are a living people." But your particular proposal would not give American Jews the communal autonomy to "formulate its own laws." Were you wary of

---

[37] This phrase had some currency in the early 1900s. The first usage I found was from *The Times* of London, Dec. 15, 1865.

dual loyalty charges, the kind of allegations we see nowadays against American Muslims and *sharia* law? Your proposal also does not consider how Jewish law or ethics might influence U.S. legislation. Granted, the legislative route to social change may be more associated with my generation, with our experience of civil rights, environmental, consumer, health and other legislative reforms. After working on environmental policy, I myself started studying rabbinic law. I fantasized about applying *halakhah* [Jewish Law] to improve American law or to deepen a culturally-grounded environmental advocacy. For example, in my dissertation, I argue that a rabbinic concept of socially-determined risk (*shomer peta'im ha-Shem*) would fit with risk reduction for environmental and occupational health hazards.

Unfortunately, there's a social dynamic that forms an obstacle to your proposal to reinvigorate Jewish civil courts. In my Jewish environmental efforts, I ran up against a kind of social paradox that might make sense to you, given the attention you pay in your "Self-Determination" sermon to different Jewish movements. I observed that the Jews who are most active on environmental threats are non-Orthodox, who have quite limited interest in rabbinic teachings, while Orthodox Jews, who tend to care most about halakhic discourse, were less attuned to environmental problems. This mismatch does not bode well for relying on *halakhah* to spur Jewish environmental activism.

Likewise, as a rabbi and advocate of Conservative Judaism, you are situated in a way that doesn't quite fit your vision of revitalized Jewish courts. Why? Because most Conservative Jews today (even more than in your time) do not share your dedication to and confidence in rabbinic law. Nor would they agree with your opinion that it's a scandal (or desecration of God's name, *Hillul ha-Shem*) to resort to non-Jewish, i.e., ordinary courts.

To be sure, your proposal would be even more of a mismatch with Reform Judaism. You presumably realize that the large Reform Jewish population is unlikely to turn to rabbinic courts. Indeed, you speak rather harshly against Reform, which you see as a dangerous route for American Jews, and Jewish ethical humanism. I suppose your polemics are consistent with your valorization of rabbinic law, which Reform tends to see as advisory rather than obligatory. (I've read similar polemics in the addresses of Solomon Schechter, the Conservative Judaism leader who died about a decade before you were ordained.) But isn't this kind of divisiveness unhelpful to American Jews and *davka* to the purpose of the Jewish courts you envision (i.e., to resolve conflicts among Jews)?

You distance yourself from Orthodoxy, too.[38] Yet Orthodox Jews are *precisely* the constituency that could be most attracted to your proposal for Jewish courts.

---

[38] "I'm not advocating a return to orthodoxy nor even a return to the Shulhan Oruh."

It fits their preoccupation with Jewish law and their strategic separation from gentile and secularizing culture. Not only have American Orthodox Jews trained rabbis with the necessary expertise you knew would be needed for Jewish civil courts, they do make some use of Jewish courts. Granted, this private judiciary has tangible shortcomings, such as an inability to truly enforce law the way it's done in governmental law. I saw this flaw in my neighborhood, where the local Jewish court (*Beis Din*) ruled that a *haredi* [religious] business owed a hefty payment to a Modern Orthodox family—but the business refused to pay.

When I first saw your sermon title, "Self-Determination," and the Ahad Ha'am opening, I assumed that you'd advocate for Zionism and Jewish autonomy in Palestine. But even with an almost unrelated goal—rabbinic arbitration—your sermon nods to Palestine as a "source of hope." You ask whether Jews in (what has become) the State of Israel would increase the role of rabbinic courts. You predicted that they will, "but it may take two centuries."[39] Well, you'd be pleased to know that there's been an influential *hevre* [cohort] of Israeli rabbis and scholars who share your enthusiasm for a renaissance of rabbinic civil law (i.e., *mishpatim*). Under the umbrella of *Mishpat Ivri* [lit. "Hebrew Law"], they've especially worked to integrate rabbinic responsa and other legal sources of responsa literature into Israeli law. They've had some successes, through jurists such as Menachem Elon, who was an Orthodox rabbi, university professor, and Supreme Court Justice.[40] To be sure, their injection of rabbinic law into secular judicial reasoning is the obverse of your proposal to implement secular law via a rabbinic judiciary. You likely would praise them as performing a *kiddush ha-Shem* [sanctification of God's name], by drawing upon the ethical wisdom of our *halakhic* [legal] heritage, and you'd be proud of the expertise they've gained as "rabjurists" who are enabling Jewish religious culture(s) to self-determine their own laws. I hope this *hevre* will read your "Self-Determination" sermon and add it to their reading lists of pioneering *Mishpat Ivri* writings.

Hillel Gray serves as Assistant Teaching Professor for the Department of Comparative Religion at Miami University of Ohio. He received his PhD from the University of Chicago, a master's degree from Harvard University, and previously worked at the Investor Responsibility Research Center and as Policy Director of the National Environmental Law Center. He is a former chair of the National Havurah Committee. His research has examined the interplay of Jewish law with Christian and secular ethics, Jewish bioethics, rabbinic approaches to gender assignment,

---

[39] In a prescient aside, you write that Israel's (Palestine's) "problems for the next century will engross all their attention and absorb all their energies."
[40] See Elon's biography in Wikipedia.

and religious responses to the COVID pandemic. He leads the Empathy and Religious "Enemy" project, fostering nonjudgmental interactions with groups such as the anti-LGBT Westboro Baptist Church and anti-Zionist Neturei Karta.

Ethical Judaism

Delivered in Morristown, New Jersey at
House of Israel, May 25, 1923, for *Parshat Naso*

1. Jewish custom prescribes the reading of the Mishnaic treatise of Aboth.[41]

Importance: Second to the reading of the Scriptures each Sabbath. Chapters of the Fathers include various maxims and precepts of the great *Tannaim* or authors of the Mishnah.[42] These maxims [are] distinctly ethical in contrast with the legislative character of the rest of the Mishnah.

2. Maxims hold our interest far more than either the prayers or the legal opinions produced by the same *Tannaim*.

3. This preference for ethics is only a *phase* of the wide-spread preference that is often voiced as an excuse for indifference or hostility to Jewish worship and ceremony, and for the failure to affiliate with Jewish communal activities.

4. The great achievement of Ethical Culture[43] is not in acquiring adherents to its program and organization but in furnishing an excuse for being disloyal to Judaism and for leading individualistic lives. Thousands of our people whom, if you were to ask [them] to join a Congregation would at once tell you that *they* do not believe in ceremonies and ritual, they believe in being ethical and speak in the highest terms of the Ethical Culture Movement, though they have not the slightest intention of joining it.

5. This preference for the ethical, although it does not lead us to cast off Jewish interests and affiliations altogether, *does* however render us half-hearted in our Jewish efforts.

6. It is therefore essential to see to what extent this preference is justified.

7. Preference based on a *popular conception of ethics*. According to that conception Judaism is supposed to prescribe to its followers two types of conduct:

a) The type that sets the individual right with his God. This kind of conduct, they say, is of little or no consequence to the rest of the world. Under this

---

[41] *Pirkei Abot* (often written *"Avot"* in modern orthography), literally "Chapters of the Fathers" but also called "Ethics of the Fathers," is part of the rabbinic compilation of the *Mishnah* (200 BCE-200 CE).

[42] One of the earliest written collections of rabbinic laws, opinions and stories, compiled 200 BCE-200 CE. The *Mishnah*, written in Hebrew and the later rabbinic discussion of its contents, called the *Gemarah*, comprise the *Talmud*.

[43] The Society for Ethical Culture, a "non-religious" Jewish organization, founded by Felix Adler (1851-1933).

head[ing] are included the various rites and ceremonies, such as observance of the Sabbath and Festivals, and taking part in religious services.

b) In contrast with that is the type of conduct which has to do altogether with one's neighbour, conduct which makes for self-control, honesty, fair dealing and kindness.

The first type is considered *religion*;
the second is considered *ethics*.

8. This distinction is entirely untrue to fact. There is no such thing as conduct which is purely a matter between an individual and his God. If observances and ceremonies have any effect upon the individual, they make him a better or a worse neighbour to get along with. There is no so-called religious act that is not at the same time social, or that does not affect the welfare of others besides the welfare of those who practice them. Take the dietary laws, and note their effect in maintaining Jewish group life—how many social consequences flow from these observances!

9. Justification for the feeling that some acts are ethical and others are not. But the contrast to "ethical" is not *religious* but *conventional*. This means acting in conformity to social usage or custom, without stopping to think as to the meaning of that usage, conforming to tradition or to fashion without realizing the who and wherefore of what we do, this means acting mechanically like an automaton. Whether we pay our bills, tell the truth, give charity, eat Matzos or go to the Synagogue—so long as these are done merely because we are expected to do them, they are purely conventional acts, they are neither ethical or non-ethical. They have no special meaning for us. CHURCH scene in The Hairy Ape.[44]

10. These same acts become ethical when we reflect upon them and attach to them certain values. Appeal to K.H. Prayer for Zion.[45]

11. Herein lies the importance of the Ethics of the Fathers. This is the significance of the teaching these ethical maxims and precepts try to drive home to us. They take the conventional acts and assign a value to them, i.e., they point out some of the consequences of these socially accepted standards, or indicate their

---

[44] "The Hairy Ape" was a play written in 1922 by Eugene O'Neill. The protagonist is called a "hairy ape" by someone who doesn't understand his behavior and he is so affected by this remark that his behavior degenerates into animal-like conduct. In the "church scene" that Signer alludes to (Scene 5), the protagonist accosts churchgoers in Manhattan, insults them and is arrested for assaulting them. It is unclear what relation there is between this scene and the point Signer is making in his sermon.

[45] Signer is alluding to part of the blessing said after reading the prophetic portion (i.e., "K.H."—*k'riat haftarah*) during the Sabbath service. The Prayer for Zion includes two sentences: "Have compassion on Zion, for it is the source of our life; save the humbled soul speedily in our days. Blessed art thou, O Lord, who makest Zion rejoice in her children."

relative importance by naming the extent to which we must exert ourselves in living up to them. Thus when Antigonos[46] says [Abot 1:3]:

אל תהיו כעבדים המשמשין את הרב על מנת לקבל פרס אלא הֱווּ כעבדים המשמשין את הרב שלא על מנת לקבל פרס—"Be not like servants who minister to their master upon condition of receiving a reward but be like servants who minister to their master without the condition of receiving a reward" we are to understand that he implies that a good deed is *so* worthwhile that no thought of reward must enter one's mind. If therefore a good deed is done in a spirit of such an evaluation, it is an ethical deed. This method of evaluation applies to all the departments of life in business as well as in ceremonial observances.

12. By giving a value to every action of ours in this way we become moral or ethical beings, and it further gives rise to that element of responsibility without which no action has a moral value.

13. The life of the average man is unethical not because it is steeped in vice and sin but simply because it is humdrum and thoughtless. Even the virtues are not virtues.

The Adding Machine.[47]

The drab conventionality and lack of all individual thinking is what renders the life of the average man unethical.

14. Hitherto we Jews have stressed the need of either Orthodox or Reform Judaism. Neither one is enough. We must develop an ethical Judaism; we must cultivate that spirit of evaluation—giving a religious value to every one of our actions in all the fields in which we may be interested. Judaism must today as it has always done in the past—must make ethics devolve upon every Jew. In that way more than in any other can Judaism become the source of salvation to the individual Jew, so that it may be said of us once again:

ועמך כלם צדיקים—"Thy people shall all be righteous (Isaiah 60:21)."

---

[46] Mentioned in the first chapter of Abot, where he is called "Antigonus of Sokho" and quoted in chapter 1 verse 3.

[47] *The Adding Machine* is a play written in 1923 by Elmer Rice. The play details the experiences of the protagonist, Mr. Zero, who kills his boss when told he will be replaced by an adding machine, is executed and carries out similar work in the afterlife. Mr. Zero is notable for his lack of insight into his feelings and desires.

response from
Barry Schwartz

Dear Rabbi Signer,

Though we never met, I am honored to reply to your sermon "Ethical Judaism" delivered over a hundred years ago!

The sermon was delivered on May 25, 1923, at House of Israel in Morristown, New Jersey, not all that far from my Congregation Adas Emuno in Leonia, New Jersey.

I am connected to your family, specifically to your granddaughter Aliza Arzt, in that my cousin Ellen was married to Rabbi David Arzt, who you will recall was the son of Rabbi Max Arzt.

I'm a rabbi and publisher; the director and editor-in-chief of The Jewish Publication Society, which I know you are familiar with, since it is the nation's oldest Jewish publisher.

I'm also an author, including a book, *Path of the Prophets: The Ethics-Driven Life*, which relates directly to your sermon. If I can figure out how to master the challenge of time-travel I would be happy to present it to you!

I once heard someone define "coincidence" as "God's way of remaining anonymous." It is quite a coincidence that I received this invitation from Aliza just as I was working on a chapter entitled "About Ethics" for my new book, and dealing with the very same concern of your sermon.

I perceived a veiled reference in your sermon to Jews who leave the fold, or stop practicing Judaism, in the name of universal ethics. I think you had in mind the same example I was writing about—the Society for Ethical Culture, an organization founded in 1876 by Felix Adler, who as you know was the son of a prominent Reform rabbi, and who himself was studying to be a rabbi before taking a secular humanist turn. The Society, which still exists, has lofty and laudable goals; there is nothing to object to. But it is devoid of religious practices.

I share your concern that while humanism may be philosophically enticing to Jews who do not hold to traditional theology, when it leads to a completely secular lifestyle, something precious is lost. It's not only about losing members of the tribe, though with the skyrocketing rates of intermarriage which have occurred in the last several decades, coupled with non-observance, the demographic decline of the non-orthodox Jewish community is highly concerning. Without a religious commitment many Jews don't stay Jewish, and fail to pass on their Jewish line to the next generation.

It's also, as you write, about the loss of meaning. You are right that divorcing religion from ethics is unfortunate. Most people are not abstract, philosophical thinkers. They do not pause in their daily lives to contemplate a systematic code of ethics, and whether they are living up to it. Their lives, as you say, are conventional. I suppose there's nothing bad about conventional unless one takes a morally wrong turn. Religion helps guard against that.

But religion does more than keep us out of trouble. Judaism challenges us to aim higher and do better.

The Torah does not call us to be conventional. It calls us to be exceptional.

The Torah commands us neither to embrace the profane nor settle for the mundane, but to strive for the sacred.

The Torah proclaims, "you shall be holy," not "you shall be mediocre."

Judaism gives us an ethical vocabulary—in clear commandments.

Judaism gives us memorable stories that reinforce those values every time we read the Torah.

Judaism gives us rituals that embed those values every time we celebrate the Sabbath and holidays (or even recite a blessing of gratitude before a meal).

We may not stop and appreciate the fact that the rituals of religion bring us together as families and as communities. Around the table and in the sanctuary, we elevate the commonplace with blessings, prayers, songs and stories that extol the worthy life, in the words of Micah [6:8] "to do justly, to love mercy, and to walk humbly."

So thank you, Rabbi Signer, for your ever timely reminder, in the spirit of the ancient prophets of Israel, that ritual and ethics together point us to holiness and that the escape to platitudes about principles without commitment to commandments is a mistaken course.

You were very young when you gave this sermon; actually, still a student rabbi at the time. But your insights and wisdom are already evident. Little could you have known that you would also be graced with a family that appreciates and remembers you a century later. Well done!

Rabbi Barry L. Schwartz is the director and editor-in-chief emeritus of The Jewish Publication Society in Philadelphia, and rabbi of Congregation Adas Emuno in Leonia, New Jersey.

He is the author of books for adults, teens and children, including Open Judaism: A Guide for Believers, Atheists and Agnostics *(2023);* Path of the Prophets *(2018); and* Judaism's Great Debates *(2012). One of his children's books,* Adam's Animals *(2017), was a PJ Library selection. His next book,* Biblical Israel: A Family History, *traces the three dynasties that shaped ancient Israel and the Bible.*

When Are Laws Just?

Delivered in Bethlehem, Pennsylvania at Brith Shalom Community Center, January 28, 1927, for *Parshat Mishpatim*

We have in this week's weekly portion fragments of the ancient criminal and civil code of laws of the Jews which today are obsolete. Their true merit can only be seen when compared with other codes of antiquity. Place the Code of Hammurabi[48] alongside of *Mishpotim*[49] and the spiritual originality of Israel becomes evident.

But what interests us more is the fact that these laws were to be placed before all Israel: ואלה המשפטים אשר תשים לפניהם [These are the rules which you should place *before them*—Exodus 21:1]. Not for the student, the expert, or the lawyer or the archaeologist, but for all Israel were these laws given.

It seems inconceivable for a people to exist without its own code of laws. And so this code which is found in the Torah became later the basis of the חשן משפט [lit. "breastplate of judgement" Exodus 28:15, meant here to refer to codified law] which for 2,000 years actually functioned among Jews. For even after the Jews had been exiled from their native land and had lost their political rights as a people to govern themselves, they had left to them their social autonomy. Until 1605 the Jewish code of laws marched hand in hand with Jewish life and received its changes and its interpretation and its modifications at the hands of our Jewish leaders and lawmakers. Jewish education also followed hand in hand with Jewish life. The Jewish child at the age of 8 or 9 would actually study Jewish law, which he saw practiced and lived all about him—[50]שנים אוחזים בטלית / ארבעה אבות נזיקין not to become a lawyer or a Rabbi but merely to call himself an educated man familiar with the viewpoint of his people and the management of their affairs, i.e., to become a better Jew when he grew up to man's estate. Jewish law at that time was the content and substance of Jewish education.

Today we are living a life that is enough to call forth wonder even on the part of our own Jews, let alone other peoples.

---

[48] A Babylonian legal document, believed to have been composed 1755-1750 BCE. Many of the laws found in this code are also found in the Bible.

[49] The weekly portion, Exodus 21-24, that deals with civil law.

[50] שנים אוחזים בטלית—*lit.* "two [people] taking hold of a prayer shawl," which is the first line of the *Mishneh* (rabbinic law compiled 200 BCE-200 CE) tractate *Baba Metziah*.

ארבעה אבות נזיקין *lit.* "four categories of damages" which is the first line of the *Mishneh* from *Baba Kamah*. These were often the first rabbinic works studied by children.

Today Jewish law is defunct, i.e., criminal law and civil law is dead as far as Jewish life and conduct are concerned. Even among Jews who claim to be staunchly orthodox in tendency and viewpoint, Judaism or Jewish law has become confined only to ritual law—that is, law affecting our prayers, the kind of food we eat, the way we observe on holidays and holy days. Here is a problem that is a very vital one. Can Judaism survive if our own code books are a dead letter, if they are of interest only to the archaeologist? I believe that Judaism can retain its vitality only if and when Jewish law as a whole will be reinterpreted to meet our modern conditions and our modern needs and requirements.

We hear people say that one must be a law-abiding citizen; that the better [the] Jew, the better the American does he become. For the Jew to be a better Jew or a better citizen being merely law-abiding is hardly sufficient. The Jew must also be law-shaping.

To be in a position to shape the law we must know what the תוכן—the meat of the Law, the kernel of the Law has always been—what Judaism has always striven to put into practice and to preach: צדק צדק תרדף ["Justice justice you shall pursue" Deut. 16:20] and that is Justice. What is [the] nature [of] justice? Any number of answers may be given to answer this question. Perhaps the simplest answer is this: The nature of justice is a double one. First we have political justice and second spiritual justice. POLITICAL JUSTICE was first clearly stated by one of the early Greek philosophers, Plato, who believed that a country should be governed with the intention behind everything that the state or the country can do no wrong. The state must be the strongest thing in the world. All people in the country should be divided into three groups or classes. At the head of the list should come the thinkers or the actual lawmakers, the administrators, the governors, the judges—then should come the soldiers who shall carry out the laws and orders and commands of the statesmen and lawmakers, and last of all the laborers who are not to think for themselves, who are to be governed by another class completely, who must obey their superiors without question and who must be content to supply their country with the means—whatever they might be—to keep their country supreme higher than any other country. This is the theory of political justice.

Opposed to this theory there is the other one of spiritual justice. This lays its emphasis and stress on the individual. Spiritual justice aims to produce not strong states but spiritually strong human beings. Souls. By soul we mean that which makes you and me different from a mere animal. Have you a true soul?

Have you the power to think? The power to see clearly the difference between appearance and reality?

Have you a true soul? Have you the power of sympathy? Can you put yourself in another's position?

Have you a true soul? Have you the power of exercising self-control when confronted by strong passions?

And now we come to the question contained in the topic of this sermon. When are laws Just? Only when they aim at spiritual justice when their purpose is to make men think constructively, to feel for their fellow-man and to exercise self-control. That is our test!

If the recital in the Synagogue of portions of laws which we don't practice any more is to have any value for us Jews today it can have value only when we shall learn what was the purpose [in] back of these laws that it was not to create a strong political government or state where political justice should be the guiding force, where men should say 'my country right or wrong' which I believe is a false teaching, but the purpose of Moses and the lawgivers was to establish peace on earth and brotherliness through the cultivation of spiritual justice to do everything to bring man nearer to God to develop in him the passion to be willing to use his God-given intelligence, a passion to learn the divine quality of sympathy and to exercise self-control over his baser nature. There you have the formula—the only prescription for right relations with God and man. It is the same formula uttered by that master among men, Isaiah, who looks forward to a time when Israel shall practice the teaching that פקודתך שלום ונגשיך צדקה . . .—your governor shall be Peace and your ruler, Justice, no sound of violence shall be in your land, nor ruin nor rapine in your borders; your ramparts you shall name protection and your gates renown (Isaiah 60:17-18).

response from
Ray Arzt

Dear Rabbi Signer,

If I were your congregant when you delivered the sermon "When are Laws Just?" I would have been inspired and would have agreed with you wholeheartedly. Your sermon is, I am sure, an articulate expression of your deeply held values and viewpoints. My comments will, therefore, not address the content of the sermon in terms of its spiritual quality, but will rather apply some analytic tools to ferret out a few underlying problems.

A few templates guide my thinking.

1. A legal system, as such, exists only when there is a recognized legislative body (פוסקים) and a method of enforcement (שוטרים). Methods of enforcement can be applied either as a function of state authority ("stop at the red light or you will be fined") or as a strong community norm (if a woman dresses immodestly, she will be ostracized).

2. Justice and Law are related but are not the same. The delicate balance between Justice and Law has been maintained in the past within slowly shifting historical contexts. Today, the rapidly shifting contexts of post modernity (taken at its best), have made it harder to maintain that balance. Justice is an open-ended value orientation constantly seeking what is right in a particular historical context. Law, on the other hand, is the necessary application of Justice in a specific historical contextual moment. A sense of Justice serves as a critique of existing Laws which, as contexts change, have become obsolete. Justice calls for a change in the Law (e.g., civil rights legislation in the 1960s).

3. Quotes of passages from contextually defined sacred pieces of literature, authored in specific historical periods, may inspire a person. It must be kept in mind, however, that any such quote was first uttered in a specific context—in the past, a context that cannot be recovered and, therefore, ought not stand as an absolute defining principle or proof text.

Your sermon was delivered in 1927, before the establishment of the State of Israel. As a Sovereign state, Israel is now governed through a legal system which grants authority to the ultra-Orthodox rabbinic courts. These courts no longer have to rely on communal enforcement alone, but can rely on official state enforcement as well. Many laws, under their jurisdiction, relate to one's personal status such as rights and requirements pertaining to status at birth, marriage, divorce, death, religious conversion, religious rituals, etc. As an Israeli citizen and as a liberal Conservative Jew, I consider many of these restrictions obsolete. I must, nevertheless, abide by them in the public domain as they are state-sanctioned laws, which will be enforced by the state.

I join those groups who oppose these laws, hoping that our sense of Justice will in some way bring about a correction. Whether they succeed or not will be purely a function of whether general political interests, when applying our sense of Justice to change the Law, will win the day.

Finally, the notion of law when applied in post-modern, pluralistic, individualistic and western styled societies, without the enforcement methods of a sovereign state, or those of a closed charisma-led community is, to a large degree, irrelevant. Law, in an open voluntaristic setting, can only be understood as a recommendation. Without serious enforcement, Jews will act as they see fit.

Judaism, as such, cannot talk and therefore cannot say anything. Only Jews can talk. As they talk, Jewishly, they may or may not convince others. If they succeed in convincing many "others," they may form a "plausibility structure" and then use political, economic and educational methods to attract more "others." If, however, they slip into the trap of automatically knowing what is best for the "other" and consequently use methods of indoctrinating "others" with absolute solutions, they will, unwittingly, form an Orthodoxy which will be cult-like and narcissistic.

I, for one, may have been inspired to act after hearing your sermon. I would hope, however, that what would follow would move well beyond the somewhat Messianic urging that cries out in your words. A meaningful follow-up must be rooted in interdisciplinary knowledge, varied sensitivities, multifaceted ways of education, constant clarification and rebooting. This will be nothing less than a dynamic work of art in progress.

Sermons may have worked in the past and brought about change. Today, sermons try to find in the wisdom of the past solutions for the present. This is not enough. At times it can be even dangerous, cultivating a feeling of warmth rather than a readiness to act in a context of complexity.

Ray Arzt is not an academic, therefore he is free to think as he wishes. Though professionally active in a variety of educational endeavors over the years, he is particularly grateful to have been the director of Camp Ramah in Palmer, Massachusetts during the turbulent 1960s. It was during this period that he was able to help generate many of the contemporary liberal frameworks that are now commonplace on the Jewish scene. This was done by inviting stimulating people to serve on his staff and creating an atmosphere of a free confrontative intellectual climate which enabled some to think outside the box and act. His approach to the challenges facing Jewish education is covered in his doctoral dissertation: Towards an Existential Model for Jewish Education.

RAY Arzt

Ray made Aliyah in 1971 and as a volunteer, was a driving force helping to establish all the institutions that make up the Masorti movement in Israel. He will be 92 this year but his thinking still focuses on the future. Ray has been married to his beloved Roz for 67 years, has 4 wonderful children and 8 loving grandchildren.

What's in a Name?
(The Meaning of Your Name)

Delivered in Manhattan Beach, New York at
Temple Beth El, January 24, 1930, for *Parshat Shemot*

In ancient times the belief was current that the essence of one's personality was indicated by his name. Thus Adam gives the names to the animals because he was presumed to know their essence, their characteristics and quality. In the story of David and Nabal,[51] David's protagonist is pictured as living up to the connotation of his name. In Jewish speech the proverb has come down כשמו כן הוא [he behaves according to his name]. This explains why incantations of all kinds depended on the knowledge of the name of the person over whom prayers were to be recited, or curses uttered, or blessings invoked. In the naming of children, the same practice is followed today. Children are named after ancestors, parents or relatives. When a child is given a relative's name out of sentiment it is perfectly laudable, but all too often superstition governs that action, as when a name is given to a child under the mistaken belief that the personality of the dead will fall upon the living. It is undoubtedly a superstitious practice—that of changing the name of a sick person.[52] It is very much like transferring one's property to his wife's name to escape the hand of the law.

Similarly with the gods of ancient days. It was necessary to know the names of the gods in order to know their essence. Gods therefore received names which indicated their functions. Thus Rimmon in the Bible is the god of thunder and lightning, wind, rain and storm because for the Arameans, *Rammanu* meant thunder and storm and rain. Moses as we are told in the Bible wants to know God's name; he makes this request because he is of the belief current among all the people of his time that he will thereby know God's essence. And he is told that the characteristic of the Deity is eternity.

Now while thinking people don't accept the belief that the name which a person bears broadcasts his essence and personality, yet we must admit that the name which he carries is an INDEX of the civilization to which he belongs. To the same

---

[51] In First Samuel chapter 25, King David requests aid from a rich property owner named Nabal and is turned down rudely. Subsequently, Nabal's wife aids David and Nabal is struck down by God. The word "Nabal" in Hebrew (נָבָל) means "scoundrel."

[52] It was a custom to change the name of a person who was deathly ill in order to thwart the Angel of Death and preserve the person's life.

extent to which a civilization determines the characteristic and life of a person, to that degree does one's name reflect the civilization of which he is a member. One's civilization shapes a man's thoughts and ideas and colors his mental outlook and intellectual perspective. Just as the physical environment determines the life of everything in each locality so does the civilization of a person determine a Man's whole life. Now that civilization, to a great extent, is reflected in a man's name.

In commenting upon the names which the children of Jacob bore in Egypt in the midst of a foreign civilization, the Sages point with pride to the fact that they did not change their names [לא שנו את שמם]. And the Rabbis seem to deduce from that, that Jews were always conscious of their names. This however is not borne out by the facts of history. Because as a matter of *fact*, there is no better way of judging the vicissitudes of the Jewish people in its passage thru various civilization than a study of the type of names borne by its men and women throughout the ages.

The first stage at which we meet Jewish names is in Bible times. Then the bulk of names were God-bearing names. The worshippers of the God of Israel indicated their loyalty to their God by incorporating His name within their own. Thus every name which contains the letters EL, IAH or JAH is distinctly Hebraic. Elkanah, Jeremiah, Isaiah, Israel, Daniel, Hezekiah, Jehoram, Joshua, Judah.

After the Exile in Babylonia, we find foreign names already. It is most interesting to comment on the fact that the Jews were there only one generation and in the very family of David, the royal family, we find a name like Zerubabel. Then came the *Persian influence* which is reflected in such names as Mordecai (*Marduk*) and Esther (*Ishtar*).

Alexander the Great early let his influence be felt in Palestine in such names as Antigonus and Alexander and Sender. And in the Egypt of that time, a batch of documents has been discovered, called the Elephantine Papyri,[53] which are full of Greek names. Philo, which means God-lover or beloved of God, dates back to this time. It is the height of irony to reflect that the descendants of the Maccabees, who fought so valiantly to stem the tide of Hellenization but a short while before, succumbed to the same influence in having Greek names such as Alexander Jannaeus, Hyrcanus Aristobulus, Salome, Alexandra. Names like Petros, Rufus, Pappus and Toderos (which is used to this day) tell of the Roman influence; while אביי, רבא, פפא, אשי, רבינא [*Abaye, Raba, Papa, Ashi, Rabina*] show the influence of the Aramaic, when Jews lived in Chaldea and Persia, in the first five centuries of the common era.

---

[53] Documents discovered in Egypt in the 19th and early 20th centuries, which dated from the 4th and 5th centuries BCE, many of which detail Jewish life of that time period.

Then came the Judaic contact with the Arabic civilization and some of the greatest figures in our history bear the impress of that culture in their names. Maimuni, Ibn Ezra, Ibn Gabirol, Nagdela, Shaprut, Migash, and Dunash ibn Labrat are names to conjure with.

Spain and Portugal and France each affected the names of their Jewish inhabitants as Mendoza, Mendes, De Sola, Jarchi, Anatoli, Don Meyer di Malea, Palkera, Chiquitilla, Moses da Leon, Moses Narboni, Duran, Alami and Sarco testify.

Nor was Italy backward with its contribution of Donollo, Sforno, Lazzato and Padveh.

The giving of names was thus an unconscious process until the period of the emancipation began. By emancipation we refer to the first steps which were made by European governments to reckon with Jews as individuals. (Explain: matter of taxation previously taken care of by each Jewish community or Ghetto).[54]

Thus, in the Teutonic countries, from which the vast majority of our names originated, the adoption of hereditary surnames by Jews is comparatively recent. It was not until 1845 that the governments of the last of the German states took measures to compel their adoption. The decree of Napoleon, and the measures subsequent to it, were considered by those toward whom they were directed as savouring of cruel persecution. Recourse was had to subterfuges, but they proved of no avail. Attempts were made to evade the decrees, but they were unsuccessful. The last day fixed for the adoption of surnames arrived, and none were allowed to escape the ordeal. Patronymic surnames like Israels, Jacobs, names ending in "sohn" like Mendelssohn and "mann" like Lippman were accepted in many places and when these Teutonic Jews went further East to Russia and Poland, they added -sky, -itz, -itch, -off, -vitch and their variants, frequently to their Jewish or German names. Others took merely fancy names derived from trees, plants, jewels or natural features. In some cases chance was called to the assistance of the undecided. The Bible was opened and the first name hit upon [was] adopted as the future surname or patronymic of the family. In one instance at least, the congregation assembled in the Synagogue, the Rabbi opened the Prayerbook and the first word on the page was taken by the first family, the second by the second family and so on. One holy man, immersed in his studies, heeded not the injunctions of the authorities and when at length asked for the name he had chosen, replied in the

---

[54] Signer is likely referring to special taxes levied on the Jews which were collected in the ghettos and other Jewish communities. There were some temporary measures taken by the governments in 1848 to eliminate these taxes in a short-lived attempt to increase the equal treatment of all residents.

language with which he was most conversant אנחנו לא נדע ["we do not know"].⁵⁵ Without hesitation the official recorded his new name as NEUDA and by that appellation his descendants are still known. Another in similar circumstances, when asked for his name, said YANKELE and in reply to remonstrances repeated POSHET YANKELE [i.e., "simply 'Yankele'"]. His name was entered as Poshet. Many people like the Schiff family took their name from their calling, *schiff* in Middle High German, meaning a vial, to show that the founder of the family was an apothecary or physician; or from some visible symbol about them like the Rothschilds from the *red shield* upon their house-door; or from the town they came from like Eybeschutz, from Ebenschitz in Moravia or from the abbreviation of their name like Katz for כ"ץ [k"tz];⁵⁶ Sachs for זרע קדש ["*zerah kodesh*"—holy seed] Goetz or Yates for גר צדק ["*ger tzedek*"—righteous stranger, denoting a convert to Judaism], Segal for סגן לויה ["*s'gan l'viyah*"—officer in charge of accompaniment], Brown for "Ben [i.e., *son of*] Rabbi Nachman"; Schatz for שליח צבור ["*sheliach tzibur*," often abbreviated as "*Sh'tz*" and pronounced "*Shatz*"] or from their trade like Snyder/Schneider [cutter], Steinschneider [stonecutter], Wechsler [money changer]; Spielman [storyteller].

But cruel Austria in 1787 forced the Jews to adopt certain names as a badge of shame and mark of disgrace. Names like the following were unwillingly bestowed upon Jews. Eselskopt, Rindskopf, Gottlos, Hunger, Fresser, Pferd, Nashorn, Kussemich, Schnapser, Elephant, Trinker, Grauberklotz, Todtschlager⁵⁷ are the mildest among a list of degrading names.

At the present time the matter of giving names can no longer be left to chance but is decidedly one that will be determined by the extent to which the Jew will want to do one of three things:

1) To disguise his Jewish identity.
2) To accentuate his Jewishness.
3) or to express his desire to identify himself as a Jew with the non-Jewish civilization in which he lives.

To disguise his Jewish identity: Here we have the common example of what we are doing now to a large extent. The Americanized generation of Jews of today is hungry for American names, given and surnames, and the process of modification of names goes on from Canada to Mexico. The process is rather simple. Usually

---

⁵⁵ A liturgical phrase from the weekday *Tahanun* and High Holiday liturgy ("We do not know what to do, but our eyes are upon You"), taken from II Chronicles 20:12.
⁵⁶ Abbreviation for *Kohen Tzedek*: a righteous priest.
⁵⁷ Respectively: donkey's head, ox's head, godless, hungry, glutton, horse, rhinoceros, kiss me, boozer, elephant, drinker, grayblock, blackjack [literally "death blow"].

a Jewish child is named after some ancestor. It has become a recognized custom to take the first letter of the ancestor's given name and give the newly-born an Anglo-Saxon name beginning with the same letter. Whence come the numerous Irvings, Irwins and Isadores for Isaac;[58] Rhea, Rae, Ruth, Reba, Ronda, Irene, for Rebecca and Rachel; Shirley, Sylvia, Serena, Sybil, for Sarah; Morris, Maurice, Max, Marmeduke, Marshall, Malcolm, Mortimer, Marsters, for Moses, Menahem and Mendel and etc. Some of these adaptations have become standardized, and in the eyes of the Gentiles such names as Isador, Louis, Morris etc. are JEWISH names. Hence they are being abandoned by the richer Jews who are forever alert to the latest in Anglo-Saxonism. Kenneth for Akiba still appeals to them. Likewise they favor Dittmar for David, Laura for Leah and so forth.

As to the surnames, the process of dissection is popular among the middle classes; the richer groups favor a complete change. When the process of dissection is resorted to, the suffixes -SKY, -OFF, -BERG, -WITZ, -MANN, -ESCU etc. are dropped. In general, short names are preferred. Anglo-Saxon names are looked on as a mark of distinction; they hardly ever fail to follow increased annual incomes. The immigrant father became Goldberg, JACK GOLDBERG. Then the God of Israel made him prosperous. Under the name of Jack Goldberg he took a deed to a million dollar piece of real estate. He rather thought that he was playing fair by keeping the Jewish name of Jack Goldberg, regardless of his wealth. He sincerely believed that Jack Goldberg was a good Jewish name. His son now has an assured income of over $20,000 per annum, and Jr. changes his name of Harry Goldberg to Hallsworthy Gilbert, and his brother Isaac has become Hitchcock. Nobody but his closest relatives knew that the late Conrad Hubert[59] came to these shores from Russia bearing a name suspiciously like Getsel Horowitz.

Some people on the other hand go to the other extreme by over-emphasizing their Jewishness. When done in America, it seems in some cases quite foreign. When, as happens, the change takes place in Palestine it is the only natural thing to do. Because one becomes a new person in Palestine, and therefore a new name is necessary. And so, quite properly, the Official Gazette records such changes going on every day like the following:

Dov Abrami or Benavraham from Berl Abramowitz; Johanan Even-Ari from Hans Lowenstein; Chaim Malchi from Carl Salzburg. Goldstein becomes Ibn-za-

---

[58] "Isaac" was Isador Signer's Hebrew name. He does not spell his English name the same way he wrote it in his sermon.

[59] Conrad Hubert (1856-1928) was an inventor, born in Russia, who emigrated to the United States in 1890. He was best known for the invention of the flashlight. According to Wikipedia (https://en.wikipedia.org/wiki/Conrad_Hubert) his birth name was Akiba Horowitz.

hav.⁶⁰ In almost every case the Hebraized form is prettier and more euphonious than the original. They are far more pleasing to the ear in the soft Sephardic pronunciation than their foreign counterparts, and beyond that, children as well as grown-ups are always called by their full given names so that Yaakov never becomes anything like Jakey. Nor is Rivkah lacerated into Becky. Disguises for Hebrew names are of course unthinkable. Names, like personalities, are respected.

But what about the rest of the world? What about us in America? Our problem, your problem, is to find a happy medium. Hebraic names to be sure are AMERICAN. We have only to turn to any American History Book from the first Puritan to the late Gamaliel Harding,[61] to see the impress of the Biblical background upon our country. Names furthermore must be well-sounding. Therefore instead of the haphazard method of giving names which is current today, it seems to me that a more deliberate and conscious approach should prevail in the giving of names. Remembering that we want to be American, that we are American to the very core of our being, we want to identify ourselves with our civilization. But what should be the criterion? How [can we] be American and Jewish at the same time? As time goes by, the Jewish civilization of our fellow brethren in Palestine will influence our Jewish life in this country. Indeed, it is already doing so. Already we have people giving their children Palestinian names like Carmel, Ezri, Bat Ami, Ben Ami, Hadassah, Ziona, Edyah,[62] Shoshanah and so on. How should that influence be felt? The past provides the answer for us. The past teaches us that when there are other factors involved to identify us as Jews, there is no danger to our Jewishness if we adopt the names current to the civilization in which we belong. By all means let us adopt as surnames Anglo-Saxon names. There is no particular virtue in stubbornly insisting that one comes from Vilna or Cracow, or Bukovina, or Kletsk. Nor is there anything to be gained by retaining "itch"es, or "burg"s or "sky"s or any other Teutonic or Slavic appellations. I see no objection at all to changing a Grosberg to its equivalent (Larchmont—big mountain) or Kornfeld to its equivalent Hawkin. That's the name by which you are known to your world but as far as your given name is concerned, there is little room for a Seymour, or Stanley, or Sanford, or a thousand other such names. Somehow a Gerald Schuchatowitsky is far more grating to the ear and harsh-sounding than Gershon Sackton would be. Schuchatowitsky conjures up no Jewish picture to the mind of child or adult, but Gershon does. Let us therefore remember that

---

[60] These are all the translations into Hebrew of German-based names.
[61] President Warren *Gamliel* Harding.
[62] Signer named his first child, born in January 1929, "Edya," from the Hebrew for "ornament." This name has never been commonly used.

as long as we will be inspired by Israel and identified in some personal way—as one's given name does with its hopes and ideals there will be no danger to the continuation of our Judaism. Let us follow the advice of the prophet who looks forward to the time when: "One shall say I am the Lord's, and another shall call himself by the name of Jacob and yet a third shall name himself by the name of Israel." (Isaiah 44:5)

response from
Ronnie Levin

Dear Rabbi Signer,

As you say, "The name we carry is an index to the civilization in which we belong." Indeed, names identify us by time, location, and gender.

For Jews, the Bible is the most common source of our names. Many early Biblical names have a single component. Abraham, Isaak, Joseph, Reuben, etc., and many of the male names are based upon a verb: Isaac ("he will laugh"), Joseph ("he will add"), Reuven ("Look! A son"). Many Biblical female names were the names of animals—Rachel ("ewe"), Tzipporah ("bird"), Deborah ("bee"); or objects—Peninah ("pearl"), Sarah ("officer"), Michal ("power"). There are some male names of animals: Achbor ("mouse"), Shaphan ("rabbit").

It is hard for us to notice this, but even within the Bible, names evolved to reflect the contemporaneous culture. Egyptian names entered the Bible while we sojourned there. Although Moses' name is given a Hebrew derivation in the Bible, it is probably derived from the Egyptian word for "son" and related to other Egyptian names such as Ramses, Thutmose and Ahmose. Similarly, the name Miriam (Moses' sister) is probably from the Egyptian word *mr* ("love").

Later Biblical male names had two elements, one a verb and the other a theophoric (god-related) element; for instance, Yehoshua/Isaiah ("Yah will save"), Michael ("who is like God?"), Daniel ("God will judge"). There are also a few female composite names, such as Hephzibah ("I delight in her"). Not all names occur in the composite form. It's possible that with names that only retain a verbal element, for example, Natan ("given") or Asaph ("collected"), the divine component dropped off.

In the later biblical writings, Aramaic forms (with an *aleph* ending, e.g., Ezra) begin to appear, as do foreign names (Mordechai related to Marduk; Esther related to Ishtar).

As the Jews found themselves dispersed throughout the world following the destruction of the First and Second Temples, Jewish names increasingly took on the forms of the countries in which they lived. Aramaic forms are common in the Talmud, and Greek and Roman names are frequently used for both men and women (e.g., Hyrcanus, Dosa, Alexander). Greek translations of Hebrew names also occur, e.g., Theodorus for Nataniel, as well as shortening—for instance, Eleazar becomes Lazar. This would later happen in Europe where a Biblical name like Solomon could become the Yiddish Zalmen.

These adaptations continued in both Sephardic and Ashkenazic communities. Some Hebrew names took their Arabic forms (Daoud for "David," Musa for "Moses," Salman/Suliman for "Solomon"), while in Ashkenazic communities, they took a Yiddish form (Dovid, Yoshele, Shuli). Some Hebrew/Jewish names are translated ("blessed" is *Maimun* in Arabic) or take the form of the colloquial language ("son of" *ben* in Hebrew becomes *ibn* in Arabic).

Few biblical names repeat within the Bible. In particular, neither descendants nor others reuse an ancestor's name. This is in sharp contrast to the Jewish tradition that began in the Talmudic period of naming an infant after a deceased relative. This naming practice has since proliferated extensively and is now virtually ubiquitous throughout the Jewish world. In most of the modern Jewish world, it is even considered bad luck to give a child the same name as someone in the family who is still alive.

Another Talmudic innovation was changing the name of a person who became ill—especially a newborn or young child—to disguise that person from the Angel of Death (R. H. 16b).[63] Both Ashkenazi and Sephardi Jews have such traditions, and the person was often renamed Chaim ("life"), Raphael ("God heals"), or Azriel ("God is my help") for a male or Chana ("beloved"), Chaya ("life/living") or Sarah ("officer") for a female.

In the Western world, surnames began to be used in the Middle Ages. Jews previously were identified as "someone the son/daughter of so-and-so," and the name changed with every generation. Boys were the sons of fathers and girls were the daughters of mothers. This is still the religious custom and the early preferred Jewish surnames reflected Jewish practice: Mendel son of Avram became Mendel Abramson or Avramowitz. Surnames appeared first within Sephardic communities while Ashkenazic Jews were among the last Europeans to take them.

Historic and professional circumstances influenced family names. Many Russian Jews changed their names to hide in plain sight to avoid being conscripted into the Czar's army. Surnames might refer to place of origin (Deutsch, Frankel), profession (Schneider is German for tailor), or an aspect of nature (Greenbaum is German for green tree). In the United States in particular, these names became as Jewish as the name Cohen (or Levin!) but in Germany they would have been accepted as generic—and German. Thence began the move in the U.S. to shorten surnames (Rosenzweig to Ross) and especially to de-Jewify last names (Epstein to Eastman, Horowitz to Howe, etc.).

---

[63] Talmud *Rosh HaShana* 16b: ". . . a person's [death] sentence is torn up on account of four types of actions. These [include] . . . a change of one's name . . ."

RONNIE Levin

At the beginning of the 20th century, many names became popular with American Jews as male first names such as Morris, Norman, Morton, Isidore, Stuart, Gordon, Robert and Maxwell, that were originally English, French or German surnames. Interestingly, those names are again increasing in popularity in the early 21st century, along with some common female names from a century ago, too, such as Sadie, Isabella (or just Bella), Eva, Maya/Mia, Hanna and Leah.

So, yes, Rabbi Signer. Names identify us by culture, time, and family. They simultaneously bind and differentiate us. They can disguise or proclaim our heritage. There is a story behind every name, as well as the story to be written by the holder.

The *b'rachah* (Jewish blessing) recited when one sees a multitude is:

> Blessed are You, LORD, our God, King of the Universe, knower of secrets.
> *Baruch ata Adonai, Eloheinu melech ha-olam, chacham harazeem.*

The Talmud (Brachot 58a) explains that the secret of the universe is that no matter how many people you will ever see, each is unique and unlike all the others. And the same is true of our names: part of a long chain of Jews, but each distinct from all others.

Ronnie Levin, after graduate school at Brandeis in Near Eastern and Jewish Studies, worked at the U.S. Environmental Protection Agency for 38 years, retiring as a Senior Scientist. She now runs the Water and Health Program at the Harvard T.H. Chan School of Public Health. She is a national expert in lead exposures, particularly lead contamination of drinking water, and in monetizing health damages; she has been instrumental in federal policies to reduce lead contamination of U.S. public drinking water and to remove lead pipes. Her interests remain in Jewish texts, especially Bible and Tefillah (liturgy).

Prophets of Peace: Woodrow Wilson

Delivered in Morristown, New Jersey at House of Israel, February 8, 1924, for *Parshat Trumah*

The last week has seen the world shocked out of its habitual indifference by the death of Woodrow Wilson. This passing of ex-President Wilson is a matter of especial grief to us Jews. To many of us, the news that Wilson was in large measure responsible for the Balfour Declaration and was one of its heartiest sponsors will come in the nature of a surprise. We can well say that the statement of the Rabbis חסידי עמות העולם יש להם חלק לעולם הבא[64]—"The righteous of the world have a portion in the world to come" (*Mishneh Torah Repentance* 3:5) applies to him. He is indeed worthy to be counted among the righteous men of the world. Indeed, we honor ourselves in honoring his memory and paying respect to this great man in the world's history. For the Rabbis well say in the case of the daughter of Pharaoh: אמר לה הקב'ה לבתיה בת פרעה, משה לא היה בנך וקראתו בנך. אף את לא את בתי ואני קורא אותך בתי שנאמר 'אלה בני בתיה בת יה [The Holy One of Blessing said to Bityah, the daughter of Pharoah, "Moses was not your son and you called him your son. Even though you are not my daughter I call you my daughter as it is said, (*I Chronicles 4:18*) 'These are the sons of Bitya [daughter of Pharoah] Bat-Yah [*Vayikra Rabba* 1:3]."[65]

It is not only formal adoption of the Jewish religion that puts Wilson into the fold of Judaism but the special interest in the life of Israel that he displayed and the help he gave in promoting the existence of Jewish life. These place him in the front ranks of the benefactors of the world. These qualities make of him one of a line of חסידי עמות העולם ["The righteous of the world"] revered by Jews as they do their very own.

It has been said, "it is pitifully true of some men that they must die to live." These men are the prophets who preach something new, the men of vision who

---

[64] Signer has misspelled the word for "nations" in his handwritten Hebrew quote: עמות instead of אמות.

[65] First Chronicles 4:18 states, "These are the sons of Bitya daughter of Pharoah." The *Midrash* (Rabbinic exegesis of the Bible) revocalizes the name "Bitya" as "Batya" which means "daughter of God." In the rabbinic text, God asserts that just as Pharoah's daughter calls her adopted son Moses "my son," God has called her "my daughter" because of her charitable actions. In the same way, although Woodrow Wilson is not himself a Jew, Signer states that the Jewish people have accepted him among them due to his charitable actions.

struggle with the unwilling spirit of man to imbue him with an ideal and a goal in life. But in the history of the world we find that these men have been scorned and mocked at and their teachings derided and unheeded. The idea that Wilson preached is not a new one. It is as old as the prophets of Israel. It is as old as Amos; it was preached by Hosea. From Isaiah came the clarion call: וכתתו חרבותם לאתים וחניתותיהם למזמרות. לא ישא גוי אל גוי חרב ולא ילמדו עוד מלחמה—They will beat their swords into plowshares and their spears into pruning hooks; nation shall not lift up sword against nation, they shall not learn war anymore" (*Isaiah* 2:4).

Micah repeated it, (*Micah* 6:8): Justice between man and man, fairness between nation and nation.[66]

But were these men listened to? No. Their ideals were mocked at:

... חזה לך ברח לך אל ארץ יהודה ואכל שם לחם ושם תנבא. ובית–אל לא תוסיף עוד להנבא כי מקדש מלך הוא ובית ממלכה הוא

[... Seer, off with you to the land of Judah! Earn your living there and do your prophesying there: But don't ever prophesy again at Bethel; for it is a king's sanctuary and a royal palace] (*Amos* 7:12-13).

And Isaiah was killed, the Rabbis say, for his doctrines. At that time the mass of the people did not long for universal peace. It was not an ideal that they looked forward to and so they stoned the preachers of peace and heaped contumely and shame upon them.

But, my friends, it was an *idea* these men advocated, not themselves. Had the prophets been organizers of men, inciters to revolt, dashing personalities with their power depending on personal magnetism and contact, the backbone of their movement might have been broken, perhaps, by their removal from the scene. But they were none of these. Their weapons were *ideas* and ideas cannot be *killed*. They can kill themselves but they cannot *be* killed. And so long after these prophets were dead, men came to revere and respect their teachings. And no more did they say we don't *believe* in a world peace and a democracy of nations. The world had thus advanced, yes, but only in looking to the era of universal peace and the abolishment of war as a dream to be realized only בימי המשיח—when the Messiah should come.

---

[66] Micah 6:8—[God] has told you, O man, what is good, and what the Lord requires of you: Only to do justice and to love goodness, and to walk modestly with your God.

But along came a man in our own day who gave the same idea a color of novelty because it was powerfully repeated, because it was preached at a time of universal bewilderment and despair by the highest seat of political authority in the world and now the man was not scoffed at, nor ridiculed any longer. The human mind had developed within the last 2,500 years. But his idea, though admittedly a good one, was not thought possible of realization. It was called *impractical*, impossible to realize and another man was thus offered up as a sacrifice on the altar of ideals—yet another man was left to die of a broken heart because of our lack of faith in the possibilities of the human mind.

Wilson is dead, you say? No, my friends, Wilson is alive in the hearts and minds of the people whom he imbued with his idea. Wilson is alive because his idea LIVES. And he will live forever in the cause he has made his own. Cynics may sneer, materialists jeer and politicians punily continue yet awhile their battle against destiny, but the cause that has thrilled with hope the hearts of the masses in the humble cabins of the earth will prevail. He has raised a standard that people will not let fall. He has awakened a hope that the masses will not let die. He has harnessed his claims on immortality with the truth that is immortal.

And the suggestions of people now, who are without vision and without faith, that Wilson failed are answered by his words: "I would rather fail in a cause which I know some day will triumph than win in a cause I know some day will fail." The prophets are almost invariably stoned but soon men come along to gather up the stones to build the monument. The men and women kneeling in prayer before the house where he lay dying, the men and women weeping in Madison Square Garden are a symbol, and a prophecy of what is bound to come sooner or later when come it must.

Now how can we Jews who have always been ready to take up the cudgels on behalf of a just cause and to fight for the right, how can we hasten the coming of the ideal of Peace for which this martyr laid down his life?

Peace, like war, my friends, is simply a *state of mind*. Habits of thought, of feeling, of sentiment, of action make war while there is yet peace. True, we say that we hate the thought of war and in a vague abstract way we [are] like other nations and are by no means opposed to them and when war comes, it *seems* to break upon us like an electric storm, it *seems* to come upon us with no warning as does an earthquake, it seems to happen *to* us in some sudden and unaccountable fashion. But in reality it happens *within us* as a long series of events closely connected— the call to arms, the wearing of a uniform, the actual fighting—these are merely the culmination, the climax of that series of events. If we are not aware that it is so, it is because we are not in the habit of thinking along those lines consciously.

But suppose that we did think along those lines consciously. Suppose that all our children in the schools of the country today were trained so that a generation later the American mind should have a deep hatred of the inhumanity of war, realization of the futility and uselessness of war, at least a little understanding of the causes of international strains and of the ways in which people who do not want to fight are nevertheless *made* to do so.

Again suppose that the educators of this country were granted a free hand to reeducate the children along the lines just mentioned. Don't you think they could "turn the trick"?

Suppose that instead of having the American Legion and Hirschfield[67] trying to have new history books written that shall make the US out to be lily-white in its actions in the past or that shall make national heroes out of the kind of leaders Fall and Daugherty[68] have proven themselves to be, suppose that in its stead we were to have our children taught the unvarnished truth of our past. Suppose that in place of making our children study the lives and sayings of our soldier heroes they be taught that war thrives on prejudice, misunderstandings and half-truths. Don't you think they would grow up to hate the idea of war and all the horrible things it implies?

Suppose that in place of learning our national virtues *only* so that our country is made to appear as the paragon of all homelands and the salute to the flag as it is now taught which results in a readiness to rise, follow and fight whenever any administration sounds the alarm. Suppose instead of this we teach a new kind of patriotism, suppose we salute the flag because of the use made of the Boxer indemnity fund,[69] the unfortified Canadian boundary, the tasks of world-helpfulness and world peace that are still ahead of us. Will that kind of patriotism make for war? I think not.

---

[67] David Hirschfield, New York City Commissioner of Accounts, published a report stating that recently revised history books used in the New York City public schools were part of a conspiracy on the part of Great Britain to recover her American colonies. Information taken from the article "Pure History and Patriotism" by Albert Kerr Heckel PhD, Dean of Men, University of Missouri, which appeared in *The Historical Outlook, A Journal for Readers and Teachers of History and the Social Studies*, Philadelphia, March 1925.

[68] Harry M. Daugherty, Attorney General during Warren G. Harding's presidency and Albert Fall, Secretary of the Interior, were both members of the "Ohio Gang" and were indicted for corruption after President Harding's death in 1923.

[69] At the end of the Boxer Rebellion in China, 1899, the Chinese government was forced to pay indemnity money to the eight North American and European nations who crushed the rebellion. When this led to a Chinese boycott of American goods, Theodore Roosevelt proposed to use the funds to educate Chinese nationals in the United States. The program began in 1908.

[The following is a handwritten addendum to the typed sermon and may have been the actual ending.]

Today State and Church [are separated]. Unfortunate yet in many respects fortunate. The Synagogue has not yet given up its right to criticize conditions since the State is purely materialistically governed. It is our duty to study these facts here to do all in our power through our vote and our influence to teach the true state of affairs.

If we succeed in doing so we all, like Wilson's parents, succeed in giving the world at least a few prophets of peace who, even if their own generation stone them will, as I am sure will be the case with Wilson, from their graves lead the forces of good-will to victory.

response from
Jonathan Sarna

Rabbi Signer,

You, like many Jews of your day, admired Woodrow Wilson. You felt particularly inspired by his pacifism. Following his passing, you described him here as a "prophet of peace." You judged him a visionary who looked to abolish war and establish "justice between man and man, fairness between nation and nation."

History has not been kind to this view of Woodrow Wilson, Rabbi Signer. Many argue today that Wilson's pacifism, eloquent as it was, paved the way for World War II. You were not alone, of course, in extolling Wilson in World War I's wake. "Idealism, cynicism and disengagement were understandable responses to World War I," a standard work by Hal Brands and Charles Edel[70] concedes. "All, unfortunately, did more to weaken than fortify the constraints on future aggression." Tragically and in ways you could not have predicted, the liberal anti-war sentiments that Wilson, you, and so many others espoused in the 1920s were exploited a decade later by Adolf Hitler. Secure in the knowledge that many in America and Europe opposed *all* war as futile and useless, he invaded his neighbors. The United States and its allies could not muster the will to stop him until millions already lay dead.

Rabbi Signer, history has looked even less kindly upon your view of Wilson as "worthy to be counted among the righteous men of the world." Really? Today we are more apt to view him as the most racially insensitive of our 20th-century presidents. He was a child of the Deep South, raised in Georgia and South Carolina, and he absorbed the prejudices of his surroundings. He staunchly defended segregation. He espoused racism, characterizing Blacks as "an ignorant and inferior race." He sought to disenfranchise Black Americans, calling them "unfitted by education for the most usual and constant duties of citizenship." As President, he dismissed as many Blacks as he could from government service. His policies reversed advances made by African Americans after the Civil War, and strengthened the hands of their White oppressors.

Admittedly, Woodrow Wilson was good to the Jews. He endorsed the Balfour Declaration that viewed with favor "the establishment in Palestine of a national home for the Jewish people." While modern scholars doubt that he was "in large measure responsible" for the declaration, as you contend, it would never have happened without him. He also nominated the first Jew ever to sit on the US Supreme

---

[70] Hal Brands and Charles Edel, *The Lessons of Tragedy: Statecraft and the World*, 1st edition (New Haven, Connecticut: Yale University Press, February 26, 2019).

Court, Louis Brandeis. He continued to back him in the face of widespread opposition from prominent businessmen and lawyers, and succeeded in pushing his nomination through the Senate. In addition, Wilson repeatedly vetoed restrictive immigration legislation, thereby enabling hundreds of thousands of Jews to enter the United States. He also personally befriended a slew of notable Jews, including Bernard Baruch, Samuel Untermeyer and Rabbi Stephen Wise. "Perhaps more than any other president," scholars David G. Dalin and Alfred Kolatch conclude, "Woodrow Wilson had the utmost respect and admiration for the Jewish people."[71] Your sense that he took "special interest in the life of Israel," was correct.

I suspect that you would have found it disconcerting to learn that Wilson was, at one and the same time, so bad for American Blacks and so good for American Jews. Rabbis of your day usually heralded "perfect" heroes and role models, not those sullied by great sin. They feared that complex figures like Woodrow Wilson, so easy to valorize and to demonize, would promote discord and confusion.

Realistically, though, flawed heroes like Wilson have much more to teach us than the impossibly "righteous" Wilson you described. Flawed heroes, Rabbi Signer, are human beings we can relate to: complex figures who combine good and bad elements; visionaries with blind spots. They remind us that good people can do very bad things—and vice versa.

Jewish history is actually replete with flawed heroes, dating all the way back to the biblical patriarch Jacob, who deceived his father, stole his brother's birthright, and played favorites among his children. Perfect heroes, for obvious reasons, have been few and far between. Indeed, the more closely we probe, the more flaws even the greatest of our heroes inevitably display. Such was the case, Rabbi Signer, with Woodrow Wilson.

It is easy to kick flawed heroes off their pedestals, deface their images, and bury old sermons extolling their memories. But perhaps, keeping in mind your own treatment of Woodrow Wilson, it would be better to learn from once-praised heroes' disappointing shortcomings. Probing their flaws more deeply may invite us to think harder about our own.

Jonathan D. Sarna is University Professor and Joseph H. & Belle R. Braun Professor of American Jewish History at Brandeis University. He also chairs the Academic Advisory and Editorial Board of the Jacob Rader Marcus Center of the American Jewish Archives in Cincinnati, and serves as Chief Historian of the National Museum of American Jewish History in Philadelphia.

---

[71] David G. Dalin and Alfred Kolatch, *The Presidents of the United States & the Jews*, 1st edition (Middle Village, NY: Jonathan David Publishers, 2000), p. 133.

Jonathan Sarna

He is the author or editor of more than thirty books on American Jewish history and life. His most recent books include Coming to Terms with America *(JPS, 2021); his annotated edition of Cora Wilburn's previously unknown 1860 novel,* Cosella Wayne *(University of Alabama Press, 2019); (with Benjamin Shapell)* Lincoln and the Jews: A History *(St. Martin's, 2015); and* When General Grant Expelled the Jews *(Schocken/Nextbook, 2012).*

Dr. Sarna is married to Professor Ruth Langer and they have two married children and three grandchildren.

Jews, History and Return to Israel

Science And Faith: What Effect Has Science Upon a Belief in God?

Delivered in Bethlehem, Pennsylvania at Brith Shalom Community Center, December 12, 1926, for Parshat Vayigash and in Manhattan Beach, New York at Temple Beth El, December 30, 1927, for Parshat Vayigash

Dramatic story of Joseph leading up to the climax: ועתה לא אתם שלחתם אותי הנה כי האלהים, וישמני לאב לפרעה ולאדון לכל ביתו, ומושל בכל ארץ מצרים ("So, it was not you who sent me here, but God; and He has made me a father to Pharoah, lord of all his household and ruler over the whole land of Egypt"—Genesis 45:8). [It] Opens up the interesting question of belief in God. What did the ancients believe? What do we believe? Do we differ from them and how? [According to the] Ancient point of view: God is EXTERNAL. The physical world is so constituted that everything in it is in some way calculated to benefit man, and is a means to his spiritual growth. All living creatures of earth air and sea are regarded as contributing to his well-being: את הכל עשה יפה בעתו—["He brings everything to pass precisely in its time"—Ecclesiastes 3:11] "Nothing of what God created in his world is in vain."

Furthermore God was believed as manifesting Himself in the external world through the prosperity and peace with which virtue and piety were rewarded. Whatever natural calamities befell man, such as earthquakes, pestilence, famine and wars, were regarded as punishment for sin. Thus, everything that happened was in fulfillment of justice. If, now and then, there seemed to be an exception to that law, there was always some way found to explain away the incongruity. If the wicked prospered, it was in order that they might be punished the more in the hereafter.

With the rise of science and the scientific outlook on life another point of view took shape and supplanted the first. I refer particularly to the evolutionary theory. [It] Took away the emphasis laid on man and his place in the scheme of the universe. [It] Resulted in confusion in some minds. The effect has been to give rise to a different conception of God. The evolutionary theory has by no means taken away the belief or faith in God. It has merely turned our search for God from the physical world about us to the soul within us. It has emphasized the truth that it is only as we come to recognize God's immanence within man that religion can influence man's actions in the proper way.

As a matter of fact it didn't require the evolutionary theory to bring this truth home. The Jew in time of old began to recognise the indifference of nature to human needs, desires and wishes, and so he looked about for the manifestation of God in human life rather than in the world about him. They felt that even if man is not the purpose of the whole of creation the fact remains that within man himself there burns the desire to give purpose to his own life, to find a goal for the struggles of the race and feel that his own efforts contribute to the accomplishment of some faraway end which redeems even the most obscure life from futility.

Furthermore the belief in God as immanent implies that while we cannot regard nature as conforming in its phenomena to what we understand by justice, there nevertheless is a passion for justice in every normal human being, a restless urge to suppress violence and to establish righteousness. These promptings to live a life of purpose and to establish justice should satisfy us that this world is not a thing of blind chance, but that there is an order and plan of some kind, though we happen to be too insignificant to grasp it.

In Judaism this directing of the search for God within man gave rise to the conception of the *Shekinah*. The belief in the *Shekinah* is the belief in God dwelling within Israel, or as showing Himself through those things which happened during Israel's career. In order for God to show Himself completely, Israel, or the Jewish people, had to be in a position to give full play to its spiritual powers. This was conceived as possible only so long as Israel was in its own land. But what of Israel in the *Goluth* [in Exile]?

The answer is implied in the words of encouragement uttered by God to Jacob:
אל תירא מרדה מצרימה כי לגוי גדול אֲשִׂימְךָ שם. אנכי אֵרֵד עמְּךָ מצרימה ואנכי אַעַלְךָ גם עלה
"Fear not to go down into Egypt, for I will make of thee a great nation. I will go down with thee into Egypt, and I will surely bring thee up again" (Genesis 46:3-4). This, say the Rabbis, implies that wherever Israel might happen to be in the course of its wanderings, the *Shekinah* would always be with them.

The world needed us badly at one time when we were ready to give to a waiting world the idea of God. The world today does not need, however, our philosophy or our science to demonstrate the reality or the existence of GOD. But the world does need us today even as it needs every people or every person who is dominated by a sense of purpose in its life and by an urge, an impelling urge for justice; the world certainly needs every person or people that earnestly feel they have something to live for. If they are bending their every energy upon living a life of purpose and justice, in other words, the righteous life, they are demonstrating by their lives the reality of God.

During the long dark days and nights of the Middle Ages as we Jews looked forward to the time of the restoration of our people to Zion, as we gave expression to that thought in our prayers and sighs and in our conversation, we were animated by a sense of purpose. We felt that we were not living and suffering in vain. We were certain that somehow, some time our claim would be vindicated and that we would again be able to be of service to mankind. In this manner were we witnesses of God throughout the many centuries of persecution.

But if we are to surrender our hope for the restoration of Israel, the feeling of purposelessness and futility in attempting to live as a distinct people is bound to chill our hearts. With no creative task to look forward to, we are bound to feel that there is nothing for us to live [for] as Jews. Thus, instead of demonstrating the reality of God in the world, we become a living denial of God's existence.

Or take the other evidence which we have of the existence of God in the world, namely the urge for justice. Throughout their existence until recently the Jews had occasion to give expression to that urge in some form or other. If it was not as a people in their own land that the Jews demonstrated justice, they did so in lesser and smaller communities throughout the *Goluth*. The Jewish system of justice, the Jewish judges, and above all the unwritten law of fair dealing that was so completely characteristic of Jewish life hitherto, they were all concrete expressions of the sense of justice which points to the existence of the Divine in the world. If that sense of justice is not to have an outlet, if it is not to have its expression in a Jewish Homeland, it is bound to run to seed and spoil by expressing itself in the unregulated and wild protest against the *status quo*. The prevalence of radicalism among Jews is due to the fact that Jews have not the opportunity to give expression to the sense of justice in a normal way, that is, through their own communal life.

If it is our plan to play a part in the spiritual life of the world about us, if we mean to remain a force regulating mankind which shall in any way approach the part played by our people in the past, then we must foster and develop the inherent, basic, underlying sense of purpose and the urge for justice. This, in large measure, can be accomplished here, but it can reach its highest development only in Palestine, for it is only there that Jews can hope to have the opportunity of exercising their creative powers as a people. Only then can Jewry the world over begin to feel that they are not living their life as a people in vain. And it is only in Palestine that Jews can expect those manifold and countless opportunities which come with a commonwealth and a government and a land to demonstrate to the world and to themselves their inherent underlying passion for righteousness.

And thus too may the *Shekinah*, which has ever been with us in the *Goluth*, return with us to the land where it first revealed itself.

"Faith is the pencil of the soul
That pictures heavenly things."⁷²

---

⁷² This quote, handwritten at the end of the sermon, is found on page 108 of *Many Thoughts of Many Minds* edited by Henry Southgate, published by Charles Griffin in 1872, and attributed to "Burbridge." No other information about the editor or the putative author of the quote is available.

response from
Betsy Forester

Dear Rabbi Signer,

It was a privilege to read this sermon, and I am honored to have been invited to share a brief reflection.

You present the historical discontinuity between Science and Faith effectively. I have a feeling you sensed that some of your congregants struggled to reconcile Science and Faith. I sense that in my work, as well. Yet I also find that belief in Divine reward and retribution, and to some extent the rationalizing of apparent exceptions by means of conjecture about the hereafter, die hard. I often encounter people who yearn for those beliefs to be manifest, even as their experience argues otherwise, leading many to crises of faith.

Therefore, I appreciated your stating explicitly that our ancient sages experienced a similar conflict and endeavored to resolve it. I wish that their attempts to understand humanity's place in the cosmos and the problem of suffering were more widely known. I find that many Jews turn away from synagogue life, lacking awareness of the more convincing idea, as you aptly state, that "it is only as we come to recognize God's immanence within man that religion can influence man's actions in the proper way." Since the Holocaust, new theologies have expanded convincingly from the notion of a more internal God. It seems to me that many people are either unaware of or reluctant to explore these newer theological ideas, but they are drawn to Hasidic masters whose writings are congruent with notions of the Divine within, which can be awakened and help people to experience transcendence and unity with all of Creation. There is something that appeals to people when those ideas are expressed by Hasidim. I suspect that people sense an inviting authenticity and an ethnic connection in those Hasidic teachings that they do not find in less thickly pious writing.

I suspect that when you speak of "faith," you are referring to spiritual attunement. In the last decade, science has identified a difference between religious practices and attunement to the Divine, or "spirituality." Organized Jewish life has focused almost exclusively on the former, to the near exclusion of the latter. Conflating the two probably worked well enough for those who fervently used post-Temple rituals as replacements for the spiritual connection they imagined their forebears to have experienced through the sacrificial cult. It may also have sufficed for generations of their descendants, who kept faith in the dream of a rebuilt Temple. I wonder if you, like myself, decades ago, conflated religious experiences with soulful experiences. Did you sense that religious services in your congregation met the spiritual needs of your congregants? If so, then your sermon would have been intellectually interesting without raising troubling questions about the utility of religious ritual.

Today, many Jews feel perfectly comfortable discarding synagogue ritual in favor of spiritual practices found in other contemplative traditions, outdoor adventure, physical exercise, and the arts. Only in the past decade or so have Jewish organizational leaders and funders begun to turn serious attention to people's spiritual or "faith" needs, as distinct from ritual needs. I find this shift in attention helpful, albeit overdue and unrefined. We have much to learn about how to use faith practices in ways that feel authentic to our tradition and help people cultivate the rich inner lives they seek.

Despite a fast-growing decline in religious identification across the religious landscape, people crave identity and connection that helps them experience transcendence. In an age where personal meaning, rather than duty, drives religious behavior, I believe that our practices continue to provide a reliable scaffolding for a life of purpose and that through authentic and soul-stirring Jewish experiences, we can yet cultivate rich inner lives and be moved toward justice and compassion.

I agree with you that the Jewish People are called to make a particular type of contribution to the world through our way of life; specifically, by working for a world of justice and compassion. As religious leaders, we are called to help our congregants use the tools of religious practice to support human thriving. We tend to imagine that in ancient Israelite religion, mission and faith were intertwined more tightly than they are today. Whether or not such was the case, I have seen that praxis can inform on-mission ways of being in the world even in the absence of strong faith.

Contemporary research sketches a path toward achieving our mission, regardless of where we live and independent of the Jewish State. People will gather to experience positive emotions and to share life's difficult moments; to explore ultimate questions of purpose and meaning; to feel soulfully engaged; to matter to others and be held accountable; to strive for greatness; and to link themselves to meaningful purpose beyond themselves. We have not lost the rabbinic creativity that characterized post-exilic Judaism. What we need to recover is our courage and readiness to create the next, thriving Jewish future.

That assertion leads me to reflect briefly on the latter part of your sermon, in which you change focus from the subject of Science and Faith to your belief that Jewish sovereignty in the Land of Israel is a necessary requirement for the Divine Presence to manifest fully and for the Jewish spirit not to wither into oblivion. I do not share that tenet of your theology, but how I wish that our people's righteousness had reached its full flowering with the establishment of the modern State of Israel. Sadly, I do not find that to be the case. Today, Israel stands in violation of international law in its treatment of conquered Palestinians. The tremendous good Israel does goes largely overlooked in the face of unjust policies and practices perpetrated by the strong upon the weak. We, the strong, are off mission in our homeland, defying Torah and rabbinic law. Despite that heartbreaking reality, I pray that we will yet live out the Torah's vision that we be a light unto the nations.

May we engage our vitality in pursuit of a vision of a just and compassionate world in which the Divine Presence delights to dwell.

Rabbi Betsy Forester is a congregational rabbi who shares a dynamic, spirited, and scholarly approach to living an observant Jewish life in the Midwest. Her Torah centers on mindful practice, a passion for compassion, and an earnest desire to heal our society and our world. Prior to becoming a rabbi, she was a master teacher and Jewish educational leader for many years in the Chicago area; prior to that, she worked as a certified speech-language pathologist. Since 2018, she has served as sole clergy for Beth Israel Center, a Conservative synagogue of about 275 households.

When Evil Hastens Good

Delivered in Manhattan Beach, New York at
Temple Beth El, January 11, 1929, for *Parshat Va'erah*

Evil wastes itself, one of the wise has declared. In childhood violent tempers are very quickly spent and in society the more vicious elements arouse enemies more quickly than they can overcome foes. Somebody has written that in the history of man it has been very generally the case that when evils have grown insufferable, they have touched the point of cure.

Unchecked wrath and violent will, rushing forward under a free rein, defeat their own purposes. Joseph's brothers had no idea of creating a prime minister when they sold him to the merchants bound for Egypt but their jealousy made a prince instead of a prisoner. Pharaoh's crafty policy in putting yet heavier burdens upon the Hebrews caused him to lose them, although for a time, he may have secured more bricks. In the end, slaves, who, under a more generous servitude, might have remained with the heathen fleshpots forever, went on famine rations to discover a promised land beyond the wilderness.

Haman's wrath which erected a scaffold and planned an execution for Mordecai, hung Haman. In the Franco-Prussian War[73] one nation ground another into what she believed was permanent physical inferiority, stripped her of land and resources, executed a terrible judgment, but now we know that she was mistaken in her conclusion. She possessed certain fruits of victory for two generations but they were heavily mortgaged and foreclosure was inevitable. It will be well for other nations not to forget the lesson of Alsace-Lorraine.[74]

Human judgments are always in danger of overreaching themselves. In the long run mercy is a finer quality and more potent than wrath. As the years pass the glory of [General Ulysses] Grant at Appomattox grows upon the eyes of the world. His military triumph was complete but immeasurably less than his moral victory. In the one he defeated an army; in the other he reunited a nation. His cannon have been silent for half a century but the voice of his graciousness sounds louder today than when it first spoke.

---

[73] A war fought between France and the North German Confederation led by the Kingdom of Prussia, 1870-71.
[74] French territory given to the Germans at the end of the Franco Prussian war according to the terms of the Treaty of Frankfurt.

Does evil hasten good? Dueling was never outlawed by special organizations established to overthrow it. It shot itself to death when Burr slew Hamilton.[75] Salacious plays that just now seem to be our principle import from Paris and pestilential books, whatever anti-vice societies may accomplish, will at last smother themselves in their own lewdness. There is a homely maxim which runs as follows: Give a calf enough rope and it will choke itself. The same principle applies far beyond the barnyard.

Turnus Rufus,[76] he who plowed over the Temple Mount and was responsible for the inhuman persecutions of Jewry during the Hadrianic Wars; he who impiously declared and vaingloriously boasted that he could and would exterminate the Jews came at last to the conclusion that the Jewish will and not the Roman engines were victorious.

All of this may indicate that humankind is not the mere sport of fortune, that we are not at the mercy of the ruthless, whether these be passions within or foes without. Life is not a great game of chance, for chance is negation of purpose and purpose is but another name for God. An Unseen Hand is turning all things to a great end. Life is an ordered destiny. There does exist a self-corrective force in the Universe—a force which shows its greatest strength in times of greatest evil. No night is so dark but that a morning is in prospect. There could be no sunrise were suns never to set. Darkness merely hastens dawn.

Shakespeare, in Macbeth and Hamlet, has immortalized this truth in words and action which neither language nor setting can limit.

כי חמת אדם תּוֹדֶךָ — The wrath of man shall praise Him says the Psalmist [Ps. 76:11].

It is a sublime text. Somewhere I have read that the musician's harp comes from the warrior's bow.[77] We do not always live to see great principles vindicated for man is a creature of generations, while truth is an eternity. History, which gives to thought an existence immeasurably greater than the span of one life-time, teaches us that in its most unchecked excesses, man's wrath works toward the ultimate purpose of the self-corrective forces of life.

Of this the supreme example perhaps is Judaism and the Jew. Man's wrath laid the blame for all catastrophes at Israel's door. Persecution, self-immolation, *auto-da-fé*, expulsion, forced conversion, civil disability, pogrom made an ever-recurring

---

[75] The duel was fought in 1804 between political and personal rivals Vice President Aaron Burr and former Secretary of the Treasury Alexander Hamilton. Hamilton was shot during the duel and subsequently died.

[76] Quintus Tineius Rufus (circa 90-131 CE), Roman provincial governor, who failed in his attempt to subjugate Judea during the Bar Kochba rebellion.

[77] This comparison is found in the *Odyssey*.

hecatomb to the gods of envy, hatred and greed. From those awful days of 70[78] until now, man's most terrible doings have had their share in setting in motion and keeping steadfast the Jew's devotion to his people, his loyalty to Torah and his identification with his God.

The blood of martyrs is the seed on which Judaism flourished. Russians or Roumanians, in blind fanaticism destroy a few dozen Synagogues, desecrate a dozen cemeteries, ruin the Jewish quarters, torture some hundred men and women, drive the rest homeless from their hearths bereft of their nearest of kin—and then? An indifferent easy-going somnolent Synagogue awakes. Our people's hearts are moved. They open their purse, speed their aid and help establish the national homeland.

Thus does the self-corrective force of life operate—slowly, ponderously, lethargically—sometimes. At other times, with such rapidity that men call it a miracle. Thus does evil hasten good; thus distaste points the way to victory. Thus hardship strengthens limbs to master mountains and in ways that beggar description, because of their suffering men achieve faith in God—faith in themselves—faith which overcomes the world:

> Right forever on the scaffold
> Wrong forever on the throne
> But the scaffold rules the future
> And behind the dim unknown,
> Standeth God beyond the shadow
> Keeping watch over His unknown[79]

Now, my friends, with the experiences which we Jews have stored up through the ages, is it not a pitiable waste of human life—a deplorable loss of possible happiness—a wanton neglect of communal well-being—to wait, as alas we do, until conditions are become so bad that they must take a turn for the better? Must Jewry wait until another holocaust break out against our brethren before we will recognize the crying need for unity within our ranks? Must we Jews wait until the Balfour Declaration[80] will be twisted out of all semblance to its original declared

---

[78] Signer is most likely referring to the destruction of the Second Temple and the exile of the Jews from Judea in 70 CE.
[79] Paraphrased from the poem "The Present Crisis" written by James Russell Lowell (1819-1891). Also see footnote 82 in Rabbi Gordon's response below.
[80] A British public statement made in 1917 by British Foreign Secretary Arthur Balfour, stating that a "national home for the Jewish people" should be created in what was then called Palestine.

purpose ere we realize that all parties, Revisionists, Mizrachists,[81] Zionists, antis and Agencies must unite to recover ground lost through our mutual bickerings? Must we of Beth El wait until we raise up—as so many of us are now doing—a generation that knows not the Lord [Judges 2:10] ere we awake to the paramount necessity of providing adequately for our children's education—in facilities and staffs of competent teachers and above all the cooperation of parents? I have a firm faith in God, that is, I have an utter trust in the self-corrective force of life. These desiderata ultimately WILL come about. But why should the sweetness of their arrival be tempered with the bitterness of the losses which will have hastened their coming? Must sorrow be the concomitant of happiness? Is it an axiom that tears precede and accompany joy? *I* don't know. I *don't* know. I hope not.

---

[81] Members of the Mizrachi, religious Zionist movement, founded in 1902.

response from
Debora Gordon

Dear Rabbi Signer,

    I've been re-reading your sermon "When Evil Hastens Good." It has grown on me until I hear a deep *Ani Ma'amin*: I believe! that echoes my own—a cry of faith and a testament to hope. And oh, do we need hope and faith at this moment.
    Some 800 years ago when Rambam wrote his 13 statements of *Ani Ma'amin*, his principles of faith, I imagine that splendid rationalist believed them literally. The most famous today, outside of traditional Jewish circles, is—

> Ani ma'amin be-emunah shleymah b'vi-at ha-mashiach;
> v'af al pi sheh-yitmah-meyah,
> im kol zeh a-chakeh lo b'chol yom sheh-yavo.
> I believe with perfect faith in the coming of the Messiah;
> and although he tarries,
> despite this, I await his coming every day.
>   (my translation)

Given your *milieu* and this sermon, I can make some guesses concerning your beliefs about the idea of messiah. You were a contemporary of my grandfather, who was ordained as a Reform Rabbi in 1933 in Cincinnati (though raised as a Conservative Jew), and like him your faith lives soundly within the bounds of reason. I think you both would say, as do I, that humans are constantly working toward a time of true peace and justice but not awaiting a man on a white horse to usher in that age. As you write, "I have a firm faith in God, that is, I have an utter trust in the self-corrective force of life." What a marvelous definition of God! I hear the same faith in the words of martyred 20th-century Black prophet Rev. Dr. Martin Luther King, Jr.: "We shall overcome because the moral arc of the universe is long but it bends toward justice."[82]

---

[82] Dr. Martin Luther King, Jr., "Remaining Awake Through a Great Revolution." Speech given at the National Cathedral, March 31, 1968. When an excerpt was read at this year's interfaith MLK commemoration in Troy, NY, I learned that a few lines later Dr. King also quoted the 1845 poem that appears toward the end of Rabbi Signer's sermon! Dr. King wrote:
    "We shall overcome because James Russell Lowell is right—as we were singing earlier today,
        Truth forever on the scaffold,

But this begs the question of whether "An Unseen Hand is turning all things to a great end" because "Life is not a great game of chance for chance is negation of purpose and purpose is but another name for God;" or whether, to quote former Attorney General Eric Holder, "the arc bends toward justice, but it only bends toward justice because people pull it toward justice. It doesn't happen on its own."[83]

I think one can believe both: That positive change only happens because human beings work and struggle for it, but in the vast statistical universe of human existence, this struggle always occurs. Ultimately, people will not put up with what harms us. In addition, an increasing body of research tells us that compassion is instinctual.[84] So in a very long view, one can have faith that movement toward the greater Good is built into us.

I hear this faith reflected powerfully in the words of your older contemporary, poet Shaul Tchernichovsky, in his 1892 poem also titled *Ani Ma'amin*:

> Laugh,[85] laugh at the dreams,
> As I the dreamer laugh.
> Laugh, because I believe in humanity,
> because I still believe in you....
> > Humanity's spirit will cast off ephemeral chains,
> > Raising itself to heights:
> > Workers will not die of hunger;
> > Freedom for the soul, bread for poor people....
> I also believe in the future:
> Even if that day is far away,
> It will come—then peace will carry

> Wrong forever on the throne.
> Yet that scaffold sways the future.
> And behind the dim unknown stands God,
> Within the shadow keeping watch above his own."

In 2022 I can quickly look up origins and compare versions, but in 1929, if Rabbi Signer didn't know the source of the quote, he could only repeat it as he remembered it, perhaps popularized by the Christian hymn "Once to Every Man and Nation."
  https://seemeonline.com/history/mlk-jr-awake.htm
  https://en.wikipedia.org/wiki/The_Present_Crisis
  https://hymnary.org/text/once_to_every_man_and_nation.

[83] https://www.wnycstudios.org/podcasts/the-stakes/episodes/the-stakes-pulling-arc-justice-eric-holder.

[84] See, e.g., *Psychology Today*, "Compassion: Our First Instinct." https://www.psychologytoday.com/us/blog/feeling-it/201306/compassion-our-first-instinct.

[85] Some contemporary translations suggest "Rejoice" instead of "Laugh"! Quite a different reading!

blessing from nation to nation...
        (my translation)

I too believe in the future. So my question, as yours, is not *whether* things will get better again, but *when*, and *how much* suffering will occur first. With you, I ask:

> Is it not a pitiable waste of human life—a deplorable loss of possible happiness—a wanton neglect of communal well-being—to wait as alas we do until conditions are become so bad that they must take a turn for the better? ... Must sorrow be the concomitant of happiness? Is it an axiom that tears precede and accompany joy?

You apply your questions to three issues:

> Must Jewry wait until another holocaust break[s] out against our brethren before we will recognize the crying need for unity within our ranks? Must we Jews wait until the Balfour Declaration be twisted out of all semblance to its original declared purpose ere we realize that all parties, Revisionists, Mizrachists, Zionists, antis and Agencies must unite to recover ground lost through our mutual bickerings? Must we of Beth El wait until we raise up—as so many of us are now doing—a generation that knows not the Lord ere we awake to the paramount necessity of providing adequately for our children's education—in facilities and [with] staffs of competent teachers and above all the cooperation of parents?

It's January 1929 and you are 28 years old. It's a mere ten months before the stock market crash that will usher in a worldwide depression, which in turn will contribute to the rise of dictator Adolph Hitler in Germany and the mass murder of European Jewry from 1939-1945—now commonly referred to as the Holocaust. That's all in your future. To what past holocaust were you referring? Perhaps the terrible anti-Jewish pogroms in Eastern Europe which were carried out again and again during your childhood and teen years. Would Jewish unity have prevented that? Could it have prevented the coming Holocaust? Your concern about the British government walking back the 1917 Balfour Declaration was eerily prescient;

not until after the aforementioned Holocaust was the modern country of Israel established (and without, I am sorry to say, a country of Palestine as its neighbor).

I write at a moment when systemic injustice (the unequal distribution of privilege, opportunity, and oppression purposefully "baked in" to our sociocultural, political, financial, etc. systems) is being named and brought to the foreground, so I must also ask: *Who* will suffer most? While antisemitism is a growing threat, the most glaring injustice in the United States today is racism. Limiting our unity to the borders of the Jewish community not only cuts off allies in the struggle toward justice, it makes no sense when an increasing proportion of American Jews (including some of my children) are People of Color. If we intend to "bend the arc,"[86] unity must mean working in coalition with *all* people who are facing oppression and injustice.

In January 2022 we are also two years into a global pandemic, with no certain end in sight. Even those of us with plenty of resources are exhausted and dispirited. But as you say, Jews have stored up experiences through the ages that help us affirm that darkness is followed by light. I routinely think about 3,000 years of Jewish history; it's not a stretch to remember that our "pre-pandemic normal" was *your* "post-pandemic." There will be "normal life" again.

But currently the United States, comprising less than 5% of humanity, accounts for nearly 20% of cases and perhaps 15% of deaths worldwide—over 800,000 Americans dead. How, you may well ask, could such an advanced country so spectacularly fail to protect its inhabitants?

Our inability to unite in the face of this terrible pandemic is symptomatic of dark and destructive forces within our country. Individuals and groups are being targeted with information, misinformation and disinformation in ways so powerful that we have come to disagree about what is fact. Additionally,

> "the most passionate differences ringing through American history are now organized directly into the parties. For the first time, all the so-called minorities are on one side." Black Americans, immigrants and liberal women are crowded into the Democratic Party, while white [Christian] Americans are more likely to be Republican. And so a debate about health care policy or how to resolve inequality easily devolves into irreconcilable conflict. "Both parties are deeply enmeshed in feelings

---

[86] Bend The Arc is "a movement of progressive Jews across the country who are fighting for justice and equality for all." https://www.bendthearc.us/.

about identity because each draws people who see themselves as fundamentally different from those on the other side."[87]

This quotation is from the review of a recent book, *Republic of Wrath: How American Politics Turned Tribal, From George Washington to Donald Trump.* Its title resonates with your sermon text, "The wrath of man shall praise Him,"[88] which you expound to mean that "in its most unchecked excesses, man's wrath works toward the ultimate purpose of the self-corrective forces of life."

Halevai that the wrath of today will be a way station to a better tomorrow! Indeed, if I look closely at your text, I see that the word translated in the 1917 Jewish Publication Society text as "wrath"—*chamah*—comes from the same root as "heat" and "sun." So I might translate *chamah* as "passion:" the anger provoked when injustice is brought into the sunlight, the fiery response that moves us to take a stand and make a difference. Let it refer to the fierce compassion that insists that every human being is created *b'tselem Elohim*, in the divine image, and is therefore worth listening to and trying to understand. These passionate energies, generated in response to evil, can <u>indeed</u> hasten the good.

Rabbi Debora S. Gordon is the second-longest-serving rabbi of Congregation Berith Sholom in Troy, New York, a small, warm, diverse, tikkun olam-oriented congregation. It has been a rare privilege to partner for nearly three decades with this 158-year-old community. For ten of those years, her "other congregation" of dairy goats taught her practical lessons about the lives of our pastoralist ancestors.

Reb Deb's rabbinate is filled with family legacies: music, history, love of Hebrew, the ruach (spirit) of Jewish summer camp, and a deep commitment to justice and ethical behavior. Her wife Judy Wienman has loved and challenged Reb Deb to become the rabbi and person she's still trying to be. Together they have raised four children adopted through foster care.

Micah 6:8 declares the values Reb Deb holds dearest: "Do justice, love tenderly, and take up the right amount of space in the world."

---

[87] Jia Lynn Yang, "Are We More Divided Now Than Ever Before?", *New York Times* book review, quoting author James A. Morone. https://www.nytimes.com/2020/09/08/books/review/republic-of-wrath-james-a-morone.html?smid=url-share.

[88] Psalm 76:11. Another translation: "The fiercest of people shall acknowledge you"—and naturally, [in the footnote of the New JPS Translation] "meaning of Heb. uncertain."

Seeing Judaism Whole

Delivered in Manhattan Beach, New York at
Temple Beth El, January 11, 1930, for *Parshat Vayigash*

The prophecy contained in the chapter of the Bible we have just heard[89] was preached by Ezekiel to the Jews in Babylonia. At that time the ten tribes had been exiled for at least 125 years and the two tribes on the other side of the Jordan had for even a longer period forsaken the beliefs and teachings of their people. Those that remained Jewish in Babylonia, even many of the tribe of Judah who had but recently come, hung on to Judaism by the merest thread. The general belief was that as long as there would be a שאר ישוב—a remnant steadfast to the faith, salvation could be looked for in them. From this point of view Ezekiel radically differed, by insisting that it would be impossible for Israel ever to attain its spiritual goal so long as only a *part* of Israel remained Jewish. He regarded it as essential that all those who still had the faintest spark of Jewishness left within them must be reckoned with as part of the future Israel. Even with regard to those who cut themselves off from the main stem of Jewish life—so long as they were still thinking of themselves as Jews, they had to be included in all plans affecting the Jewish people.

In this aspiration, the prophet first voiced the thought which animated the Sages much later and which gave rise to a beautiful Midrash [*Talmud B'rachot* 6a]. One of the Rabbis raised the following question: What is written in the *Tefillin* [phylacteries] which the Holy One Blessed Be He wears? He was told: מי כעמך ישראל גוי אחד בארץ—"Who is like Thy people Israel a nation ONE in the earth."[90]

—Does God then take time to rejoice over Israel?

—Yes, for it is written: "This day you have avowed the Lord to be your God, and this day the Lord has avowed YOU to be His own people" [Deuteronomy 26:17-18]. God said, "You have refused to treat any part of my world as complete by discovering My completeness in saying: שמע י׳ [Shema Yisrael].[91] I, too, as a reward, will think of you only in terms of completeness, as it is written: 'And

---

[89] Ezekiel 37:15-28, the *Haftarah*, or prophetic reading, following the weekly reading from the first five books of the Bible. Signer's sermon was most likely given immediately after the *Haftarah* was chanted.

[90] Quote from I Chronicles 17:21, also included in the *Tahanun*—the supplication prayer—recited on some days during the morning service.

[91] שמע ישראל ה׳ אלהינו ה׳ אחד—Hear O Israel, "Adonai" is our God, "Adonai" is One. Deuteronomy 6:4. One of the central declarations of belief in God in Jewish liturgy.

who is like Thy people Israel a nation *one* in the earth.' Even the unity of God is a reflection and personification of the ideal, namely, the UNITY of Israel."

Both these passages, the prophetic and the Rabbinic, have usually been taken to refer to the physical unity of Israel. And the theory has been that only when Israel will be, organically or politically, united as one people—only *then* will salvation come. Even if we subscribed to this belief, it is very doubtful and wholly in the realm of speculation as to whether such an ideal can ever be attained. We are rather inclined to interpret these passages into a more correct generalization—one which is within the bounds of realization. And we would therefore say that both prophet and sage voice in these aspirations the central truth about Judaism, *viz*, that the success of Judaism depends, and the maintenance of Judaism hinges, and the continuation of Judaism will be assured, not so much upon whether all Jews will ever be physically united into one organism, to think alike, and believe alike, and work even for the rebuilding of Zion in the self-same manner but rather that the success of Judaism, the reclamation of all Israel depends upon the idea that no PART of Jewish life must play the role of being a WHOLE. The continuation of Jewish life is endangered by the evil of fragmentation, that is, the tendency of any one phase or aspect of Jewish life assuming to constitute itself the whole of Judaism. Fragmentary Judaism, partitive Judaism, spells the death-knell of Judaism.

The tendency of taking a part of a fragment of life and considering it as the whole of life is a tendency affecting everybody about us. It is in the air and everybody breathes its spirit. It is due to the complexity of life in general today. There are so many distracting interests, so many preoccupations, so many claims made upon our attention, so many demands made upon our activity, that inevitably some one phase of life or activity appeals to us to the exclusion of the others and each one of us comes to feel that that is the whole of life. To cite but one instance which will make our point clear: This is the great age of specialization, let us say, in medicine. The family physician or general practitioner is rapidly becoming a thing of the past. Specialists have grown up in every branch. That doubtless is a great advantage to the human race since such specialization leads to the preservation of human life on a scale never before attained. But there are two kinds of specialists—the little and the big. The little specialist sees only his own specialty to the exclusion of the rest of the body, while the big specialist looks at his own branch, ALWAYS keeping in mind its relation to the whole body. Thus correctly have I been informed by a dentist that most dentists ruin the teeth by thinking only in terms of teeth, by not taking into consideration the rest of the human frame. Thus too with life, we can't see the forest because of the trees. We become like a camera faultily focused on the landscape so that that which is immediately in front of us becomes foreshortened and our whole picture is out of focus, spoilt, fit only for the trash-basket.

With Jewish life the same tendency prevails. With the growing complexity of Jewish life all about us, the majority of Jews take up one special phase of Judaism and treat it as though it were the whole of Judaism. In this way do we work incalculable harm on Judaism, for it embraces not only one part of life or a fragment of life and its interests; but Judaism is the whole of life, Judaism is our civilization.

WE ARE very much like the blind men of the fable[d] (elephant).[92] In a similar Fashion are we blinded today by following the tendency of cheating the nature of Judaism by isolating one element to the exclusion of all and emphasizing it beyond all proportion. Sometimes this tendency is done maliciously or it may have immediate results which are ruinous to the body of Jewish life and which are readily noticeable. The *first* evil feature of this tendency is discernable in the tendency to treat the past as all-important. Little thought is given to the present other than to contrast it with די אלתע צייטען ["the olden times"—Yiddish] and to glorify the past. Thus, e.g., we have a multitude of Jews who believe that in Judaism only CONDUCT counts. It makes no difference what you believe. There is no need felt of squaring their actions with their beliefs, but it is merely a blind worship of the past. That is bad, since in overemphasizing the past, with present-day needs, or point of view or beliefs neglected and the future not reckoned with, we have the main reason for Jews escaping Judaism. Such over-emphasis makes for pseudo-intellectualism which is the defense mechanism employed by those who would overemphasize the present as a protest against overemphasizing the past. Then there is that vicious worship of the past which is known as SENTIMENTALISM—that gushing over the past, which is noticeable where, e.g., people come to the Temple to attend a service once a year on *Yom Kippur* [Day of Atonement]. Then they would for one day become Jews exactly like their fathers were before them. They would divorce themselves from the life they live and put themselves in the same attitude of mind of their fathers from שניפישאך[93] and you hear them gushing over the way their parents *"davened"* [prayed] or how this or that *Baal Tefillah* chanted the *Kol Nidre*, or *Unsaneh Tokef* or הנני [*Hineni*].[94] They witness

---

[92] A famous fable where a number of blind people discover an elephant using their sense of touch and come to very different conclusions about what the elephant must look like, since each is exploring a different part of the animal.

[93] It is unclear what Signer intended with this Hebrew word. Presumably it was the name of a Jewish village in Europe, or a name he made up to represent a location in the "Old Country."

[94] A *Baal Tefillah* is the prayer leader, or Cantor, who was known to chant the High Holiday prayers in an oratorical style. *Kol Nidre*: introductory prayer of the Day of Atonement service;

the service in the Temple and declare: עס האט ניט דעם זעלבעם טעם ["it doesn't have the same taste"—Yiddish] and they gush over the past. I've no objection if these same people would be loyal to the same Judaism the rest of the year which they avow a liking for on *Yom Kippur*; if they would be consistent in their beliefs as at least their fathers were before them; but that attitude of overemphasizing the past one day a year and wanting the Synagogue to cater to it is pernicious and vicious and un-Jewish. The same viciousness is evident in the emotional Jews, in the *"z'miros"* [song-singing] Judaism, such as our Young Israel Synagogues indulge in. They exorcize the past by singing *"z'miros"* and magnify its importance in our modern Jewish life. Likewise the lack of the right perspective is vicious. It is the tendency exhibited in a case such as this one:

> Nathanson's coming to the beach.[95]
> Child whom I asked why not attend Hebrew School.
> "I live in Sheepshead Bay."
> "Do you go to the Hebrew School there?"
> "No."
> "Then why not come here? your friends here etc."
> "'If I don't go to my own why should I go to yours?"

These tendencies to treat the past as all-important and the lack of the right perspective are vicious and pernicious. But the same tendency of taking a part of Judaism and considering that as the whole of Judaism is also evident in our other activities. Although they are done with the best of intentions, they fall short of their purpose and accomplish as much harm to Judaism as they do good.

Take the practice of Jewish ceremonies. For example, a great many Jews take hold of this practice of ceremonies and think that that is all-important in Judaism. [They pray] ותחזינה עינינו "And may our eyes behold Thy return to Judaism." They are called up to the Torah—*daven* [pray] the Torah—Read ואלה המשפטים ["these are the laws"][96] but don't relate it to life. Live that as a part by itself. Merely a ceremony and no more. Like the story of the man who was studying הלכות צדקה [laws of charitable giving] in the *Yeshivah*, when a poor man stept [*sic*] in to ask for charity. [The student responded] אלען די שייגעץ שטערסט מיר מיין לערנען ["all

---

Unsaneh Tokef: important prayer from the High Holiday Additional service; *Hineni*: Prayer recited before the Cantor's repetition of the Additional service.

[95] Reference is unclear, most likely a made-up place in Europe, connoting some generic Old-World location.

[96] First few words of the Biblical portion (Exodus 21) detailing civil law among people.

these pieces of filth disturb my learning"—Yiddish]. That man certainly didn't relate his ceremony of studying to Jewish life and right action.

When do the Sages say תלמוד גדול [study is great] only when שמביא לידי מעשה [when it leads to action]. We must apply our ceremonies to the whole of Jewish life, to see that ceremonies are only a means to the larger whole of life.

Or take the philanthropic Jew who contributes liberally to hospitals, and asylums and homes for the aged, etc. All very fine and estimable. But when, as so very often, philanthropy becomes the only expression of Judaism—when it becomes the formula for being a Jew then it defeats its own purpose. There are homes where children never hear anything Jewish except when they hear of a Federation drive or the slums of the East Side and the efforts made to alleviate their lot. Gives them the picture of Judaism outside of their own home as beggary. Now what conception of Judaism can people have, when all that Judaism means to them is NEED and APPEALS. (And this isn't the only distorted view of Judaism which philanthropic Jews have.) What conception can they have of Judaism when all they hear discussed is the abnormal, the maladjusted, the delinquent, diseased, uncommon, exceptional, the halt, lame and blind. Judaism is distorted when EDUCATION is ruled out—when the Jewish Education Association has to be organized to make *Shabbos* for itself, to replace and fill the need which the Federation has left out? Waste of energy and money. Danger of becoming provincial: Philanthropy saw only the poor of America. Result: Only Jews in America count. Then came the [First World] war and Jews realized that other Jews all over the world needed help. By taking in all of Jewry the charity of our philanthropists has become of great value, because there is the possibility of joining with others in giving and in receiving. It took the war and the breakdown of provincialism to bring about closer contact with other Jews all over the world. It took the war ultimately to bring about the Jewish Agency[97]—that which no amount of discussion and argument could accomplish before.

Or take all forms of ETHICAL IDEALISM. People say that ethics, moral behavior, is the key-note of Judaism. And *that* they will practice and believe in. Speak to a man and ask him to join you in a Jewish movement for doing some good and he says: "I'm a good Jew at heart." That statement is as un-Jewish as is the attitude of the expatriate American. People say: "I don't believe in organizations. I believe in doing good," and use that as an excuse for not joining Jewish movements. The

---

[97] The Jewish Agency for Israel was established in 1929 with a mission to "ensure that every Jewish person feels an unbreakable bond to one another and to Israel no matter where they live in the world, so that they can continue to play their critical role in our ongoing Jewish story."

result is that they may be doing good to everybody except their own people. The Ethical Culture Movement is an example of what we mean by a part of Judaism breaking away. People subscribe to the Ethical Culture Society because of the fine Jewish sentiment and doctrine ואהבת לרעך כמוך ["You shall love your neighbor as yourself"] which Dr. Adler[98] translates into the principle: So live as to elicit the best in your neighbor. But this doctrine, which is only part of a larger whole, has driven Dr. Adler away from Judaism until he doesn't even care for a Jew. He is loyal to everybody and everything except his own people and his own past.

There is a larger principle of which "live as to elicit the best in your neighbor" is only a part and the larger principle is this: So live that in each part of your life the inspiration of some greater totality functions as the guiding force and the motive power.

Or lastly, take NATIONALISM. [There may be a] Jew who says: "I'm a nationalist. I believe in Palestine and I want Palestine to be a political country just as Mexico is. I want the Jews to be in the majority in Palestine and to regulate and be in full control of the country. This is the sum total of Judaism." The one who subscribes to this belief is again committing the same error of having a part of Judaism and Jewish life monopolize the whole of Jewish life and attempting to become a totality by itself. It is the wrong kind of nationalism. It leads to chauvinism, false, unreasonable, exaggerated patriotism with all its evils of hatred and suspicion, bitterness and intrigue. It leads to the development of those very qualities which in America led to restrictive immigration, to the policy of isolation, to self-centered flag-waving and even to prohibition. If we persist in such a nationalism we will be flying in the face of the very doctrines of liberty and minority rights and the practise of justice for which Jews always have been *ready* and *willing* to lay down their lives and in which movements Jews have always been identified in large numbers. Dr. Magnes,[99] despite the criticism which is being levelled upon him from all sides, correctly sees nationalism in its right perspective when he says that provided the League of Nations guarantee to the Jews three cardinal rights, in other words, that regardless of what government Palestine will have, the questions of the right of immigration, land settlement, of the Jews and the official status of the Hebrew language shall never be left to any legislative interference by any local government, then the sooner we think of Palestine as a possible home for the Hebrew and Arab civilizations and cultures, like Canada or Switzerland are, the truer will we be to the doctrines and teachings of Judaism, for nationalism,

---

[98] Felix Adler (1851-1933), founder of the Ethical Culture Movement.
[99] Judah Leon Magnes (1877-1948), a reform Rabbi who was known for advocating a binational Jewish-Arab state in Palestine.

sacred as it undoubtedly is, must nonetheless be seen in its true perspective. It is only a part of which Judaism is the whole. This attitude is not new by any means, despite the prominence it has now achieved. It is the teaching and platform of the society called Brith Sholom,[100] which has been consistently ignored.

Now, my friends, don't mistake what we have just heard for the last 20 minutes. We are not now advocating, by any means, that the salvation of Judaism will come about only when all Jews will be united and unified. We are not arguing or advocating at this time uniting the various parties of Judaism. That is well-nigh impossible. It may not be desirable. Nor do we mean that the success of Judaism and the Jewish life will not come about until all of us become dilettantes—dabbling a little in everything and being superficial about all Jewish interests. We *must* have specialization, if only because all branches of Jewish interest do not appeal with equal force to all men alike. It's desirable to have our interests diversified. It makes for a broader, deeper, sounder Judaism. But with the modern tendency towards human complexity and the subdividing of human interests we must become conscious that that which we are interested in is like the arc of a circle, that *ceremonies*, or *philosophy* or *ethical idealism* or *nationalism* or any other activity which claims our attention and calls forth our devotion are each an arc of the larger circle of Judaism, and that we must ever maintain the bent, the curvature of that arc. In everything which claims our interest and arouses our activity we must be careful consciously not to permit any part, fragment, or arc of our life to monopolize or to become at any one time a totality by itself. Let the spirit of the whole of which it is a part prevail. This realization is what the prophet means in his symbolic act of uniting the two sticks.[101] It is the reflex of the picture given in the *Sidrah* [biblical reading], of Joseph and his Brethren united after long years of estrangement. The result is not merely a political reunion, but a spiritual regeneration. Israel united in so living that in each part of our lives, we would be governed and moved by the ever-present thought of the greater whole—Judaism.

תמים תהיה עם ה' אלהיך ["You must be wholehearted with the Lord your God" Deuteronomy 18:13].

---

[100] An organization founded in 1925 in Mandatory Palestine and active until the 1930s that advocated the founding of Israel as a peaceful Jewish-Arab joint country.

[101] Ezekiel 37:15-28: Ezekiel is commanded to take two sticks, to write "Judah" on one, and "Joseph/Ephraim" on the other and to hold them together in his hand so as to unite them. This is the Haftarah, the prophetic reading, which is paired with the weekly biblical reading (Genesis 44:18-47:27).

response from
William Kavesh

Dear Rabbi Signer,

Your observations on the nature of Jewish identification touch on areas that remain relevant for many of my contemporaries, and remind me of the timeless nature of the questions involved, especially the issue of Jewish unity which you discuss in your sermon, SEEING JUDAISM WHOLE, on *Parshat Vayigash*.

Both *Parshat Vayigash* and the *Haftarah* from the book of Ezekiel provide an apt stepping-off point for your observations. The Torah narrative describes the emotional reunion of Joseph with his family, especially his elderly father, Jacob, who travels from Canaan to Egypt, where Joseph has risen to a high position after being sold by his brothers to a caravan of traders who bring him there.

The Haftarah deals with the same issue, only on a tribal level. The Jewish people have reestablished themselves in their homeland after an extended stay as slaves in Egypt and decades of transition in the desert on their way home. Here they establish themselves as an agrarian society with a religious center in Jerusalem, the core of which is a sacrificial cult administered by priests at the Temple built by King Solomon. After many years of relative stability, the Jewish people are again uprooted by foreign invaders and have fractured into two sets of tribal units. Ezekiel, described by your Reform rabbinical contemporary, Solomon Freehof, as one of the "favorite prophets in Jewish tradition," is told by God to take two sticks, representing the fractured tribal units, and "join them in your hand as one. . . . and they shall be one in My hand. . . . I will gather them on every side and bring them into their own land."

You emphasize that Ezekiel intended this rebirth of the future Israel to extend to those who "still had the faintest spark of Judaism left within them," but you find this a problematic model. You have particular concern that "the continuation of Jewish life is endangered by the evil of fragmentation," and, in particular, with "the tendency of any one phase or aspect of Jewish life assuming to constitute itself the whole of Judaism [which] spells the "death-knell of Judaism." You bring an Aggadah from *Brachot* 6a that references sources in Torah and Chronicles emphasizing the linkage between Israel, "a nation ONE in the earth" and the ONE God affirmed by Israel. But you, at least at the beginning of your sermon, question whether such an ideal is possible, and then express your concern that Judaism has fragmented into a number of disparate parts, each of which you feel claims to "constitute the whole of Judaism," although *Brachot* 6a does not raise this concern, nor use your language of "completeness" in three translations I consulted. (According to the translation with added traditional gloss by renowned Talmudic scholar Rabbi Adin Steinsaltz, z"l, *Brachot* 6a focuses on the oneness of God and the uniqueness of Israel as "a single entity in the world...a treasured nation, chosen by God" [See Sefaria edition]. The translation in the Soncino Talmud and the Braude translation of *Sefer HaAggadah* is similar to that of Rabbi Steinsaltz. I am curious how you came to translate *Brachot* 6a the way you do.)

It is interesting to ponder your concerns about fragmentation from the perspective of the 21st century.

As a specialist in geriatric medicine, my point of departure in responding to your provocative analysis of the state of Jewish life is informed by the analogy you bring to medical specialization. Medical specialization has brought great advances to the care of complex illnesses. Unfortunately, the amount of knowledge required to keep pace with the continued developments in these fields is often vast. In the case of the elderly, the geriatrician plays the important role of integrating the inputs of various specialists, explaining the meaning to the patient, and setting out a plan of action that may need to take into account the input of multiple specialists. The geriatrician also assists the patient and family in understanding the cognitive and functional impacts of their illness, as well as the interactions between various organ systems, not just what the heart or kidney is doing in isolation. I wrote an article called "How Geriatricians Think," which you might find interesting because it identifies the problems that can arise when the patient as a whole is not considered.

I am unsure how this analogy applies to the examples you have chosen to illustrate your concern that "the continuation of Jewish life is endangered by the evil of fragmentation." You suggest that the medical specialist model applies, and that "In a similar fashion, are we blinded today by following the tendency of cheating the nature of Judaism by isolating one element to the exclusion of all and emphasizing it beyond all proportion." I find it a bit ironic that you note that "the first evil feature of this tendency is discernable in the tendency to...glorify the past...[where] only CONDUCT counts." When I think of where Judaism was moving in the late 19th and early 20th century, what comes to mind is Reform Judaism, which had precisely the opposite tendency. "Historical," now Conservative, Judaism was, in part, a reaction against Reform, which deemphasized conduct. The Conservative "Committee on Jewish Law and Standards," which was created three years before your sermon, provides guidance on proper conduct based on an integration of traditional Jewish thought and values, using literary and historical analysis where appropriate and "with care to ensure that the law embodies the highest of moral standards" (Rabbi Elliott Dorff, *United Synagogue Review*, 1998). Orthodoxy, at that time at least, was on the defensive.

Likewise, I could imagine your congregants might not respond well to a sermon that denigrates the behavior of Jews who come to the "Temple to attend a service once a year on *Yom Kippur*" as "vicious worship of the past which is known as SENTIMENTALISM," "pernicious, vicious and un-Jewish," without a more nuanced attempt to understand why that is happening in the first place. Your animus toward "the emotional Jews, in the *z'miros* Judaism such as our Young Israel Synagogues indulge in" has a similar negativity. But it sounds as though the "*z'miros* Judaism" may at least be attracting people. I must admit, with all due respect, that the thought crossed my mind to inquire what the attendance is at *Shabbat* services in your synagogue. Beginning in the 1960s, there was actually a rebellion of thoughtful, knowledgeable young Conservative Jews against a synagogue life that seemed stale and unemotional. "*Z'miros* Judaism" seemed a lot more attractive than sitting in a pew observing the choreography on the bimah. This rebellion, which incorporated intensive observance, celebration, and study, had a significant impact in drawing a cadre of younger Jews into serious Jewish commitment.

You raise an important concern that has exercised thoughtful Jews from the time of the prophets to the present: namely that our religious practices not exist in isolation from ethical behavior. You observe, "A great many Jews take hold of this practice of ceremonies…but don't relate it to life." Traditional *Midrash* is preoccupied with moral behavior and the fact that *Pirkei Avot* [Ethics of the Fathers] is included in the traditional Conservative *siddur* [prayerbook] reflects an awareness that the linkage between religious observance and moral behavior is a long-standing Jewish concern—not just in contemporary America. One of the difficult jobs of the rabbi is to remind congregants of this connection.

At the same time, I do not share your concern that philanthropic Jews are to be chastised for making financial support of the poor and needy the main feature of their Jewish identification. In my community, there are a multitude of organizations—far more non-Jewish than Jewish—dealing with "NEED and APPEALS." I applaud those fortunate enough to have significant wealth who want to share some of it with organizations identified with the Jewish community. They certainly have plenty of other options. The story of the poor man who is ignored by a man busy studying in the Yeshiva makes the point well. The miserly Jew is the butt of many Jewish jokes precisely because this kind of behavior—whether by a banker or the man you describe who is unwilling to interrupt his studies—is so frowned upon. It is the job of the *shul* [synagogue], in my opinion, to offer those of a philanthropic mindset various opportunities within the *shul* setting that will draw them in and expose them more deeply to Jewish values and Jewish community.

    I mention the element of Jewish community because we are now experiencing a worldwide pandemic caused by a virus at least as bad as that of the 1918 influenza pandemic you experienced. It has killed almost a million people in our country alone. We have the benefit of technological advances since your time that allow groups to actually see and talk to each other electronically. I remember growing up with a "party line" on my telephone, where several people from different households could pick up the phone and, typically to their chagrin, hear the conversations of one another. Things are better now. Because of technological advances that allow individuals to both hear and see each other on a small screen in each person's home, our synagogue has been able to establish support groups for people with disabilities and psychological stress, and also for study of Jewish texts. We do not require that any of these people commit to coming to *shul* (although we ask for membership dues from those able to pay), and we certainly welcome their financial support to pay for necessary equipment and the "telephone" bill.

    I see no evidence that Jewish philanthropists have developed the "distorted view of Judaism" that you attribute to them because "all they hear discussed is the abnormal" features of the lives of those whom their philanthropy supports. If so, we would expect the Jewish employees of the organizations that provide such services to be tarred with the same brush—and I see none of that among the many colleagues who have chosen their careers in communal service.

    As far as the Ethical Culture movement goes, you needn't worry. According to contemporary sources, it currently has less than 10,000 followers worldwide.

    Your final concern about the negative aspects of NATIONALISM is, unfortunately, prescient in some respects, but not exclusively because it will become the "sum total of Judaism." Since you wrote this sermon, the State of Israel has come to fruition as an independent country, in part, sadly, because of the decimation of the European Jewish community in multiple countries energized by a German demagogue who championed a movement known as Nazism that blamed the Jews for the ills of society, and exterminated 6 million of them in the early 1940s. Israel, established in 1948, was warmly embraced by the Conservative Movement of which you are a part.

    But, independence did not occur in a vacuum. As you know, the movement championed by Theodore Herzl just prior to your birth had already resulted in a steady immigration to Palestine prior to the time you wrote this sermon. Unfortunately, this immigration was met with violent resistance by the Arab population, energized by the Mufti of Jerusalem, who eventually joined the Nazis. Your noble suggestion that Palestine could be "a possible home for the Hebrew and Arab civilizations and cultures like Canada" as suggested by the "teaching and platform of the society called *Brith Sholom*" never came to fruition because of this persistent violent hostility of the resident and surrounding Arab communities. *Brith Shalom* never found Arab partners that might share its vision and withered well before the establishment of the State of Israel in 1948 following the War of Independence.

This intransigence sadly continued after Israel's establishment and resulted in more wars, the second of which resulted in the conquest by Israel in 1967 of the Jordanian occupied portion of the Palestine Mandate west of the Jordan River. I recall joining an American organization, *Breira*, in the 1970s that advocated a collaborative approach. The leader appointed by the surrounding Arab countries to represent the West Bank Palestinian Arab population was invited to speak at an international forum of nations in 1975. *Breira* took an ad in the *New York Times* welcoming him. He showed up at the podium with a gun in a holster, and I quit *Breira*. In the late 1980s I visited Israel and met with the leader of a Jewish movement for Jewish-Arab reconciliation who discovered I was a geriatrician and asked me to meet Palestinian dignitaries who wanted to set up a rehabilitation hospital in the West Bank. I met with them with the belief that medicine transcends boundaries and can build cooperation. Likewise, I also support organizations like the Arava Institute, an organization based in Israel but with Jordanian and Palestinian members and leaders addressing environmental issues that cross artificial geographic borders. But, despite these efforts at building communal bridges by a number of organizations based in Israel, broader minded leaders in Arab countries immediately bordering Israel have not emerged since Egypt's leader, Anwar Sadat, made peace in the 1970s and was then assassinated. The King of Jordan renounced his claim to the West Bank, but that has not improved matters. The situation of the Palestinians remains in limbo 50+ years after the 1967 war and this vacuum in peacemaking has unfortunately facilitated a gradual growth of Jewish communities in the West Bank, some of which are occupied by religious ideologues opposed to returning any land in exchange for peace, vastly complicating the task of constructing borders for a potential Palestinian state. The spirit of the *Brith Shalom* model is nowhere in evidence, and a solution based on it does not seem viable.

I read the summation of your sermon with great interest, because, perhaps on reflection, you walk back some of the things you just said: "Now, my friends, don't mistake what we have just heard for the last 20 minutes. We are not now advocating, by any means that the salvation of Judaism will come about only when

all Jews will be united and unified...That is well-nigh impossible. It may not be desirable." You indicate that the various aspects of Jewish life you discussed earlier should rather be seen as "an arc of the larger circle of Judaism...[and] we must maintain the bent, the curvature of that arc. This realization is what the prophet means in his symbolic act of uniting the two sticks [and]...the picture given in the *Sidrah* of Joseph and his brethren united after long years of estrangement."
Amen.

Dr. William Kavesh joined Havurat Shalom in Somerville, Massachusetts in the early 1970s and has maintained associations with Havurah communities since that time. Dr. Kavesh, a specialist in Geriatric Medicine, has published multiple articles and book chapters on aging issues as well as the interface between medicine and Jewish tradition. He is now semi-retired after many years of full-time practice at the Philadelphia VA Medical Center, where he also taught medical residents and students as a faculty member of the University of Pennsylvania Perelman School of Medicine.

And He Lived

Delivered in Manhattan Beach, New York at Temple Beth El, January 6, 1928, for *Parshat Vay'chi*

I.
The text of the sermon consists of the first word of the Sidrah[102] recited in the Synagogue tomorrow: ויחי "and he lived." The "he" in this instance was Jacob; the chapters that follow tell of his last injunction to his children and grandchildren and the solemn story of his death. Let us take this phrase, which is but a fragment of a sentence, and separating it from its context treat it as a complete thought and as an ideal.

Can these words be said of everyone at life's close, that he lived? That depends on our interpretation of life. We live as long as the heart continues to beat, registering its alternate systole and diastole and our temperature stays in the neighborhood of 98 degrees. Would we call that life, even though we continue it for three score years and 10? Such is the meaning of life at its lowest terms. So lives the beast that prowls over the fields. So live all the plants and all vegetation. But when a man so lives he is said to vegetate. A complete rebuke of a mode of life is here conveyed in a single word.

One of the great sentences in Moses' farewell address reads:

ראה נתתי לפניך היום את החיים ואת הטוב ואת המות ואת הרע, ... ובחרת
בחיים למען תחיה

See I set before you this day life and death, good and evil; choose life and live (Deuteronomy 30:15,19).

Its counterpart can be found in Ezekiel 18:4:

"The soul that sinneth, it shall die." הַנֶפֶשׁ הַחֹטֵאת הִיא תָמוּת.

Here life and death have altogether a moral significance, and he most *lives* who is most worthy.

There is a popular phrase known as seeing life. It means often embarking upon a round of debasing pleasures; enjoying its dazzle and its dissipation. The moralist

---
[102] Weekly biblical portion.

would call that *death*. How the same word can have opposite meanings when used by different men! Here in these surroundings we would teach life in terms of morals. We are concerned with its quality and not with its quantity. The world has ever produced men and women who lived more than the average allotted span of life only to beget sons and daughters. The world has ever produced Methuselahs, complete nonentities who deserve well only because they fathered worthy children. That is their sole excuse for living. To one who has had to officiate at burial ceremonies the most difficult thing is to avoid giving voice to that dreadful epitaph which alone could characterize the life of so many individuals who have passed away, the awful truth: that it would have made no difference had they never lived at all. Yet there were generations of such in the Stone Ages, who as far as we know now, just marked time. They lived, they hunted to sustain life, and they ultimately passed away.

Yet there is a class far worse than this one. Those who made the world worse for some by living than had they never lived at all. I have not so much in mind the out-and-out wicked men from whom their own age shrank in horror; the evil they did has long been forgotten. I have in mind some individuals who, though long dead, their influence still mars the lives of some and whose example has been unfortunate for many. I think of those whose pernicious standard has become a precedent and model. There is Epikuros the Greek, who made pleasure rather than duty the aim of life. People forget that he really taught that the nobler our pleasures the longer they would last. And Epicurean has come to be the standard for thousands אכול ושתו כי מחר נמות – eat and drink for tomorrow we die (Isaiah 22:13).

There was *Calvin*.[103] Thoroughly upright and sincere, his gloomy theory of the elect, the chosen and the doomed has saddened the lives of thousands of people; and, in another direction, there was Schopenhauer,[104] who in the same spirit made his appeal to the unbeliever—who diffused throughout the world the doctrine of pessimism, that life is essentially evil and that hope lies only in its ultimate disappearance. There was Loyola[105] the theologian, and Machiavelli[106] the statesman, both in their different spheres of activity practically teaching the doctrine that the

---

[103] John Calvin (1509-1564), a French theologian, active in the Protestant reformation.
[104] Arthur Schopenhauer (1788-1860), German philosopher.
[105] Ignatius of Loyola (1491-1556), a Spanish Basque Catholic theologian and philosopher. He was instrumental in founding the Jesuit order, and was beatified in 1609. It is unclear why Signer feels that he taught "the doctrine that the end justifies the means."
[106] Niccolò di Bernardo dei Machiavelli (1469-1527), Italian Renaissance era philosopher and historian whose seminal work, *The Prince*, advocates use of whatever means are necessary for a ruler to ensure he remains in power.

end justifies the means. Many unrighteous deeds have been done by religious cults in the name of the former, and many outrageous acts by governments in the name of the latter. There was Eisenmenger,[107] and Pfefferkorn the Apostate,[108] whose hatred of the Jews resulted in formulating against them a series of slanders that, alas, have long outlived them and remain the arsenal of the anti-Semite even to this day. Domitian[109] and Herod,[110] Louis XV[111] and Ivan the Terrible[112] are old tyrants whom the world wishes had never lived. But there may be living today nameless enemies of society, dangerous and disturbing spirits, still cumbering the earth, provoking rebellion and sowing the seeds of discontent.

II.

ויחי, "and he lived." Our first concern is to live—to live thoroughly and completely throughout all our years—to live on all sides of our richly-endowed natures. Not only should we avoid living the mere physical lives of the cattle, leaving the mind dead. We should not live exclusively the life [of the] intellectual, leaving the emotions dead. We must avoid drifting in a narrow groove of *one life interest* with which we earn our daily bread. Everyone should have in addition to his vocation an avocation. Alas, to think that there are many latent possibilities in some lives, the doors of which are never opened; springs of capacity never touched. Like the

---

[107] Johann Andreas Eisenmenger (1654-1704), German orientalist who studied Hebrew, Aramaic and Jewish sources extensively. He ultimately turned his knowledge into criticism of Jewish sources, presumably in order to stop Christian conversions to Judaism, and encourage Jews to convert to Christianity. His most well-known book is *Entdecktes Judenthum* (*Judaism Unmasked*).
[108] Johannes Pfefferkorn (1469-1523), German Catholic theologian who converted from Judaism and pursued the conversion of Jews to Christianity. While he defended Jews against blood libels, he advocated their conversion to Catholicism and the forcible removal of the Talmud, and prohibiting them from practicing money lending.
[109] Domitian (51-96), son of Roman Emperor Vespasian and brother of Titus, who crushed the Judaean rebellion in 70 CE and destroyed the Second Temple. Domitian, who had a peripheral role in the Roman-Judaean War, ruled as Emperor from 81-96 and was not known during that time for carrying out specific actions against the Jews.
[110] Herod the Great (72-4 BCE). Descended from Edomites and Nabateans who had converted to Judaism, Herod was nominally a Jew. He maintained a good relationship with the Romans and was declared "King of the Jews" by the Romans in 41 BCE. He was considered by many to be a cruel and despotic leader.
[111] Louis XV (1710-1784), King of France from 1715-1784, known as "Louis the Beloved." He was a relatively benign monarch, though some historians later considered his rule to be ineffective. The period of his rule was generally positive for the Jews of France.
[112] Ivan IV (1530-1584) Czar of Russia from 1547-1584. He was called "Ivan the Terrible." Although he did preside over some reform and modernization of Russia, his rule was also characterized by persecution and paranoia. He was known as an anti-Semite who persecuted the Jews.

rudimentary legs of the serpent, or the eyes of the mole, unused, they never come into action. Let us set going all our powers. Do not play upon one string only; tune up every fibre—a full orchestra.

Moreover it is our duty to live even when life, because of age or infirmity, ceases to give us pleasure. Self-preservation is not always the first law of nature but it is always the first law of religion. It is sad indeed to think that for some life is such a tragedy that they can no longer face it and they escape. Judaism condemns suicide; Paganism condones it. When the Roman was tired of life he opened his veins in a warm bath and that was the end of it. Of all brave souls who dared to live even when life was continued pain I think of Rabbi Zadok of Temple days,[113] of Robert Louis Stevenson[114] almost of our own time. You say it requires courage to die! There are times when it requires courage to live!

III.

Now our duty to live must be applied further in that we should live fully to the very end. When the senses begin to decline, never say die. Let us learn like Moses to live fully to the final year his eye undimmed, his natural force unabated—לֹא כָהֲתָה עֵינוֹ וְלֹא נָס לֵחֹה [Deuteronomy 34:7]. One of Verdi's[115] masterpieces, Otello, was written after he was 70 and another after he was 80. Goethe[116] wrote his second part of Faust, which is philosophy as well as drama, in his 81st year. The late President Eliot of Harvard[117] still is a vibrant spirit and Rockefeller[118] the charity giver a commanding figure. Clemenceau[119] helped decide the fate of Europe in

---

[113] Rabbi of the Talmudic era who was said to have fasted for 40 years in an effort to avert the destruction of Jerusalem, which occurred in 70 CE. He was brought before the Emperor Vespasian by Rabbi Yochanan ben Zakai who successfully pleaded with the Emperor to arrange to heal him following his lengthy fast.

[114] Robert Louis Stevenson (1850-1894), a Scottish novelist and poet who suffered for much of his life from bronchial illness.

[115] Giuseppe Fortunino Francesco Verdi (1813-1901), Italian composer.

[116] Johann Wolfgang von Goethe (1749-1832), German poet and playwright.

[117] Charles William Eliot (1834-1926), who served as President of Harvard University from 1869-1909. Signer refers to Eliot in the present, even though he died 2 years before the sermon was delivered. In his manuscript, Signer hand-wrote the words "The late", suggesting that at the time he initially wrote the sermon he didn't realize that Eliot had already passed away. It's likely that when Signer actually delivered the sermon, he said that President Eliot was a vibrant spirit until the end of his life.

[118] John D. Rockefeller Sr. (1839-1937), wealthy businessman and philanthropist who founded the Rockefeller Foundation.

[119] Georges Benjamin Clemenceau (1841-1929), a French statesman who served as Prime Minister from 1906 to 1909 and again from 1917 until 1920.

his late 70s. Let us avoid the attitude of the great artist Thorwaldsen,[120] who once said, "My best work is done." These men might well serve as examples to those of us who are in our prime, or who are beginning to get along in years, that they should avoid acquiring the habit of looking backward as though life was chiefly retrospective, as though the best were already left behind. Life is ever a climb; our desire should be to reach some higher peak ever to the end. Well does the Midrash[121] commend the man who lived full of the hope of ultimate achievement, who never grew old; the man of 90 who planted a palm tree and expected to eat of its fruit. Says Koheleth [Ecclesiastes] (11:6): בבקר זְרַע אֶת זַרְעֶךָ וְלָעֶרֶב אַל תַּנַּח יָדֶךָ "In the morning sow thy seed, but in the evening withhold not thy hand."

Some do not begin to live in the best sense of accomplishment until far on in years. The call of Abraham came in his 70s and of Moses in his 80s. Some wake up to life's meaning only long after maturity. Morgan[122] wrote his first novel after he turned his 60th year. Grote,[123] our best authority on Greek history, began to study Greek at the age of 30. Others may have begun early but were recognized late. Browning[124] the poet, Hawthorne[125] the *litterateur*, and Wagner[126] the musician were neglected till they had long passed middle life. There are some who wake up to life's possibilities after youth has gone, and take up new tasks even when the snow has begun to whiten on their heads.

There have been all too many who have lived on heights so exalted that none could reach their plane. The great misunderstood; scorned and scoffed at when they should have been crowned. *Galileo* and *Bruno*[127] tortured—the former because he declared that the earth moved, the latter that there was a plurality of

---

[120] Bertel Thorvaldsen (1770-1844), Danish sculptor. He was said to have stated after the Thorvaldsen Museum was completed in 1844, "Now I can die whenever it is time . . ." and died that very day.
[121] *Midrash* refers to collections of rabbinic material which served as a homiletic and legislative commentary to the Bible.
[122] It is unclear to whom Signer is referring.
[123] George Grote (1794-1871), British historian who authored a 12-volume collection on Greek history 1846-1856.
[124] Robert Browning (1812-1889), British poet.
[125] Nathaniel Hawthorne (1804-1864), American novelist.
[126] Wilhelm Richard Wagner (1813-1883), German opera composer.
[127] Galileo di Vincenzo Bonaiuti de' Galilei (1564-1642) and Giordano Bruno (1548-1600), Italian early scientists. Galileo was condemned for heresy in 1633 for his theory that the earth orbits the sun; Bruno was burned at the stake in 1600 for his views which were considered to be antithetical to Catholicism.

worlds. Servetus and John Huss[128] were burned because they pleaded for a simpler religious life.

Some, in the world's estimate, had not begun to live till long after they were dead.

Of some we must transpose our text and say – יחיה—he will live! Spinoza[129] was one of those. His first name means blessed but he was cursed for two centuries, referred to by many scholars with contempt, and styled an unbelieving atheist. Not till nearly 200 years after he passed away did a great man, Lessing,[130] have the daring to reveal him and show to a doubting world that he was not a materialist to be shunned, but an idealist to be praised; that he was not a man who banished God but that he was saturated with God. From that time on he continued to influence all great philosophers, and influences them still. For Christendom, Mohammed[131] did not begin to live, other than as an imposter, till the 19th century. Carlyle[132] showed that he deserved to be called one of the great prophets of man.

Here then are five stages. Some never live—mere living automatons. Some live in their prime and vegetate in their maturity. Some only begin to live in their later years. Some only after death; and some never die... Some there are who have an immortality of worth. [The biblical prophet] Elijah is given a blissful immortality of service to the oppressed. There is an interpretation of actuality to the deathlessness of Elijah and others like him. We live as long as our influence endures. The influence of the prophet liberator who turned the tide of Baal worship [First Kings 18] is with us still. Humanity will gratefully keep alive in its remembrance another liberator, Lincoln, as well as the geniuses whose scientific researches made life safer, such as Jenner and Koch, Ehrlich and Pasteur.[133] Geniuses of literature

---

[128] Michael Servetus (1511-1553), Spanish theologian and scientist, and John Huss (1372-1415), Czech theologian, both burned at the stake for renouncing tenets of Catholic theology.

[129] Baruch ("Blessed") Spinoza (1632-1677), Dutch philosopher of Spanish-Portuguese Jewish descent. He was excommunicated by his congregation for his heretical views, including his belief in an early form of biblical criticism which maintains that the scriptures were not written word for word by God.

[130] Gottholt Ephraim Lessing (1729-1781), German playwright and philosopher who identified with the European Enlightenment. Although not Jewish himself, he was a friend and associate of Moses Mendelssohn and published essays sympathetic to Spinoza's beliefs.

[131] Muhammad ibn Abdullah (570-632), founder of Islam.

[132] Sir Thomas Carlyle (1795-1881), Scottish educator, philosopher and essayist. He wrote favorably about Muhammad, founder of Islam, in his work *On Heroes, Hero Worship, and the Heroic in History* (1840).

[133] Edward Jenner (1749-1823), Robert Koch (1843-1910), Paul Ehrlich (1854-1915), Louis Pasteur (1822-1895), physicians and researchers who contributed to the field of microbiology.

who have given us gems in prose and in verse will continue to live long after you and I are forgotten.

But we must all try to live so that apart from our belief in the soul's immortality, something of us, if not our actual name and record, will live in the coming years, after we are laid away—in a service we have rendered to our fellow man; perhaps in such a service as will couple our names and link them with the generation now growing up and those yet unborn whose spiritual growth and development we shall have been directly responsible for.

Just one more final application of our text: "and he lived." Let us not postpone our word of approval for our fellow man until they live no longer. Let them enjoy our appreciation. Why should all eulogies be elegies? Why should the world's diploma to a good man be an epitaph on a tombstone? We hear so often of the good which men and women do only when they are lying stretched out before us in their coffins and cannot be warmed by our praise. "Can eulogies soothe the dull cold ear of death?"[134] Bring them flowers in their lifetime, commendations and approval in their living years, while they can enjoy it with their children instead of only to be enjoyed by their children after they have passed away. The poet [Thomas] Gray had a splendid monument placed over his grave, but he starved before he entered it. Of Him we might say: He asked for bread; they gave him a stone.[135]

In conclusion we must realize that although we cannot all be great and render remarkable service, deserving fame, we nevertheless can learn to show appreciation now to the humblest workers in our midst. Grant them, therefore, not flattery but deserved commendation. That will give new hope to those who may be otherwise dispirited in life's struggle. Your unexpected endorsement to the unselfish, modest toilers may give them new confidence in themselves. That praise may even be productive. In that praise they will live again joyously, gladly continuing to the end, lives of useful service. The knowledge that their work is aiding the lives of others will make them feel that verily they live still achieving, still pursuing, even to the very end.

> Life burns us up like fire,
> And Song goes up in flame:
> The radiant body smolders
> To the ashes whence it came.

---

[134] Based on a line from the poem *Elegy Written in a Country Churchyard* by English poet Thomas Gray (1863-1928). The original line reads "Can Honour's voice provoke the silent dust, Or Flattery soothe the dull cold ear of Death?"
[135] Matthew 7:9: "Which of you, if his son asks for bread, will give him a stone?"

Out of things it rises
With a mouth that laughs and sings
Backward it fades and falters
Into the clear of things
Yet soars a voice above it—
Love is holy and strong;
The best of us forever
Escapes in Love and Song.
            —John Hall Wheelock[136]

O well for him who lives at ease
With garnered gold in wide domain,
Nor heeds the splashing of the rain
The crashing down of forest trees.
O well for him who ne'er hath known
The travail of the hungry years,
A father grey with grief and tears,
A mother weeping all alone.
But well for him whose foot hath trod
The weary road of toil and strife,
Yet from the sorrows of his life
Builds ladders to be nearer God.
            —Oscar Wilde[137]

Also: Love of Life by Tertius Van Dyke

(HR2401) in c.i.[138]

---

[136] From the poem *Life* by American poet John Hall Wheelock (1886-1978).

[137] *A Lament* by Irish poet Oscar Wilde (1854-1900).

[138] *Love of Life* by American clergyman and poet Tertius Van Dyke (1886-1958). Cited by Signer but not recorded with his sermon. The poem in its entirety:

> Love you not the tall trees spreading wide their branches,
>   Cooling with their green shade the sunny days of June?

response from
Mitchell Chefitz

Dear Rabbi Signer,

Thank you for your words. You have given us a message that transcends the generations. The general principles continue to resonate, though details have changed over time, and the style, also. In some communities we still preach sermons from the pulpit, but some rabbinic leaders stand to the side to invite *hevruta* [small group] interaction and words from the congregation.

The biblical text you cite is a favorite of mine—that we should choose to be living rather than to be dying. You adjure us to live intensely to the end of our lives, refining the full spectrum of our abilities.

Then you list those who would have been better off had they never lived. I need not mention them again nor add to that list lest I glorify them even more. Then another list, those who lived long lives and lived their lives well—nearly two dozen men: biblical figures, giants of literature, music, philosophy, philanthropy, and religion. You mention great men of medical science: Jenner, Koch, Ehrlich, Pasteur. You will be pleased to learn most all of these are remembered and revered today. But can you hear what is missing? The modern ear would hear it. There are no women on that list.

Now—how should we correct that? Should I demonstrate my erudition by compiling a list of women active before, during, and since your time?

You delivered this teaching in 1928. Fifty years later, in 1978, I was a young Rabbi with an uppercase "R" in a distinguished congregation. I might then have

---

Love you not the little bird lost among the leaflets,
    Dreamily repeating a quaint, brief tune?

Is there not a joy in the waste windy places;
    Is there not a song by the long dusty way?
Is there not a glory in the sudden hour of struggle?
    Is there not a peace in the long quiet day?

Love you not the meadows with the deep lush grasses;
    Love you not the cloud-flocks noiseless in their flight?
Love you not the cool wind that stirs to meet the sunrise;
    Love you not the stillness of the warm summer night?

Have you never wept with a grief that slowly passes;
    Have you never laughed when a joy goes running by?
Know you not the peace of rest that follows labor?—
    You have not learnt to live then; how can you dare to die?

given a similar sermon in a similar style and then felt uncomfortable afterward, not knowing whether I had done a service or a disservice to our people. In stentorian tones I might have delivered *my* lists, *my* opinions, *my* information from the pulpit to the parishioners. To the parishioners? Yes, a Christian term, but in America of the 20th century Jewish clergy were beginning to emulate Christian clergy, preaching downhill from the pulpit. In 1978 I was following suit, dressed in robes with a biretta, not a yarmulke. I preached in that style for five years, then stepped down from the pulpit and aside from the uppercased rabbinate.

That Rabbinate is still present, but alongside is an evolving style: egalitarian—egalitarian not only in gender but in recognition of the potential and wisdom of each member of our community. My task as rabbi these last forty years has been to empower small fellowships of Jews—*havurot*—to become ever more knowledgeable and responsible for their own Jewish lives. I lead from the side, not from above, and I grow along with them.

So—how might we complete the list of individuals who lived well and continued living to the end of their lives? First, we would learn your sermon as a text. We would recognize its value but also see the lacunae to be filled in—by us, by each of us. Then in *hevruta*, in study pairs, we would argue who else might be on the list, surely which women deserve to be there because of their significant contributions, but also who might rise from our personal experiences to warrant being on our personal lists. We can't all be a Louis Pasteur or a Marie Curie, but surely we know individuals whose lives are closer to the lives we live, lives we might emulate.

I am doing that exercise at this moment. Who do I know who lived a long, productive, and creative life throughout all her years, to the very end? Who lived and never stopped living? Who played not only on a single string of her being, but with the full orchestra of her soul?

One name springs to mind. Not Moses. Never again will there arise one like Moses. Not Anthony Fauci. You don't know of him, but believe me, we ordinary people can't expect to achieve what he has achieved. The name that comes to mind is Rosel Shoshana Tuetzer. You don't know of her, either, but let me tell you...

Shoshana, as we called her in the Havurah, was a Berliner. She and her family had escaped Germany on the last train to the east with visas for Japan. She was confined in the ghetto in Shanghai and admitted to the United States after the war. I recall driving her to a learning session. She was then in her 80s and active in all the worlds of experience. I asked her how she managed to maintain such vigor. She responded in her Berliner accent, "Three things. Prunes. Walking. And younger friends." I was proud to be one of her younger friends. But I knew she had omitted a fourth thing that was patently obvious. She was curious about *everything*. Her cup overflowed in all directions. Shoshana lived to be 104, curious to the end. She was living and growing to the last moment of her life.

Stories of Goethe and Galileo might inform and perhaps inspire. Stories of Shoshana have the power to inspire and transform. We do not have to go up to heaven or across the sea to find models for living. They are right here in our neighborhoods, living among us.

I'll add Shoshana's name to my list. Now to each person reading this—who are you going to add to your list? Who do you know in your family, among your friends and acquaintances who has lived or is living to the fullest? Once you add that name to your list, you will have a responsibility to that person—to tell his or her story so others can be inspired and perhaps transformed.

Rabbi Signer, thank you for your words and this opportunity to share my words with you. Your memory is a blessing—*zecher tzadik l'vrachah.*

Mitchell Chefitz is the author of a half dozen books, among them the best-selling novel The Seventh Telling. *His most recent novel is* The Rx of Dr. Z. *His story collection* The Curse of Blessings *has been widely translated. His non-fiction works include* Zoom Torah, *a collection of 50 divrei Torah;* The Kabbalist's Aleph-Bet; *and* Beyond Prayer: Eighteen Sessions to Enhance Rabbinic Prayer or Replace It. *His current writing is on Substack where he posts weekly teachings on Hasidic texts (mitchellchefitz.substack.com).*

Isador Signer's parents Malca (1859-1934) and Abraham Joseph (1857-1941).

Rabbi Signer's diploma from the Jewish Theological Seminary of America.

Rabbi Signer with his chaplain's pin and badge during World War II.

Birth and Parenting

How to Be Born

Delivered in Manhattan Beach, New York at Temple Beth El, February 1, 1929, for *Parshat Yitro*[139]

BIRTH
by Margaret Tod Ritter[140]

Nine months of bliss and pain
This miracle has lain
Beneath my heart
Nine months apart.
And now, today, they look at me and smile
And say: A little while!
A little while of agony, a stark,
Grim struggle with the long oppressing dark.
Dear Heaven
I did not dream such pain existed; seven—
Eight—nine. How slow the night how slow.
Nine months ago
My thoughts of now were dim; I could not guess
The price of happiness.
Ten—twelve. They are so lightly made
The vows of marriage. Oh, I am afraid!
The light is growing dim, and tall and queer;
The price of happiness, My dear, my dear
The road is steep and dark, I cannot see,
Come close to me.
Nine singing months of bliss,
And this!
Why did they never warn me? No one said
"Better dead . . . . . .
All inarticulate

---

[139] This sermon was preached two days after Rabbi Signer's first child was born.
[140] Margaret Tod Ritter was born in 1893 and spent much of her adult life in Colorado. She published several books of poetry.

ISADOR SIGNER

They let me wait
In ignorance; they let me dream and play
Up to the very day
This agony was due;
One—two
In very weariness I long to take
The hand of death, and yet for your dear sake
I hesitate. The tall gates swing apart,
Dear heart,
Can you not see them? Gates of amethyst
Let go my wrist,
Do you not understand
The power of your hand?
I cannot suffer longer. Let me go.
Three—four
Blackness of night
No light
No gates of amethyst, no road
No place to lay the load.
Sheer walls of agony, steep cliffs of pain
Again and again
Torture too cruel to bear
Moisture throughout my hair
Moisture upon my brow
God! It is agony now.
No shining stars, no lamp to light the way
No dawn no day
More cliffs of pain, more jagged walls of fire
Ascending higher—
A cry
Cry of the lips unsealed
Cry of my heart revealed
Nine months of waiting—yesterday—today
Oh, such a little little price to pay!

Birth is the great mystery of life's beginning. Science has charted the far country and eased the pain of the journey. But an understanding of birth is as our knowledge of the winds and lightnings.

Upon woman has been laid the burden and the pain of birth. Hers is the glory and the crown. The travail-couch becomes the greatest throne and mother is the only universal queen, whether she mothers her own children or the children of the community or of a state.

The supreme business of womanhood is motherhood; and by as much the supreme business of manhood is fatherhood.

I cannot change the facts and antecedents of my own birth, but I can influence these facts and antecedents for my child. Physically, mentally, morally, I am not so much concerned about my ancestors as I am that I shall be an ancestor, a worthy ancestor; I would rather found a line than be the last of one. Whether, as men judge such matters, I am or am not well-born, I am responsible, so far as fatherhood is concerned, for the birth conditions and environment of those who come after me. In this lies fatherhood's supreme obligations, with its supreme joy or supreme agony.

I have a friend whose parents so loved this country that before his birth they undertook a hazardous journey in order that their child might first see the light of day beneath the Stars and Stripes. Lincoln was born in a log cabin and so was Grant. Washington was born in a mansion. But the question is not where to be born, nor when to be born, nor what to be born; the question is how to be born.

Perhaps some of you may recall having lived through the experience which was mine as a lad. I would call fate cruel because I was not born in the days of King Arthur, or when knighthood was in flower, or when the Maccabees[141] led their victorious bands of heroes, or in the time of [King] David or when Indians ruled the Western plains and buffalo roamed the desert—all depending on the particular book that caught my fancy and held my interest at the moment. But no time was ever more adventurous than this time. There are tasks aplenty. Life is rich with high adventure. Where in history do you find a more thrilling career than that of Lindbergh[142] to cite but one single example? NOW is always the great moment in which to live. The question is HOW?

Thank God, if you were born strong of body, clean of blood, cheerful of disposition, and resourceful of spirit. Thank God, if you were born well. But I hear a vast company say, What of us? Whenever and wherever and whatever and however we may have been born, we are born. We cannot change the facts of our birth. Granted that we may affect these facts for others, that we may in some vital measure affect those who come after us where we are, born wrong, many of us, with weak

---

[141] Jewish freedom fighters in the second century BCE who defeated the Seleucid Emperor, Antiochus IV, which led to the establishment of the holiday of Hanukah.

[142] Charles Lindbergh (1902-1974), who made the first non-stop transatlantic flight in 1927.

bodies, with tainted minds, with sour souls. What about us? And there is only one answer to this question that I know, the answer voiced by the prophet long ago:

עשו לכם לב חדש ורוח חדשה ולמה תמותו בית ישראל

> Get a new nature and a new spirit for yourselves, O Israel, why will you die? I have no desire for anyone to die says the Lord, the Eternal. So repent and live (Ezekiel. 18:31-32).[143]

To be pulled back from the brink of spiritual death is to be born again. Here is a great mystery, a mystery more profound than that of physical birth—the birth of a new Samson, in whose heart the spirit of God could begin to pound, the birth of a new Saul, whom the spirit of God could awaken to prophecy and deeds of valor. The fact of this new birth is no less real than that of physical birth, no less real because it is spiritual, no less real because to the physical eye it is invisible. We cannot see the wind but we can record its effects and register its power. The new birth *is* subject to demonstration; it can be proved. And the proof of it is the fact of it.

We know that you were born, and we know that you were born because you are. And all about us are men and women who have been born again, who are new creatures, whose deeds are different, whose words are changed, whose very countenances have been altered. How do I know they have been born again? I know they have been born again because they exist and because they are new; because the man that was is no longer, and because the new man, the man that is now, finishing old tasks, rights old wrongs, forgives old injuries, loves even the unlovable.

Physically people may be mean and dwarfed, hopelessly deformed; but while physically a new birth may be denied them forever, spiritually they may become men and women perfected and glorified.

I have read of a young woman whom it was necessary to carry into church. Drawn and humped, limbs twisted and hands gnarled, hers was a pathetic figure. But she was beautiful; spiritually she was angelic; mentally she was an exquisite creature. She not only refused to center her mind upon her difficulties, but she insisted upon bearing the burdens of others. The young people of her church and community looked upon her as a leader, and were enriched by her friendship. Her disposition was singularly winsome; her personality attracted people who were drawn to her, not by pity, but by admiration and love. She had not always been

---

[143] Only Ezekiel 18:31 is provided in the Hebrew.

thus. There was a time when she was sullen and morose, hard with her parents and bitter against God. She seemed hopelessly afflicted in soul as well as in body, destined to be a burden until death should relieve both herself and her friends. And then she was born again. Those who knew her testify that they knew her no longer. The old had passed away; she was a new creature; and the difference between what she had been and what she had become was as great as the physical difference between two women who have no resemblance. She was reborn with a לב חדש ורוח חדשה [a new nature and a new spirit].

It was not a change of scene, nor a change of task nor a change in physical condition. She continued to go about in an invalid's chair. It was not new friends, nor the resolution of her own will; nor any physiological reaction. It was a change of heart. It was God. She was born again.

But there is no need of going so far afield for an illustration of what I mean. You of Temple Beth El have been more fortunate than most in having come into close touch with a person who must have undergone this experience. Her name is engraved on this tablet dedicated to her spirit; her memory is enshrined in your hearts. She was born some 38 years ago or so. Her youth was not directed, as far as I know, to caring for others. She was as normal a girl as most. But sometime after her marriage, when or where or how I know not, she was born again. And I who am the poorer for never having known her, I know little of her physical appearance, less of her tastes, nothing of her dress, speech, or mannerisms. But I do possess a mental picture of her soul. This Temple speaks to me of her at all times and tells me, how wracked by painful attacks, as she was in her later years, they only served to make her sweeter and dearer to all who came into contact with her. Her influence is still felt among you; Bessie Aronson still lives. Shakespeare to the contrary, one's good deeds seldom die.

This is the birth I would want for my child, this which I consider the supreme realization of fatherhood. This is also how I would want you men and women who are dear to me, to realize your fatherhood and motherhood to its fullest—to influence the circumstances of your children's bringing up—to found a line of sons and daughters who shall be much more perfect than you are. But as far as I can see it, this condition can never be brought about unless you who are fathers and mothers will first show your children the way, in your own lives. You must lead before they can follow!

response from
Noam Arzt

Dear Grandfather,

Though I never met you, my mother (z"l) always made sure you were an ever-present force in our lives. "Grandfather's picture" was a fixture in our household growing up and was used as a convenient location to leave things and pick them up. Ever since my mother's death I have had "Grandfather's picture" framed and hanging on my wall—I look at it often. How fitting that this sermon for *Yitro* was delivered just two days after my mother was born.

"The supreme business of womanhood is motherhood; and by as much the supreme business of manhood is fatherhood." Wow. I read this statement through egalitarian eyes but I wonder how *you* meant it. I suspect that this meant something a little different to you ninety years ago than it means to me. I have changed a lot of diapers in my day (and now I do for my own grandson); I venture to guess you likely never did. Gender roles in the 1920s were a little more fixed than they are now, and they had changed little when your grandchildren were being raised.

"I cannot change the facts and antecedents of my own birth, but I can influence these facts and antecedents for my child. Physically, mentally, morally, I am not so much concerned about my ancestors as I am that I shall be an ancestor, a worthy ancestor." Another powerful statement—this really resonated with me. It is very important to acknowledge—even draw strength from—those who came before us and what they accomplished, but in reality it's what comes after us that matters more. But there is a tension here. Sure, one can't change the past but we have seen virulent attempts to rewrite it. While you saw first-hand the power of Nazi propaganda, I'm sure you could never envision the power of the "invisible hand" of social media in the 21st century. In our "post-fact" age the past *can* be changed and manipulated. We need to fight against the adverse impacts of these new technologies while preserving the positive "connectedness" that they enable.

The future *is* in our hands. You felt a strong responsibility for what was to come for your children, their "birth conditions and environment." You called it "fatherhood's supreme obligations." I have always felt privileged enough to have had the means to positively (I hope) affect my sons' environment growing up. As they are now adults I think the challenge is more pulling back from those perceived obligations and letting them spread their own wings, sometimes succeed and sometimes fail. Boy, is that hard for me. We have an expression now: "helicopter parents." These are parents so involved in their kids' lives that they seem to actually "hover" around them and give them no space to act on their own. I once described my wife and myself as "suppository parents" who are so far up... well, you get the idea. While it is a "supreme obligation" to "influence the circumstances of your children's upbringing" and provide this sound environment for our children, we have to know when to let it go.

The final thought in this sermon resonates perhaps the most with me, and it's a handwritten addition to the typed manuscript. It's a desire for a parent to have children who are "much more perfect" than they are. Well, maybe that part is a little over the top for the ego in me. But I get the aspirational sentiment. But the part I like is that "...it can never be brought about unless you who are fathers and mothers will first show your own children the way, *in your own lives. You must lead before they can follow!*" (italicized section written in by hand). My wife and I have always believed that when it comes to raising children it is what one *does* that is more important than what one *says*. Children hear lots of words, lots of ideas, but the most impact comes from what they see. Inconsistencies between words and deeds are easier to spot than we think and children of any age internalize action.

But how do we "lead" our children? We lead through kindness. We lead through honesty in our words, but especially in our deeds. We lead through גמילות חסדים—acts of lovingkindness. We lead by encouraging our children to be the best version of themselves. We lead by stressing the *connection* between actions and emotions. You say in this sermon עֲשׂוּ לָכֶם לֵב חָדָשׁ וְרוּחַ חֲדָשָׁה "Get a new nature and a new spirit for yourselves" (your translation of Ez. 18:31). Our children's emotional well-being is largely driven by their satisfaction with what they have accomplished, driven by their hope in their future, driven especially by how they perceive how we as parents view *their* actions.

Through my leadership of my own children *I* want to try to be a "worthy ancestor." I never knew you, Grandfather, but you have always been a worthy ancestor in my eyes. Grandmother spoke of you always. She mentioned people you both knew, events in your lives, jokes you would tell each other. She (and my mother) spoke of your service as a chaplain in the Army Air Corps during World War II with great pride. *I* always felt that pride myself. My own children know who "Sig" was. They recognize your picture. Reading your sermons has been an unexpected surprise and has offered all of us a window into who you were and what you found important and meaningful.

I have now lived nearly ten years longer than you and I hope I am able to accomplish in my life all that you accomplished in your short one. I hope my children (and grandchildren) will recognize and remember me as a "worthy ancestor."

Noam Arzt

Noam Arzt has been an active member of the Jewish community for many years as a ba'al korei [Torah reader] and ba'al tefilla [prayer reader] in Conservative congregations from coast to coast. After nearly ten years in Palm Desert, California, Noam moved to Orange County to be nearer to his children and grandchildren. Noam holds Bachelors, Masters, and Doctoral degrees from the University of Pennsylvania. Professionally, he owns and manages HLN Consulting, LLC, which is a leading health information technology consulting company primarily serving the government and non-profit sectors. Noam and HLN were instrumental in supporting COVID pandemic response.

Are Parents People?

Delivered in Manhattan Beach, New York at Temple Beth El, January 3, 1930, for *Parshat Mikketz*

The Jewish attitude of the relationship of children to parents is, as we well know, stated positively and concisely in the fifth Commandment: Honor thy Father [and mother]. The latter half ["that you may long endure on the land that the Lord your God is assigning to you"—Ex. 20:12], the reward is not to be taken literally but is rather to be understood as referring to the race or the people. If you honor your parents you will ensure the stability of the civilization of your fathers and the continuity of the race. This doctrine is in general keeping with the spirit of Judaism which inculcates respect to one's elders, which commands obedience on the part of their offspring to those who gave them birth. The Torah, according to the Rabbis, does not hesitate to tell us that whenever this doctrine was not observed, the violators were punished. It has been said that the greatness of the Bible lies partly in its fearlessness to criticize its heroes and hold even the founders of the race guilty at times of improper conduct. Thus in our Sidrah [biblical portion] of this week, Joseph is severely criticized by the Sages for permitting the slight to his father to go unchallenged.[144]

To which the Rabbis say:

אמר ר' יהודה אמר רב: מפני מה נקרא יוסף עצמות בחייו מפני שלא מיחה
בכבוד אביו דקאמרי ליה עבדך אבינו ולא אמר להם מידי

[Rav Yehuda says that Rav says: For what reason was Joseph called: Bones, even during his lifetime, . . . ? Because he did not protest for the honor of his father, as the brothers said to Joseph: "Your servant our father," and Joseph said nothing to them in protest.—Sotah 13b].

Although Joseph, after his rise to power, treated his father and older brothers with every consideration. Although he was a paragon in the interest he, the viceroy, showed in their welfare, in the trouble he took to present them at court, in settling

---

[144] In Genesis 43:28 and 44:31, Joseph's brothers refer to Jacob as "your servant our father" which is seen as disrespectful to Jacob, since no parent should be considered to be a servant to their offspring.

them in the province of Goshen, in the respect he showed his Father on his deathbed, in the regard to his Father's memory which prompted him to arrange for so elaborate a burial in the Cave of Machpela [Gen. 50:13] in far-off Canaan, nevertheless, the Rabbis could not overlook this slight and they find his punishment meted out in the derogatory reference to himself as a bag of bones.

From the Ten Commandments all the way down in Judaism the emphasis is placed upon the honor which the child must yield to his parent. For insubordination and rebellion against parental authority, the child may merit even the death meted out to criminals. This dates back to what we moderns are pleased to call primitive forms of Society when the authority of the parents and complete control of children was not relinquished even after they had reached their maturity and their majority. That power extended even to the right of selling a daughter into marriage, or a son into slavery among the contemporaries of the Hebrews or what was even more barbaric, as in the case of Iphigenia among the Greeks,[145] or Jephtha's daughter,[146] or the devotees of Moloch among the Ammonites,[147] the parents even had the right to sacrifice their children, young and old, to the god, whether as a votive offering in payment of a debt or as a propitiatory offering to gain the favor of the gods.

This naturally sounds so old-fashioned and even antiquated and unthinkable in our day when all the emphasis is placed upon the duty which parents owe to their children. We hear on every side the need stated of training for parenthood. The modern tendency is to urge parents to respect the personality of the child by considering children *as people*. To appreciate the distance we have travelled in our education as parents since the days of Solomon [purported author of the Book of Proverbs], we need only to contrast the advice he gives with our modern attitude:

Leave not your child unpunished, if you whip him, he will not die. [Contrast this with] "Whip him with the rod and save his soul" [Proverbs 23:13-14].

חוֹשֵׂךְ שִׁבְטוֹ שׂוֹנֵא בְנוֹ He hates his son who fails to ply the rod [Proverbs 13:24] is no more considered the correct way of bringing up children. Bertrand Russell in his latest book *Marriage and Morals* [1929] points out how the dominion of the Father has gradually disappeared and the child now occupies the center of the stage. Spare the rod and spoil the child has given place to use the rod and spoil the child. Listen my son to the instructions of your Father and reject not your Moth-

---

[145] In Greek mythology, King Agamemnon is required by the goddess Artemis to kill his daughter Iphigenia in order to save the city of Troy.

[146] Judges 12: Jephthah the fighter promises that he will sacrifice the first creature that comes to meet him on his return home if he is victorious. When he returns home, his daughter is the first to greet him.

[147] An Ammonite God to whom children were purportedly sacrificed.

er's directions [Proverbs 1:8] has given place to Listen my parent to the word of thy child. It is the children who are to be considered as the people deserving of primary consideration.

Thus the modern Jewish parent who wishes to do the right thing by his child is bewildered by these two attitudes towards training the child or toward parent-child relationship. He is torn between the traditional Jewish approach and the modern approach. Is the Jewish parent on the one hand to close his eyes completely to the new ideas as some orthodox Jewish parents have done, with the sad consequences of the rebellion of their children from their authority and the tragedies in family relations which they entailed? Or is he to adopt the new as other Jewish parents have done with the result that they have resigned their parental rights and prerogatives and have become no more than the servants of their children? Can these two points of view be reconciled with each other, can they be synthesized and fused, or does the acceptance of the one point of view necessarily mean the banishment of the other?

In order to answer this question intelligently it is necessary to take into account the fact that the HISTORY OF CIVILIZATION IS A RECORD OF THE GRADUAL DECAY OF PATERNAL POWER. In earliest times the Father had complete power—the power given him by his superior strength. Later this power of his received the sanction of religion which considered him the appointee of the gods. Civilization grew to the extent and measure by which this divine power was taken away from the Father. Or take the question of marriage. Westermarck[148] shows that originally the most common form of marriage was to abduct the bride in spite of the father who was reluctant to part with another worker or slave. Then came the offering of compensation to the parent to escape vengeance and this grew eventually into the making of presents to the Father before the marriage during the courting period. It was only until comparatively recently that a marriage settlement was made directly on the bride.

A study of the array of facts must force us to admit that a philosopher and student of humanity like Bertrand Russell is correct in his analysis that the growth of civilization is directly in inverse ratio and proportion to the power which the parent could exercise over his children. But while admitting this we must also remember that which Russell forgets, [namely], that in the relationship of parents and children there are and always have been other factors involved. Russell considers primarily the factor of authority—the authority which parents formerly enjoyed. This factor functions in the element of *obedience* which the parent exacts from the

---

[148] Edvard Alexander Westermarck (1862-1939) was a Finnish philosopher and sociologist who researched and taught about early marriage practices.

child on the ground that his is a power conferred by divine right and therefore the younger MUST implicitly obey his elder. The parent is the ruler and the sovereign.

The other factors which must not be lost sight of are first: RACIAL EXPERIENCE and second: LOVE. By racial experience we mean the factor which functions in the element of acceptance of the standards of life which parents expect of children on the ground that the parents have inherited from their parents, and now possess and are in a position to transmit the accumulated experience of the race. As a matter of fact the parents represent civilization while the children represent impulse. Philosophically put, we may say that the parent represents DISCIPLINE, i.e., the conduct which the experiences of the race have proven to be best calculated to make for its preservation, while the child represents nature, the romantic element, the feeling that everything must be tried and tested and proven for himself before he will be ready to accept it. The child refuses to be guided by this discipline which the past has imposed, the spokesmen of which are the parents.

The other factor which Russell doesn't take into account is the factor of LOVE, which functions in the element of consideration which parents expect of their children on the ground that they feel toward their children love in its purest and most disinterested form. It is the love which comes about as a result of looking upon the child as a second chance. Parents want to be cleansed of all their mistakes their shortcomings and meannesses and the wrongs they have done to others by having their children a little more perfect than they are or have been. They want their children to have the opportunities which they themselves were denied. The parents want their child to be better than they are for no ulterior motive or purpose, only because they look upon their children as being an extension of themselves into the next generation, and they want that extension to be purer, cleaner, loftier, more cultured and more educated than they themselves have been. The love of parent for children is not merely physical and is never carnal. It is the realest, truest spiritual love which can be found anywhere on earth.

These three factors then have gone into making of civilization: authority, the experience of the human race, and parental love. In the past no differentiation was made between these three. These factors were not clearly distinguished from each other. Authority alone stood out. It predominated and overshadowed the other two where it did not drive them out completely as it did in many austere parents. The claim of the parents was based on this authority which had received divine sanction. That wouldn't have resulted in so great a change in the modern viewpoint if at least a time-limit had been set for the exercise of authority and of the other factors as well. If the claim of authority and social experience and love had been applied successively to the three stages of life: the first to childhood; the second to adolescence; and the third factor to maturity, I am positive that the rebellion against the old which now exists would not have been so marked nor would it have had so devastating an effect as it has had on the present structure of the family and indeed on all of our society.

But the fact remains, as Russell has pointed out, that authority was overemphasized by parents in all three stages of life and so inevitably there had come about a reaction. It is the complete abandonment of the belief that parents should exercise any control over their children. There has grown up a false theory which is doing a great deal of harm. Indeed it amounts to more than a theory. It is a cult, a religion with the younger generation which has been fostered by modern educators. It is the worship of self-expression. This stands out as a protest in the field of education against the excessive authority imposed by the older generation which tried to turn all children into one mold and one pattern. It was introduced in an attempt to consider each pupil's character and personality and train it in appropriate ways. But to suggest in education that the whole duty of the pupil or in family relations that the whole duty of the child is to express himself, and the teachers' or parents' whole duty is to help him to do so, is the direct contrary of true education whether in the school or in the home. From the uncontradicted parent the pendulum has swung around the complete arc to its opposite: the unpunished, self-expression-seeking child, and the latter, if anything is a worse state of affairs to be in than the former, though both are admittedly bad, for while the uncontradicted, authoritative parent leads to tyranny, the unpunished over-indulged child leads to a horrible selfishness. Unfortunately, in an attempt to abolish the tyranny of the parent, we seem to have run the danger of encouraging the selfishness of the children. It is too bad that there is this feeling that we must have a choice of one or the other and that it is a matter of being under the dominion of one of two necessary evils. But is this the only way?

Is there a need for our going to extremes?? The rebellion of the modern age has succeeded in pointing out to us the prime necessity as parents to train ourselves for parenthood; that we can no more fall back on supernatural sanctions about the divine right of parents or to seek to establish the relation of parents and children, which means morality on a basis which has already collapsed. We are by no means attempting to minimize the tendency of the present age to put parents on probation, i.e., to have parents really learn how to bring up their children; we take it for granted that the trend is correct; we understand that it is a good tonic for us parents to realize that children, as we are told, are *people*, and that their personality must be taken into account, BUT we must not permit ourselves or our children to go to the extreme of forgetting that parents are also people and as such deserve some consideration at the hands of their children; to understand as parents should strive with might and main to make their children understand, that for the parents to give up their parental prerogatives and exist merely for the purpose of satisfying their children's whims or desires is to destroy the internal conscience of the world which is ever striving to improve humanity and society. They must be made to appreciate that we as parents are people too and that the doctrine of self-expression may mean spiritual stagnation or even death. Self-expression! Taking nothing for granted! Why, there are experiences of the race which children simply must accept on our say-so. Otherwise the doctrine of trying everything by experiment would be as ruinous for the race as it would be for a child or an adolescent to say: 'I don't believe that arsenic will poison one. I want to try it and see for myself'. The streets of the world, its highways and byways; its prisons and detention homes; its asylums and hospitals; its dens and brothels are filled, packed to the doors with those who seek for self-expression, who take nothing for granted, who want to see for themselves. Every one of us starts life with an extremely limited appreciation of the greatness and beauty by which we are surrounded and also with a pretty confident opinion that a thing which does not happen to please us is not up to much. Just think if one generation were to be left to itself at the age of 6. I cannot imagine an education or parental training which for me personally would have been more utterly damnable than to teach me to be contented with my existing beliefs and powers and just to express myself—to take the raw untrained ME of 15 or 20 years ago as the measure of the universe and simply encourage me to go ahead my own way. I shudder to think what might have become of me then.

The human personality needs the reins of authority to hold him in check, to curb desire and bound passion, to impose a will upon his own when he is too young to see ultimate consequences by himself. He also needs the experience of the race to help him avoid unnecessary pitfalls on the one hand and on the other to bridge over at one leap all the achievements which have been made for him as the heir to his civilization; and lastly he is eminently in need of the disinterested pure and spiritual love without which the human personality would feel so utterly alone in the world. All three factors are necessary to be practiced by parents in their relations with their children. How then avoid the pitfalls? By knowing as parents when to stress each factor most. Just as we have the three factors so have we also three stages of growth toward full manhood. It is a matter of emphasis as to which factor is to be employed.

But all three are necessary.

response from
Claudia Kreiman

Dear Rabbi Signer,

One hundred years after you wrote your sermon "Are Parents People?", I know that in some ways, the questions you posed remain extremely relevant. While the conditions of my life are considerably different from yours, I share your experience of asking hard questions about my relationships with my own children and my role as a parent.

As I read your words, I hear your concern that the "modern views," which you perceive as being in conflict with Jewish views, might make people forget how parents must exercise authority. From your description, you are afraid that modernity might undermine the Jewish teachings of כבוד אב ואם *"Kibud Av V'Em"* honoring parents—that we learn from Torah and, specifically, the fifth commandment, that rabbinic literature took very seriously.

You explain that the power and authority that parents have, which you define as traditional Jewish teachings, stands in opposition to what you call the more "modern" view that urges parents to respect the personalities of the children and consider children as people. I believe, though, that the importance of honoring and respecting one's parents can coexist harmoniously with honoring the individuality and evolving needs of one's children.

It seems to me, from your sermon, that you are also fearful of how a "modern" approach could pose a threat to Jewish continuity (what you call the "continuity of the race"). I believe this question is valid, though I would frame it differently: How do we balance the importance of creating limits and anchoring our children with a moral and spiritual foundation, while appreciating that our children may view the world and their own lives differently from how we were raised?

You could have never imagined my life. I am a 47-year-old woman, mother of two, a 12-year-old and a six-year-old, and I am a rabbi. I am, what we call, a working mother. And I live my life balancing my duties as a congregational rabbi, as a parent and, of course, as a wife of another working parent, who is also a rabbi. My life is busy and filled to the brim. Parenting is perhaps one of the most challenging parts of my life, though also my most rewarding one.

As a mother, I constantly struggle with balancing what you state in your sermon. I cringed and smiled at the same time when I read your words that new "modern views" may be problematic because children would be considered individual people with their own needs. Each of my children, and all children, are people with their own sets of needs. They are little human beings created in the

CLAUDIA Kreiman

image of God. Children being people does not mean that parents aren't *also* people. But it *does* mean that relationships between parents and children can feel messy or exhausting. Indeed, they almost always do!

As a parent, I want to do everything possible to help my children to grow and become more of who they are in the world, which might not always be exactly what I hoped for or imagined. As you also write, parents are, in fact, people; I have surely felt my share of loss, frustration, disappointment, and anger when my children do not make decisions or cultivate skills or interests that I value. Regardless, I have an obligation to keep them safe and give them the best life with a healthy mix of boundaries and freedom. I am not torn between what you call the "traditional view of parenting" and the "modern view of parenting." Instead, I choose to shape my role as a parent by applying and adapting Jewish tradition to modern life.

You write about the "general decay of parental power" and I question whether the word "power" is useful when we think about the relationship between parents and children. Can we teach, educate, and yes, at times, also discipline our children without thinking of ourselves as powerful, or without the arrogance of knowing exactly what is right or wrong for our children? Perhaps by cultivating humility, we can better serve our children and also serve ourselves.

You write, "We must not permit ourselves or our children to go to the extreme of forgetting that parents are also people and, as such, deserve some consideration at the hands of their children." In my experience, what is most important is building trust, through love and connection across generations. Respecting each other and recognizing that all humans, no matter their age, were created in the image of God and that we are all people.

As a parent, I let my children know that I am imperfect. I tell them I will make mistakes and I will fall short. They, too, will make mistakes and fall short. When I fail, I make sure to ask for forgiveness. I also let them know that, as their parent, I am ultimately the person who defines the rules and makes decisions. But that does not mean I don't hear their ideas and recognize the wise teachings they have to offer.

As the 21st-century American Jewish author, Mitch Albom, wrote:

> "All parents damage their children. It cannot be helped. Youth, like pristine glass, absorbs the prints of its handlers. Some parents smudge, others crack, a few shatter childhoods completely into jagged little pieces, beyond repair. I also believe that parents, if they love you, will hold you up safely, above their swirl-

ing waters, and sometimes that means you'll never know what parents endured..."
[Taken from *For One More Day* by Mitch Albom]

Our tradition teaches innumerable times about our obligations and responsibilities for children. It is both traditionally Jewish *and* a modern value to believe that children are people and deserve the respect, care, love of their parents.

In your words, "The love of parents for children... is the realest, truest spiritual love which can be found anywhere on Earth." Perhaps that is the main teaching we find in our tradition. Parents are people, children are people, and hopefully the relationship between parents and children is based on mutual respect and love. Whether we are living in the early 1900s, the mid-2000s, or at a moment in the far-reaching future, I believe that the humanity of parents and children will continue to be enriched by Jewish tradition while also growing in new ways with the cadences of modern life.

Rabbi Claudia Kreiman is the Senior Rabbi at Temple Beth Zion (TBZ) in Brookline, Massachusetts. She grew up in Santiago, Chile and lived in Argentina. Rav Claudia is the first Chilean-born woman to be ordained to the rabbinate. Rav Claudia moved to Israel in 1996, and received rabbinic ordination from Shechter Institute of Jewish Studies in 2002. She was the first Rabbi of Noam, the youth movement of the Masorti Movement in Israel, and Camp Ramah Noam.

Rav Claudia moved to the U.S. in 2004 and became the director of the Jewish Studies program at the Jewish Community Day School in Watertown, Massachusetts. She has been part of TBZ since 2007 and is deeply invested in growing the social justice ethos of TBZ and engaging community members in meaningful experiences of prayer. Rav Claudia is also widely involved in the local and national Jewish community. She serves on the board of directors of T'ruah: the Rabbinic Call for Human Rights, is a co-convener of the Brookline Interfaith Clergy Association, and serves and supports the Greater Boston Interfaith Organization (GBIO). Rav Claudia is married to Rabbi Ebn Leader. They have two daughters, Alma and Ariel.

The Role of Parenthood in the 20th Century

Delivered in Manhattan Beach, New York at
Temple Beth El, April 16, 1935, for *Parshat Metzorah*

In the changing world in which we live, where life itself becomes a problem, the sanction for the way we act is also a problem; and human conduct, formerly based on habit and tradition, is changing to behavior based upon ethical living. The end in view and the crux of the change is the achievement of personality, which means, the synthesis in each individual human being of a maximum of self-revelation plus a maximum of cooperation, achieved in the light of reason.

With our attention focused on the breakdown of authority and its attendant morality in all human relationships, we are confronted with the difficult problem, in all its complexity, in the field of primary relationships as is illustrated in the case of parent-child relationships. So that we can speak of training for parenthood in the same sense as we think of training for a profession or industrial skill. It consists in threading one's way through a maze of scientific theories and religious dogmas.

Besides realizing how difficult it is, very few would be graduated as having the *right* to practice parenthood. For as with other professions, so with parenthood. Even sustained study is no guarantee of a successful practitioner, and many a physician, lawyer or engineer, though carrying off the sheepskin, would fill a better niche in life, perhaps, as shoemaker, tradesman, tailor or carpenter. To be sure, we have not made such a success in the other trainings to use them altogether as a model. For there is one clear-cut difference between training for any of the professions and training for parenthood. In the former, as in medicine or law or the secretarial profession we are dealing with skills. In each case it is a matter of learnings which are imparted to the student. He receives training in the manipulation of a tool or of a set of terms or to recognize outward manifestations and in each case he is taught to encounter and handle specific relationships where ability or knowledge or skill will supply the method of approach and treatment of any given situation.

However in the case of training for parenthood, it means being trained for human relationships and this, in turn, involves in a sense, the whole problem of human life, for parent-child relationships run the gamut of the whole complexity of living together.

At the very outset we come up against the element of polarity in each human being, where the achievement or personality or self-realization means the correct interplay of the maximum of individuality and the maximum of cooperation. The art of living together consists in the art of balancing these two extremes and the difficulty of attaining this state is evidenced in our inability to lay down any specific rules to guide the parent as to just what is the proper balance between the extremes of polarity. That is why we have problem children, and every problem child implies a problem parent. For psychologically it is a matter of dealing with big babies who are trying to bring up little ones. Therein lies the tragedy of human life. All other problems affecting human relationships will be delayed in their solution as long as we fail to deal adequately with undirected family relationships which are left to chance.

It really cannot be conveyed. It can only be pointed out. The proper degree of balance must be achieved in each separate act, for in the parent-child relationship the problem arises of teaching the child on the one hand respect for authority and on the other, to retain his independence and initiative. Thus the parents must strive to strike a balance between

strictness	&	indulgence
giving the child ideas	&	yet not indoctrinate[ing]
how to wean the child	&	yet hold him
how to foster cooperation	&	yet not to become subservient to the group
how to protect him	&	yet to teach him self-reliance
how to develop leadership	&	not be domineering
respect for property	&	yet not overvalue its place in the social structure
giving the child a sense of security, for that is an indispensable foundation for life free from complexes	&	yet not make him dependent but rather to teach him to learn to accept solitude, pain and defeat

Thus we see that training in parenthood is really training for the whole of life.

In Rabbinic literature the common theme of parental education is the terrible consequence of indulgence. The Bible holds up as examples, in turn, Ishmael, Esau, Hophni & Phineas,[149] Absalom and Adonijah.[150] Adonijah runs amok in

---

[149] From the biblical book First Samuel, the two sons of Eli the priest who behaved in undignified and disreputable ways.
[150] Two sons of King David who rebelled against him in their desire to succeed him instead

his frenzied efforts to wrest the kingship from his brother, to whom it rightfully belongs, while his father David lies helpless on his couch. And all because ולא עצבו אביו מימיו לאמר מדוע ככה עשית—"his father had not grieved him all his life saying: 'Why hast thou done so?'" (1 Kings 1:6a) The Rabbis emphasize the severity of the indictment against David by interpreting the seeming irrelevance of the phrase ואותו ילדה אחרי אבשלום—"And him she had borne after Absalom" (1 Kings 1:6b) to imply that: מתוך שיצא לתרבות רעה ולא רדהו אביו, וכתיב באדוניה ולא עצבו אביו' ואף הוא יצא לתרבות רעה, לפיכך כתיב 'ואותו ילדה וגו'—[since Absalom came to no good, and his father didn't take him to task, Adonijah also came to no good; for this reason the verse concludes "and him she had borne, etc.—*Shemot Rabbah* 1:1]. David should have learned from his sad experience with Absalom the effectiveness of chastisement as an aid to child training. We have moved far from the day when the only manner considered correct in child training was to exercise the rod freely. To pursue such a policy would be to accept John Wesley's principle in which he stated in one of his sermons, saying:

> "Break your child's will in order that it may not perish. Break its will as soon as it can speak plainly, or even before it can speak at all. As soon as a child is a year old, it should be forced to do as it is told, even if you have to whip it ten times running. Break its will in order that its soul may live."[151]

It is because of a lack of understand[ing] such as this.

Under these circumstances a condition to achieving such balance is for parents to give up their desire to have the child's response affected by their parental attitude, and to be sincerely interested in the child's own growth. In other words, balanced relationship between parents and children is conditioned upon the parents giving up their sense of possessiveness of the child.

There are three forms in which the sense of possessiveness expresses itself:

1. *In the desire for obedience*. A 17th-century writer points out that "children are their parents' goods and possessions and owe to them all, even their own selves. As the law our God hath created and made children through their parents so hath He also made them subject under the power and authorities of their parents to obey and serve them in His stead."[152]

---

of David's bequeathing the position to his son Solomon, Absalom in the book of Second Samuel and Adonijah Second Kings.

[151] Quoted from *Sermons on Several Occasions*, Sermon 96 ("Obedience to Parents") by John Wesley (1703-1791), minister and founder of Methodism.

[152] Despite the fact that Signer attributes this quote to "a 17th-Century writer," he is likely

The testimony from literature.

2. Possessiveness shows itself again when parents attempt to force their own ambitions upon their children.

Michelangelo's father was a lawyer who wanted his son to take over his practice. So he sent him to the academy to study law. The son was more interested in the pencil and canvas. One day Michelangelo's father became so infuriated at seeing his son draw sketches on paper that he beat him mercilessly. If his father had had his way, Michelangelo would have been lost to the world.

Darwin's father was a physician. He wanted the young Charles to study medicine. When he refused that, the irate father commanded: "At least become a clergyman." When this failed to bring an affirmative response, the father yelled, "You care for nothing but shooting, dogs and rat-catching, and you will be a disgrace to yourself and all your family." Some of us may think his father was right. But if he had had his way, the "Origin of the Species" might still have lain hidden in the shadows of the future.

Jewish parents are particularly guilty of this trait of possessiveness when, in their ambition, they insist that their children become proficient on the piano or violin and force them to pound away endlessly or to scrape away for interminable hours on pain of punishment. The same story is repeated in the parents' ambitions for their children to become members of the recognized professions.

The widespread effect of this ambitious zeal is seen in:

the overcrowding of the professions

the mediocrity of the general professional man

the loss to Jews of the hold they formerly had upon certain trades, e.g., the needle-trade

3. This possessiveness further shows itself in the tendency on the part of parents to manage their children. They seem to have an unholy fear of giving up the sense of *being wanted*. They enjoy the sense of dependence which their children have and consequently prolong the period of dependence for as long a time as they can. This sense of being wanted is carried over even when children are married and supposedly set up house for themselves. Statistics will never be able accurately to estimate to what extent and degree the marital unhappiness of young people is due to in-laws carrying over the feeling or possessiveness long after they have voluntarily given up their warrant for so doing.

In a changing world from authority to the higher level of ethical living, the relationship of parents and children can no longer be based upon the sense of

---

quoting loosely from William Tyndale (1494-1536), an early figure in the Protestant Reformation, from his book *The Obedience of a Christian Man*.

possessiveness in its various manifestations but *on the respect which parents by their behavior earn from their children.*

1. In place of blind obedience which parents demanded because they felt that the child owed them a debt of gratitude for being brought into the world, parents must begin to analyze and study their own behavior. If only they did, how often would they be brought up short when realizing that their own actions belie the doctrines they are imparting to their offspring and the adherence they demand to their own authority!

i. The little things in life which they don't give a second thought to:

Urge Synagogue attendance on their children	BUT do not attend themselves when they can
Tell the Temple Committee they are out	BUT demand absolute honesty from their children

ii. The larger interests:

Demand that children lead truthful lives	BUT proudly boast of tax falsification or of how they outsmarted their competitors
demand parental loyalty	BUT exhibit national disloyalties

How true it is that parents themselves live a lie! And in so doing they forfeit the respect of their children, for the latter soon learn that their parents are not the little gods they would like their children to believe them to be.

2. The antithesis to forcing their own ambitions upon their children must show itself by their permitting their children's own talents or wishes to be recognized and taken into account as the youngsters grow older.

3. The tendency to insist on visible proof that they are wanted must be superseded by the readiness on the part of parents to give their children the measure of freedom they are capable of exercising as their maturity and years allow. It is the parents who must insist on their children carrying responsibilities at an early age and to cease coddling them at the earliest possible time. It is here that parents must consciously make their sacrifice.

To the extent to which possessiveness will be replaced by the desire to earn the child's respect, so will balance be maintained in parent-child relationships.

The second requisite for making possible the proper balance between individuality or the development of self-hood and cooperation or living together with parents is for the latter to begin from early childhood to make clear that they, the parents, do not constitute the only authority in the world. The parents must therefore learn to evaluate the social resources which their community possesses and share their authority with social agencies. First in the experience of the child is the social agency known as *the School*. The parents should not be jealous of the school but should realize that the state shares with them the right to develop the personality of the child.

This is why poorer homes very often give the children a better opportunity because they are compelled to share with other agencies the task of bringing [up] their children, e.g., the Settlement Houses, Social Centers. The children in such cases have the feeling that they are working with the community whereas in the rich home there prevails the feeling of self-sufficiency. There is no urgent need felt to interact with other social agencies than the family and that attitude prevents a large measure of cooperation.

This is clearly illustrated in any religious school, when some of the pupils have that attitude that it is not a social agency with which they must cooperate to their fullest ability but that it is, so to speak, an extension of their own homes. (One of our pupils told his teacher that he could do as he pleased because his father was Vice President. At that time he was seven years old.) The poorer child has to cooperate with others; the well-to-do child does not.

The third requisite is to initiate the child into responsibility. While the child must not be exposed over-young to adult anxieties and perplexities, he must be spared unduly from realizing the difficulties which confront his elders. It is itself a matter of balance. If the parents knew they had to aim in the development of a sense of responsibility they would avoid the danger of spoiling him. Parents who strive to make life so easy for the child and provide him with every comfort on the pleas that when they were children they lacked so much, bring about a situation where the children become *bored with life*. In order that the child shall learn responsibilities the parents must permit him to engage in whatever work absorbs him to the point where it becomes a consuming interest with him, for in that way alone does the child really learn the meaning of responsibility. The balance is shown when the parent begins to perceive glimmerings of aptitude or desire on the part of the child.

The fourth requisite is to know the world of the child. The parents must be able to let themselves into the world of the child. When parents are dominated by their own personal interests, these fill their minds to such an extent that they cannot enter the life of the child.

Again it involves respect for the child's privacy.

And lastly it involves the whole sex problem. Parents avoid the difficulty by feeling that they have to conceal all knowledge on the plea of decency. Desideratum: wholesome relation.

But these are not the only considerations confronting the problem of synthesizing parent-child relationships. Society and its place in the relationship now looms up.

Society as a whole is interested in parents keeping the child's personality down and making him obey because it wants to maintain the *status quo* insofar as possible.

Hence, even the parents who do seriously reckon with the four requisites we have outlined and who attempt to strike a proper balance between the two extremes of developing the child's self-hood and individuality while getting him to cooperate with them and the school to his fullest capacity will often find themselves in a quandary. For when it comes to educating the child in a changing world wherein we have to change standards, whether of patriotism or of property or of any other factor which enter into the frame of social living, the parent hasn't a chance because society is against him. He is therefore in danger of crippling the child for living the life about him, e.g., if the child learns about the way business is commonly conducted and he learns to be disgusted with it and its methods, he will grow up a rebel. That is why even with the best of intentions on the part of parents it is difficult indeed, if not altogether impossible, to have the proper kind of education or schooling or teacher because education today insists upon transmitting the old corrupt and outworn ideas. The parent is hampered from interpreting the changing world honestly to the child.

With the four steps which we have outlined, however, the parent would be sufficiently conditioned to have the proper balance between the extremes and would be in a position to accomplish the development of personality in his child.

But in all of this we must expect the general difficulty of our environment.

Therefore we cannot solve the parent-child relationship problem unless at the same time we work for the improvement in the other human relationships as well.

response from
Helen Levy-Myers

Dear Rabbi Signer,

Thank you for a great sermon on a topic that is as relevant today as it was when you gave it at Temple Beth El in 1935. I hope you allow me the liberty of building on and expanding your excellent foundation with some solutions to problems you diagnose. One of the issues you spend a lot of time discussing is that some parents see their children as possessions, which leads parents to demand obedience from them, that they follow in the parent's desired professions, and that parents sometimes try to manage their children even after they are married.

Today we call these parents "helicopter parents" in the sense they swoop in to protect their children inappropriately. According to Wikipedia, "Helicopter parents are so named because, like helicopters, they 'hover overhead', overseeing every aspect of their child's life constantly. A helicopter parent is also known to strictly supervise their children in all aspects of their lives, including in social interactions."[153] Helicopter parents may not see their children as possessions, but these parents see their role as always being their advocate, sometimes almost in a lawyerly way. They do not see their role as gently guiding their children toward adulthood. If the child turned in homework late, resulting in a lower grade, they might contact the school to ask for forbearance, provide an excuse, or complain to the administration.

One of the issues I wish you had addressed is the difficult parental role of stepping back and letting one's own child fail, experience disappointment and learn from the experience that being late can have important consequences. It is very hard to watch one's child not be the success each parent dreams of, but offering parents the wisdom that experience, while a painful teacher, is often the most effective teacher. Parents also need the courage to actually step back, and your leadership and support to parents when necessary could have been truly valuable and possibly life-changing. Learning to be resilient in the face of difficulty is a lifelong skill that children need to learn, and that schools and parents collectively and repeatedly need to teach.

One can even make the case that resilience is a Jewish trait that can help explain how the Jews have survived so many difficulties. When Judaism redefined itself, after the destruction of the Second Temple, from a religion focused on animal sacrifice in a specific Temple location to worship in multiple synagogues and the

---

[153] Wikipedia. "Helicopter parent" definition. https://en.wikipedia.org/wiki/Helicopter_parent.

home, resilience helped Judaism survive. After the Spanish Inquisition, many responded by diving deep into the spiritual mysticism of Kabbalah, still today one of Judaism's great traditions. Judaism values the response to trauma or catastrophe as finding a way for new ideas, new opportunities, even sometimes new lives. Judaism reflects this resilience, even grit. Grit is that skill of getting back up and doing something again and again, even when it is difficult. Resilience and grit are what all children need to blossom and grow into caring, responsible adults who can thrive even in the face of adversity.

You do address the issue of responsibility a bit indirectly by stating that parents need to teach it to their children. But what does teaching responsibility mean? How does the modern parent do it? Of course, the very modern, 21st-century way to get answers to questions like, "How does one teach children responsibility?" is to search for the answer through Google. According to The Center for Parenting Education,[154] it turns out that many parents say they want responsible children. Some of The Center for Parenting Education's suggestions include keeping one's word, being accountable for one's behavior and acknowledging mistakes. In our modern world of almost infinite advice, I think your sermon could have built on this with some suggestions of how to instill responsibility in children rather than just calling out parents for being hypocritical by demanding children lead truthful lives while the parents boast of tax fraud. I am not sure what Temple Beth El's policy was about b'nai mitzvah or even b'not mitzvah for girls in 1935, but being recognized as an adult in the Jewish community is an excellent time to start to learn adult responsibilities. If the policy was a minimalist one with just learning the blessings and how to chant Torah, you could have suggested that they be required to give back to Temple Beth El through participation in additional services or by helping elderly or disabled members. A more ambitious policy would be to require children to consider how they could give back to their community or world, define how their project reflects Jewish values, and complete it as part of their bar or bat mitzvah. Such a tikkun project, even a 13-year-old sized one, can have a lasting impact on a child. That child will remember the time it took to conceive the project, the effort to complete it, and the satisfaction of making an impact.

Modern research on child development puts emphasis on developing rituals and structure in the child's life which make it easier for the child to navigate the world, as there are certain events, people, or traditions that ground and explain the world to the young child. According to Dr. Rebecca Lester, "One of the most

---

[154] https://centerforparentingeducation.org/library-of-articles/responsibility-and-chores/developing-responsibility-in-your-children/.

important features of rituals is that they do not only mark time; they create time. By defining beginnings and ends of developmental or social phases, rituals structure our social worlds and how we understand time, relationships, and change."[155]

I think your sermon could have provided more useful suggestions to parents and at the same time emphasized the Jewishness of your sermon by making a strong case for establishing Jewish traditions in the home, both for weekly Shabbat rituals and for annual ones like Passover and Rosh Hashanah. Your sermon notes include making a special pitch for the upcoming Religious School's Pesach Entertainment program. I am not sure exactly what you said, but you could have again mentioned the event within your sermon, and you could have emphasized that attending these events lets children know that parents value their religious education, value their participation in religious and community events, and value the joy they bring into the world. Going beyond your Temple's upcoming event, you could have even gone "wild and crazy" by suggesting non-traditional ideas like turning Shabbat into family game night. Or you might have considered suggesting that the Christmas holiday could also be a Jewish family tradition, not with a tree, but as an opportunity to help those less fortunate when often many social services are shut down.

Again, it was a wonderful sermon with a very modern feel that addressed topics that still feel relevant, and I hope you continue to speak on this topic as there are still many ways to address the problems you correctly see.

Helen Levy-Myers was a member of Havurat Shalom in Somerville, Massachusetts from 1981 to 1995 then she moved back to Northern Virginia near her parents and high school. A month later she had her first son. Now she is a member of Congregation Beth Emeth in Herndon, Virginia and an active member of the Ritual Committee. She currently works as a Data Scientist for The Dark Star Group doing what many Data Scientists do: looking for that needle in the poorly organized haystack of endless dirty, messy data. Her other interests include cooking, walking outdoors, visiting her three grown sons (one in San Diego, two in Austin, Texas), reading, and laughing at all that life has thrown us recently.

---

[155] https://www.psychologytoday.com/us/blog/anthropology-in-mind/202005/the-importance-ritual.

Value of Literature

Poetry in Religion

Delivered in Manhattan Beach, New York at Temple Beth El,
May 23, 1930, for *Parshat B'har-B'hukosei*

> The world is too much with us: late and soon,
> Getting and spending, we lay waste our powers.
> Little we see in nature that is ours;
> We have given our hearts away, a sordid boon![156]

With these words the poet Wordsworth voices his condemnation of an age that has grown prosaic and has banished the poetry of life. There is in man a spark that bursts into flame at the sight of the beautiful, an echo that responds to the voice of Nature in its wild freedom. There is in him something that thrills at the thought of the majesty of the world's pageantry as it passes before him, with its interminable succession of times and seasons. For man is by nature romantic—and it is this quality in him that tends to disappear from life today.

We live in an age of steel and stone, of gas and oil, of dynamos and motors, a century wherein all bow the head to the three great gods: Utility, Production and Efficiency. And as faithful converts to this cult we consciously or unconsciously banish from our hearts all that cannot be measured by the exact rule of practicality nor weighed in the balances of increased production. And, indeed, it is not to be wondered at if our lives, for all their turmoil and hustle, are commonplace and dull. We move in narrow canyons overhung by towering cliffs where we spend most of our waking hours. Every morning anew, we enter into the perpetual race against time—a hysterical struggle wherein, as the day goes on, and our energies are bent more and more to our tasks, we find, perchance, a sort of peace. And yet it is no real rest, only the delusively calm equilibrium of the spinning top, which seems to be still while whirring at a pace faster than the eye can trace.

Bound as we are to the wheel of life, who among us can stop but for a moment to reflect upon our lives, to turn our thoughts to the awesome universe wherein we move and have our being, and to pay our respects to the Spirit of the World, whose divine energy moves in unseen paths behind the veil of phenomena? It is because of the absence of such moments of clear reflection that life grows irrational, because of the haste with which we act that we do not see the leisurely beauty

---

[156] The beginning of the poem "The World is Too Much With Us" written by the British Romantic Poet William Wordsworth (1770-1850) circa 1802.

and order of the world in which we live and move, and because of our self-centered activity that we lose the highest moments of self-realization, in a sense of harmony and union with God. Our lives, in their hectic fevers, lose simultaneously the cool calm of repose and the peacefully heightened activity of poetic inspirations.

And here our Judaism has a function that is not often recognized, and which I want to point out at this time, the function of giving us the hours of calm which our turbulent lives demand and of bringing into the wearisome, monotonous prose of life the stimulating rhythm and fancy of poetry.

When amidst the ceaseless rush of a long, toilsome week, we come to God's house on a Friday night for the *Ma'ariv* [evening] Service, there comes to our hearts, if we will only let it, the majestic panorama of the heavens, as the might of God rolls away the light from before the darkness, and the darkness from before the light, and our souls, if they but will, may find a momentary rest in the peace that flows from the contemplation of the dignified march of the constellations as God's hand arrays the stars in their watches in the sky, according to His will. For Jewish life is filled with strains from the proud poetry of nature, the waving of the *lulav*, with the *hadasim* and *esrog*[157] or the reference to the rainbow, which is God's seal of peace. And we become again children of our world when we chant how the trees clap their hands with joy[158] and how the roaring of the breakers of the sea cannot drown out the voice of God.[159] But it is not only the poetry of heaven and earth and their fullness which Judaism brings to us, but also the fast-vanishing poetry of our homes. The heart and soul are reborn, as the eyes, weary with the ledger, look up to see the angels of peace enter the magic circle of the glow of the *Shabbos* [Sabbath] candles. Such are the moments of the richness of life. And this too Judaism can give us to keep up a task that taxes our powers to the full.

Sometimes too, the poetry of our observance serves another purpose, a much more important purpose. By taking us for a moment out of ourselves, it enables us to look upon our lives in a spirit of objective criticism. We come to challenge the value of our activities, the worth of our ends and goals, the measure of our striving and toiling; it enables us to look upon our lives in a spirit of objective criticism. We come to challenge the value of our activities, the worth of our ends and goals; we contrast them with the ideals that Judaism puts before us and we find them wanting. At such moments, we recast our plans of life, we remodel our patterns, remould our ideals and open new vistas for ourselves.

---

[157] The palm frond, the myrtle, the willow branch and the citron fruit which the Bible commands the Jews to use during the Feast of Tabernacles (*cf.* Leviticus 23:40).
[158] Isaiah 55:12.
[159] Psalms 93:4.

At that time there blow into our narrow lives the free winds from the great open world, stirring the dust and turning life once more from a safe routine into what we should always find it—a poetic adventure.

We catch glimpses of new mountain ranges, of vast, unexplored realms or dark and alluring seas, and new havens beyond them that would be won. We break the fetters that have bound us, and set out again with the same sense of enticing risk that Columbus must have felt as his ships turned westward.

Santayana[160] the philosopher has said that religion and poetry are one in essence, and while there is much in this statement liable to misunderstanding and abuse, one of the greatest functions of religion in our day is to give us surcease from our matter-of-fact lives. To be vital and relevant, Judaism must not, cannot fail in this. To be full, rich, deep and whole, our hearts should turn eagerly to the poetry wherewith religion grants to life the romance it demands.

What Emerson has said applies quite rightly to us. The Daughters of Time, as he aptly phrases it, bring diadems and fagots in their hands, offering each according to his will.[161] Of the fagots, we all must, perforce choose, for Life is a stern Taskmaster. But Judaism offers us the diadems of its beauty wherewith we may, if we are wise, crown our lives with a quickened sense of the poetry of the Universe, the beauty, the meaning, and the dignity of our existence.

---

[160] Jorge Agustín Nicolás Ruiz de Santayana y Borrás, George Santayana in English, a Spanish philosopher (1863-1952). The term *fagots* in this passage refers to bundles of sticks tied together for fuel.
[161] From "The Daughters of Time" by Ralph Waldo Emerson (1803-1882).

response from
Lawrence Rosenwald

Dear Rabbi Signer,

It feels strange to write you in this way, across the gulf that separates the living and the dead, with me in life and you *in der emeser velt*, in the true world—strange not only because of that gulf, but also because your voice in the sermon of yours I'm writing about is so alive, so present, so contemporary. I can almost hear you, and the concerns you address in 1930 are our concerns today, the mechanizing, hurrying pressure of the way we live, the turn to nature as a refuge from that pressure, as an alternative to that pressure, and then the capacity of Jewish poetry and the rhythms of Jewish life to offer us a different way of seeing, of being, a place from which to survey and chasten the lives we lead.

I have some thoughts about how you set up these oppositions, even some respectful dissents to offer, but before getting to them I should note, with pleasure and admiration, how deeply literary your writing is; you write as someone with an inward sense of great poetry, and with a poetic sensibility of your own. I savor with special admiration the analogy you make between the false peace of steady mechanical work and "the delusively calm equilibrium of the spinning top"—I'm reminded of a passage I treasure in the work of Samuel Johnson, where Johnson is writing about the Metaphysical Poets, Donne and company, and he observes that in their poems "the most heterogeneous ideas are yoked by violence together" (Johnson's *The Life of Cowley*, 1779-81). He means this as disparagement, but I take it as praise, and comparing false rest to a spinning top is such a yoking, not at all violent but inspired and fruitful.

I also love how inward you are with the language of scripture, making sentences saturated with its beautiful language; I'm thinking in particular of this luminous sentence, "we become again children of our world when we chant how the trees clap their hands with joy and the roaring of the breakers of the sea cannot drown out the voice of God"—you draw on Isaiah 55 and then on Psalm 93, but the sentence is yours, the juxtaposition yours, and all honor to you for that power.

You quote Wordsworth, then Santayana, then Emerson at the end. Santayana I've read little of, but Wordsworth is important to me, Emerson still more so, and it's by way of thinking about the two writers that I arrived at the respectful critique, or dissent, that I'm about to set out, sadly knowing that I'll have the last word here, wishing I could know what your response would be.

You quote Wordsworth as a sage, almost as a rabbi: "The world is too much with us: late and soon, / Getting and spending we lay waste our powers." So also with Emerson: "the Daughters of Time," as he aptly phrases it, "bring diadems and fagots in their hands, offering each according to his will." (Eleven years after you gave your sermon, by the way, the great American literary critic F. O. Matthiessen, in his extraordinary critical work *American Renaissance*, singled out "Days," the poem you quote, as Emerson's best work; you quoted what was best.)

Both passages are indeed full of moral wisdom, quasi-rabbinic in their force, and you draw out that wisdom beautifully. I have the sense, reading, that you rejoice in having these great writers on your side, on the side of Jewish teaching, and even, perhaps, that you feel that all wisdom is in the end one, that the teachings of Wordsworth and Emerson on the one hand, of Torah on the other, are in accord, in harmony and in synergy.

If you feel that—and you may not, of course—then I respectfully disagree. This for many reasons, but above all, in this context, because of the most troubling passage I know in Emerson's work. It's in the journals, which you may well not have read. I love them; I wrote a book about them; I edited them. They are full of life, of movement, of candor. But they also reveal Emerson's limitations, and nowhere more troublingly than in a passage he wrote in 1852:

> I waked at night, and bemoaned myself, because I had not thrown myself into this deplorable question of Slavery, which seems to want nothing so much as a few assured voices. But then, in hours of sanity, I recover myself, and say, "God must govern his own world, and knows his way out of this pit, without my desertion of my post, which has none to guard it but me." I have quite other slaves to free than those negroes, to wit, imprisoned spirits, imprisoned thoughts, far back in the brain of man,—far retired in the heaven of invention, and which, important to the republic of Man, have no watchman, or lover, or defender, but I. (from Emerson's *The Last of the Anti-Slavery Lectures*)

This is, for me, unbearable, a failure to recognize the difference between literal slavery, the legal and behavioral torment and dehumanizing of African Americans, and the metaphorical slavery, if indeed the metaphor can be justified, of "imprisoned spirits, imprisoned thoughts." Emerson was better than pretty much anyone else at freeing imprisoned thoughts; but thinking that these are comparable to imprisoned slaves is a failure of moral imagination, a failure even of poetical imagination, a failure to understand what metaphor, that essential resource for poets, can and cannot do.

And here Jewish tradition, as I understand it, dissents from Emerson and has much to teach him—because Jewish tradition, rich in metaphor as it is, beautiful as are the metaphors that you quote, never confuses metaphor with truth, never lets a love of metaphor or a reliance on metaphor get in the way of moral teaching. "Oppress not the stranger, for you were strangers in the land of Egypt" (Exodus 22:20), that wonderfully repeated and varied stern commandment, is about being a stranger for real, is about oppression for real. To treat it as if it were a commandment to govern the mind in relation to oppressed thoughts would be wrong, would be blasphemous. I can imagine how deep the desire would have been, in 1930, in the United States, in what for many Jews, though not for all, was *di goldene medine*, the golden state, to find Jewish teachings in accord with American and English ones. And of course they often are. But not always, and not here.

Having spent more of my life in the realm of literature than in the realm of Jewish tradition, I am aware of having come only gradually to this sense that the Jewish tradition is sometimes the rebuker of those literary traditions I love, and which you too love; that there are tensions as well as synergies, and that when push comes to shove, I know which side I'm on.

With every good wish to you *in der emeser velt*, and deep gratitude for having written so beautiful and thought-provoking a sermon.

Lawrence Rosenwald is the Anne Pierce Rogers Professor of English Emeritus at Wellesley College, where he taught from 1980 to 2022. He has written on diaries, the relations between words and music, translation and the multilingual world, Yiddish literature, and nonviolence. His most recent book is War No More: Three Centuries of American Antiwar and Peace Writing *(Library of America, 2016); his current large project is called* Portrait of a Pacifist Critic. *He has also published translations from French, German, and Yiddish, and has written and performed some fifty scripts for early music theater. He has been a member of Havurat Shalom in Somerville, Massachusetts since 2003, and is profoundly grateful to all who created and have sustained that community.*

Truth Will Be Crowned

Delivered in Manhattan Beach, New York at
Temple Beth El, January 17, 1930, for *Parshat Vay'chi*

Adonijah, Absalom's brother,[162] and a well-favored handsome fellow he must have been, was by his age and in seniority [King] David's successor. He had designs upon the throne; he was eager to be Israel's king. Nor were his only slightly veiled thoughts and desires rebuked by his venerable father. Knowing that Solomon was the next monarch of the Children of Israel, he nevertheless seems to have looked indulgently upon the pretender. David was ever a poor disciplinarian when his own household was involved. He seems almost invariably to have taken the line of least resistance with his children to his own grief and their disaster. No father serves his son's best [interest] by allowing him unlimited freedom, by exempting him from the restrictions of sound parental authority. The child will pay in sorrow and in disappointment for every hour of ill-gotten liberty, and society will suffer for the indulgence that was cruel instead of kind. Adonijah carried his conspiracy to such a length that his life was only saved by his direct appeal to the religious tradition, when he flung himself upon the horns of the altar. A little later, when after his reprieve and practical banishment under an agreement of good behavior, he revived his intrigue, he suffered the death penalty always meted out to traitors or conspirators.

Adonijah's ambition was a curse because it was not ruled by a righteous purpose, an unselfish motive and modified by love. He *would* be king, but not for the sake of his subjects. He would hold his father's scepter for his own glory, to gratify his own pride. Again we find pride, self-seeking lust for position, going before a fall. The most dangerous man in any age is not the ill-favored criminal of low intelligence and no order, but the well-born aristocrat of manners and station, who regards himself as the heir of a divine right, and who looks upon society as the playground of his latest fancy, if not of his vicious passion.

Adonijah's ambition, which should have been a blessing, was a curse; drove him to the depths instead of sending him to the heights, because it had no regard for others, because it respected no rights that lay in the way of his selfish will. And it was doubly a curse because it had no regard for God. As well as he knew his own age he knew what Heaven's will was with regard to David's successor. Solomon

---

[162] The story of King David's sons Absalom and Adonijah and their attempts to succeed their father can be found in Second Samuel chapters 13-19 (Absalom) and First Kings chapter 1 (Adonijah).

had been chosen. Israel was a theocracy. It was God who was the ruler. And it was only through His divine will that a monarch could reign. Not age but divine appointment named the head to wear the crown. Saul the first king had by this time no successor in his own blood. The haste with which the pretender went upon his ill-starred way is proof of his culpability. With his father lying in helplessness upon his last bed Adonijah sets up a popular spectacle which he hopes will give him the headship of the government. With spirited horses, shining chariots and abundance of feasting he puts himself into the eyes of his people, seeks to capture their imagination and pre-empt their allegiance.

And his ambition ran forward against a most significant warning. He was a full blood brother of Absalom, whom tradition says he strongly resembled. Graceful, tall, generous appearing and commanding, he looked, as did his ill-fated brother before him, the royal part to which he aspired. Daily he must have been reminded of that family catastrophe by the faraway look in his father's eyes. Daily he must have been warned against the repetition of that colossal folly. He went to his death with little excuse for his gamble.

Now Adonijah was not crowned because the crown belonged to another. There could have been no crowning with him as the principal. And the obligation upon those in authority was to crown the true one. A few leaders were faithless, a few in places of influence encouraged the young man's rashness, but faithful Nathan and the rest stood fast; they met or rather anticipated the shock of rebellion, and brought Solomon in safety to his throne. Nathan could have followed the line of least resistance also. He could have said: Oh well, what difference does it make; Adonijah looks every inch a king, his case can be given a good appearance to the people, he is popular and has the initiative. I run some risk in lifting my voice against him. Why should I, an old man, who has seen trouble and bloodshed enough in his day invite more disorder and sorrow? But Nathan said nothing of the sort because he was God's prophet and a voice of truth. The only reason for his choice of Solomon over Adonijah was the fact that Solomon was the selection of God and of David, and Nathan knew his sacred obligation to crown the true one.

Too many of us are following the easier way today, unlike the course which Nathan chose. We are following it in business, in society, in the home, in politics. I grant you that it is not an easy thing to crown the truth, to follow it unreservedly. It is not an easy thing for a college lad to go with his conscience against [the] will of his roistering mates. It is not an easy thing for a senator to vote his conviction against the command of his party. It is not an easy thing for a man to stand out among his fellows and friends as refusing to enter into crude and childish and bestial forms of amusements. It is not an easy thing for a preacher to stand in his pulpit and deliver broadsides at his congregation, no matter how rightly he feels they deserve it. It is not an easy thing for a mother to find herself alone in her purpose to bring up her children in simplicity and naturalness. But whether these things are easy or hard, it is our duty, whatever the cost, to crown only that which is true. Duty is ours; events are God's.

Adonijah teaches us that no man has a right, whatever his power, to take the rights of others. The recognition of this principle will lead us at once to see the fallacy of the personal liberty argument wherever it is applied. Only one thing, one reason, stood between the pretender and the throne he sought so eagerly—the fact that the crown belonged to Solomon. His freedom of action in the direction of that crown was interfered with and he was stopped because that crown was not his. He had no right because the right was his brother's. We want to keep that always in mind. We drive our cars on the right side of the street because of others. We clear the ice from our front door lest others fall. We do not smoke in the subway because of the inconvenience to others. We refrain from many things because of the rights of others.

Again we want to remember that Solomon would hardly have been crowned had it not been for the loyalty of Nathan and his mother. What a beautiful thing a mother's loyalty is. Bathsheba's voice, the voice of the woman David loved above all other women, rang David out of his senile sleep; challenged him up from indifference, and placed the crown upon the head of the fond mother's son. Nathan the prophet knew when a mother's voice would carry farther than any other. No son who has gone through life without it will ever know what infinite power lies in a mother's love and allegiance. Let the emphasis rest upon the woman who, with her prayers and her tears and her sacrifices and her faith, follows her son and her daughter through temptations and trials of every sort to the place of high decision to the throne of service and power, to the crown of loving favor from God and man. God bless the mothers and God bless those fathers who in these days of unusual strain and uncertainty strive to crown the true and supplant the false.

But apart from our children, what about ourselves? We too are to crown truth in our own lives, crown it by enthroning it in our minds, exalting it in our thoughts and honoring it in our actions. כִּי כְמוֹ שָׁעַר בְּנַפְשׁוֹ כֶּן הוּא "As a man thinketh so is he" (Proverbs 23:7), proclaimed the wise man long ago. As a man THINKETH, not by the fair speaking of his lips when they are contradicted by the sinister glance of his eye, but by the selfish meditations of his soul does he stand judged by the One who knoweth us altogether. When I plan against my fellow man, and prove faithless to the trust his friendship places upon me, I am crowning the base and the dishonorable within me. When I entertain unworthy thoughts of womanhood to which my mother belongs and of which the mother of my child is a part, I become unworthy of my manhood. When I fail to speak out in defense of the principles and ideals of my character, I shrivel in my moral being, and in spite of my loudest protestations, stand ashamed. We can do no better than follow the advice one old man gave his son as a death-bed legacy. "My son," said he, "be courteous and considerate, zealous for true popularity and disturbed should you find your friends growing cold to you, but my son, at whatever price and at any cost, stand true to truth."

And in conclusion, let us never lose sight of one stupendous fact—that truth will be crowned. With us or without us, truth is omnipotent. We may be responsible for delay, our faithlessness may postpone the event, but we cannot defeat the divine ultimate purpose. Indeed it is true that the greatest friend of truth is time. I have read that during the war a platoon of French soldiers was charged with fleeing from the face of danger, with cowardice and refusal. A hurried court-martial imposed the sentence of death, and these unlucky fellows with their officers were blindfolded against an ancient wall and shot. Two years after the armistice the terrible mistake was discovered too late to bring back the dead, but not too late to vindicate their honor. Now the families of these victims of the cruel war's haste and horror wear the honors which a grateful nation can never bestow upon the soldiers who should have worn them. We do want to remember that

> Truth crushed to earth will rise again
> The eternal years of God are hers
> But error wounded writhes in pain
> And dies amid her worshippers.[163]

But truth will be crowned. No earthly court could do more than torture Galileo, imprison Columbus or burn Bruno.[164] Their spirit is still alive today. The truths they have exemplified are still our crown. And so it has been with every patriot who fell on the sharp sword of freedom. And so too shall it be with every *chalutz*[165] who has become martyr to his faith and a torch for his belief. And so it has been with many a humble person unknown to fortune and unsung by fame.

---

[163] The ninth stanza of the poem *The Battlefield* by William Cullen Bryant (1794-1878).
[164] Giordano (Filippo) Bruno (1548-1600), an Italian Dominican friar and cosmologist who was burned at the stake by the Roman Inquisition in 1600.
[165] Hebrew for "pioneer," referring to the European Jews who emigrated to the Holy Land in the 19th and early 20th centuries to settle and work the land.

In the story of Adonijah the false was overthrown by the lifting up of the true. Nathan did not lead a force against the pretender, he did not attack Adonijah. He led forth Solomon. He anointed the chosen successor. Nathan's campaign was *for* Solomon rather than against Adonijah. It was positive rather than negative. The false was dethroned when the true was enthroned. Adonijah was put down when Solomon was lifted up.

Is not this as fine an object lesson as we can find? Crowd out that which is unworthy of the best within us. Crowd out the lewd thoughts and the evil passions; the hates which sear our souls; the bitterness which discolours our lives; and the neuroses which poison our minds.

Crowd them out and crown the true. How? Our fathers did it by the never-failing practice of giving themselves to God for a half-hour or so every morning. They *davened*.[166] They made themselves right with God. We however, for one reason or another, do not do so. But we must do something if truth is to be crowned. Can we not therefore make this habit our own? Let us spend a few minutes in the morning while in the train, or in our cars, with a clean idea; a verse from a poem or a line from the Bible. If we will, we may have, with but little effort, a library of inspiring thoughts, a rich storehouse to draw upon for all manner of occasions, a veritable congestion of wholesomeness that will leave no room for anything base or mean. But we must first give truth our mind, our body, our soul. We must think it; serve it; worship it. Let us crown the true and win.

---

[166] Yiddish term meaning "to engage in prayer."

response from
Chaya Rowen-Baker

Dear Rabbi Signer,

What an honor it is to be writing to you! When asked the common conversation-starter, "With whom, from any time in history, would you like to have coffee?" people's answers are often theoretical and do not develop into an actual conversation. Here I have the privilege of actually having with you, well, half a conversation.

I write my thoughts with tremor and reverence because this is not in fact a conversation. You will not answer. Still, it is an incredible thrill to feel as though we are reflecting together on eternal ideas across generations.

The topic of your sermon poses a challenge to the very idea of "speaking across generations." I wonder whether we even think of truth in the same way, you in your era and I in mine.

Two ideas resonate throughout your sermon, which in your view are bound together but which I have difficulty connecting to each other consistently. You speak of crowning that which is true, no matter how much friction or personal cost it might cause, but in saying that, you assume that truth is apparent. You combine the virtue of absolute truth with a compelling call to devote our lives to revealing it. Before we can muster the courage and stamina to do that, however, we must be able to identify something as true.

I wonder whether crowning truth is actually the hardest part. In fact, one of life's biggest challenges might just be discerning truth.

It may be an impossible task to define truth. Perhaps, to paraphrase Max Kadushin, what is not defined should not be defined.[167] Still, when major trends clash—how do we decide between them? How do we decide which parenting theory to adopt, which approach to creating a just economy should have our vote, or how to weigh conflicting rights and values?

I suppose if, like the prophet Nathan, we were told directly by God what is true, we would be faced with the "mere" task of pursuing it bravely. However, most of us are not in that position and those who claim to be are generally assumed to be charlatans thirsty for power and control. How, then, can we know what is truly true?

You cite the "line of least resistance" as the consistently wrong option taken by King David in his relationships and politics. That could be an interesting criterion:

---

[167] Max Kadushin (1895-1980) was a Conservative rabbi. The quote is paraphrased from a line from his book *The Rabbinic Mind*, p. 45.

if it is too easy, it is probably not truth. One might argue that since trends come and go, sometimes even swinging between opposite poles, truth itself vacillates and therefore cannot be identified by an absolute criterion. On the other hand, there may be merit to the claim that since many truths are time-bound and relative, they are, by definition, the path less traveled at any given time. According to this perspective, a life of meaning and significance will be a life of struggle. Such a life would not be about a specific truth but about promoting any idea, ideal or value larger than yourself, your needs and your comfort.

God, through Moses, warns us against a life of comfort: "But Jeshurun waxed fat, and kicked…" (Deut. 32:15). In its context, this verse conveys concern that prosperity would detach people from the Source of Livelihood and cause them to forget their dependence on God. Rabbinic literature, however, is more nuanced. The Rabbis tell us that God's voice spoke from Heaven, declaring that Hillel's and Shammai's *halachic* (legal determination) methods are equal in their truth—both representing "God's Living Word"—but according to that voice, Hillel's *halachic* method is to be the one practiced, not Shammai's (BT Eruvin 13b).

Hillel's *halacha* is more lenient, easier to practice, more accessible—the method that perhaps allows for more convenience. In this approach, the search for truth meets the need for comfort and seeks to dwell with it.

Perhaps this is because seeking truth makes us hard. The preference for Hillel's *halacha* may be intended to teach that truth-crowning, however strongly desired, must incorporate softness. For truthfully, "truth" can be dangerous. When taken to the extreme it is the basis of conflict. Fighting over truth has caused endless harm and suffering in our world. The claim to truth must therefore be accompanied by a measure of humility and flexibility, so that the coronation of truth does not cause disaster.

Moreover, if we remove direct Divine revelation from the equation, someone who fluctuates in their truth and wavers in their conviction may actually be more likely to "crown truth." Holding a softer concept of truth may increase our openness to information and enhance our complexity of thought and ultimately our chances of "getting it right." That intention seems clear in the determination that *halacha* should follow Hillel. The tradition in the Palestinian Talmud holds that his approach was not only the more lenient one but also was predicated on first hearing the opposing argument and sometimes even being convinced by it (PT Sukkah 2:8).

By following this notion of truth, one can pursue truth without increasing aggression in the world. It may very well be the reason our Rabbis cite the Hillel-versus-Shammai controversy as the only type of conflict which is fruitful and therefore welcome.

You say, "The greatest friend of truth is time." I love that sentence. I think you are right, but in a slightly different way than you explained. Time allows space and perspective for new facts to be revealed, but its greatest power is that it allows for a change in interpretation. It thus helps to reveal truth. It enables deeper and wider contemplation, leading to a better understanding of the issue at hand. We must bear in mind that revealing truth is not only knowing facts. It is also understanding their meaning and value within the relevant context.

That said, I must disagree with you concerning the French soldiers. I see their story as tragic, not redemptive. You understood their vindication as a triumph of truth. However, all that was achieved was clearing their name while they remain not only dead but also having died in vain. The truth revealed in this story is how war will make the military systems engaged in it rash and obtuse. But that is not redemptive for the unfortunate French soldiers.

The Hebrew word for truth, אמת (*emet*), stems from the root א.מ.נ (*aleph.mem.nun*), as does the word for faith, אמונה (*emuna*). One might think that truth and faith are opposing ideas: truth is what I know and faith is what I believe. However, the Hebrew etymology indicates that truth and faith are two manifestations of the same basic imperative; both are vehicles for interpreting life and seeking meaning. They are merely different ways of saying "amen."

Saying "amen" and embracing the ordinance to seek truth, even to "crown truth," is a way of coming to know that the more we reconsider and remain flexible, the more meaning we will find in life and the finer our faith will be.

Rabbi Chaya Rowen-Baker was ordained by the Schechter Rabbinical Seminary. Rabbi Rowen-Baker holds a BA in Jewish History and Archaeology from the Hebrew University, and an MA, magna cum laude, in Jewish studies from the Schechter Institute. She has been head of the internship program and teaching practical rabbinics at the Schechter Rabbinical Seminary since 2016, and was the rabbi of Congregation Ramot Zion in French Hill, Jerusalem from the time of her ordination in 2007 until 2023. She was the first Masorti rabbi—and the first female rabbi—ever to be invited to teach Torah at the Israeli President's residence. She is now the Dean of the Schechter Rabbinical Seminary in Jerusalem.

Rabbi Rowen-Baker lives in French Hill, Jerusalem with her husband Etai, their four children Adaya, Keshet, Clil, and Yagel, and their dog Hummus.

A Virtuous Vice:
Creative Expectations

Delivered in Manhattan Beach, New York at Temple Beth El,
December 20, 1929, for *Parshat Vayishlah*

We have seen in our reading how Jacob struggled in the night—a struggle in which he is described as having conquered gods and men: כי שרית עם אלהים ועם אנשים ותוכל ["... for you have striven with beings divine and human and have prevailed" Genesis 32:29]. As a token of his victory the name Israel is conferred upon him. The name suggests prince and victory. But at the time of the story, Jacob had not yet become a prince among men. He was a mendicant, journeying to ask the forgiveness of his brother Esau.

The idea that every man possesses a dual personality is elaborated by the Sages, who interpret for us the meaning of the vision which appeared to Jacob 21 years earlier, in his flight from Esau. He saw the angels going up and coming down [the ladder].[168] The angels, the Rabbis tell us, went up to heaven and there saw the image of this man enthroned in Heaven at the right hand of the deity—the image of an Israel, a prince among men, and then they descended and saw his likeness lying prone on the ground, a Jacob—an ordinary mortal, subject to base thoughts, strong passions, a creature weak and full of faults. They were moved to mirth and scorn. "How could such a mortal aspire to so heavenly an image," they cried and prepared to harm him, when suddenly God Himself appeared standing beside Jacob—giving to this man His divine approbation.

It is customary practice for us humans to give payment for work well done in the form of approval and praise. By the same token we are ready to condemn a man over-hastily. So common is this, that there has come into circulation the proverb: "Give a dog a bad name and hang him." We think ourselves extremely forbearing if we RESERVE our opinion until we are convinced of the merit of the person judged. We are more often inclined to pour out the vials of our criticism and scorn upon the head of him who is looking for approbation from his fellows for every act he performs. We look upon such an attitude as somehow ignoble and lacking in manliness and moral stamina and courage. We class such behavior among the vices, even though it be but a minor vice.

But have we ever analyzed it to see whether in truth it is a vice? Whether it's not rather a virtue? And if we went a step further in our analysis, would we not come

---

[168] Jacob's dream: Genesis 28:12.

to the conclusion that this desire for universal approval, if taken advantage of by society, would redound to the great benefit of society at large? In other words, if society were not to wait with its conferring of the seal of approval until after a man has performed good deeds, if society would instead first signify its approval of a man on the basis of faith in his potentialities and possibilities, would not then society serve by this attitude to elicit and evoke and bring out from him that kind of conduct and behavior and action which would make him WANT to retain the trust and affection and approbation of society?

This is what the Torah means by presenting the story of Jacob gaining the angel's approval. This is what the Rabbis meant by picturing God set[ting] the stamp of approval upon Jacob while yet he did nothing to merit it. This is the very thing the Rabbis want to teach with the legend of the conduct of the angels at the giving of the Torah at Sinai. Angels complain that God is favoring Israel by taking away from them His most precious gift. [They] want to restrain Moses from taking away the commandments. God tells Moses to give them an answer. Moses says: you don't need it. We need a pattern, an ideal by which to live in order to gain the approval of God and man. This is the meaning of the prayer they would have us recite: יהי רצון שתתנני לחסד ולרחמים בעיני כל רואי [may it be Your will to give me lovingkindness and mercy in the eyes of all who see me]

This is what R Yohanan b Zackai meant when his pupils asked for his blessing just before his death (Talmud B'rachot 28b)

יהי רצון שתהא מורא שמים עליכם כמורא בשר ודם [may it be God's will that the fear of heaven shall be upon you like the fear of flesh and blood].

Thus we see that from the Jewish point of view, the desire of a person for approval by society may well be a virtue. To see how this living up to that which is expected of us may act as a great moral force in the shaping and transforming of character, it is well to read *The Man Who Pretended* by Maxwell.[169] Oswald Raikes, the hero of the book, is the product of the urge to live up to the good opinion that people had of him.

Oswald is a young man born to a middle class family in England. His mother died while he was still a child, leaving him to the care of his widowed aunt. At no time did he feel close to his father since the latter was a cold, unemotional man, devoted to his own pursuits. In common with a number of people whose senses

---

[169] W.B. Maxwell, *The Man Who Pretended: a very clever novel of self-created dual personality* (Garden City, NY: Doubleday, Doran and Company Inc.), 1929.

are keener than the average, he possessed to a remarkable degree the faculty of introspection, of looking at himself as if he were an outsider looking in, and of analyzing himself. He found that he possessed qualities and tendencies of which he was heartily ashamed, that if left alone, these tendencies would ripen and thus make him into a person he would hate.

The story opens with the funeral of his father. Oswald goes through the outward gestures of a person sorely stricken by a loss. He feels that in so doing he is living a lie, yet his actions are motivated by the thought of what people would say were he to be guided by his instincts. He is enabled by reason of a small legacy to pursue his studies in an art school where he comes in contact with an instructor by the name of Lawrence. He sees in this Lawrence the kind of man he would like to be.

At school he has occasion to note that one of his fellow-students is shunned by the whole school. This arouses his pity. He is kind to the neglected soul and makes a friend of him. His attitude is admired by the whole school and as a result of his kindness, the student is at first tolerated and then accepted by the student-body. Oswald's personality expands by being referred to as a man full of generosity.

However, the incident that determines his moral career took place when he worked for Lawrence after leaving school. He happened to go into a room to sort some drawings and unable to help himself, overheard Lawrence speaking to his secretary. The secretary was praising someone and Lawrence was agreeing with her. Oswald thought to himself how splendid it would be if such fine things could be said of him. He receives the surprise of his life when the secretary refers to him by name. As the book puts it, that overheard conversation decided his fate. "He accepted the desire of approbation as the impulse of his whole life." This henceforth was his undeviating aim.

The reputation he gained for generosity [is] put to the test when he learns that his aunt has speculated heavily and has lost. Her brother, who could well afford to help her, would rather have Oswald come to the rescue. His best offer is that Oswald leave Lawrence for another firm where he can make more money, give up his plans for a career and support his aunt and her daughter. At this Oswald flares up with anger, but realizing that his refusal would shatter the image which people have of him, that he would lose their approval, he bids good-bye to his dreams of a career and personal comfort and accepts this new burden. He is consoled by the approval of his relative, aunt and cousin and the feeling of having done what was expected of him.

His fear of being found out a coward is put to the test when a strike threatens his firm and he comes to the rescue of his employer by arguing the threatening strikers into a conciliatory mood. This elicits more praise which ties him more closely than ever to his employer.

An illustration of the way the reputation he built up got him into more trouble, and placed upon his shoulders greater responsibilities is what happened to him in the course of a vacation. There he met an engaged couple who came to him with their troubles. He attempted to reconcile them to each other seemingly with success. On his return to work he learned that he had shouldered yet another burden because the young lady came to him asking advice and counsel in her plight. Her lover had left her. He feels that the proper thing to do is to help her make herself financially independent. The more he helps her the more she becomes dependent upon him. To her dependence is added feeling of affection for her benefactor tempered with worship for the good he does. Realizing that she is taking up too much of his time, Oswald writes her that he will have to see less of her in the future. She interprets this as meaning that he has tired of her and threatens to commit suicide. Greatly agitated, he runs to save her. He feels that the right thing to do at this time would be to marry her. This he does.

At this time his earning power is limited. His wife does not know how to budget her expenses and despite his fear of being dunned, he always manages to keep a step ahead of his creditors. His employer recognizes his ability and thrusts greater and still greater responsibility upon his shoulders, until he virtually controls the business. This enables him to live on a higher scale. After a time a girl child is born to the Raikes. But he feels strange toward his own offspring because of the possessive attitude of his wife. Since at this time he hasn't any real affection for his wife, he feels his life becoming empty. At this time however another opportunity presents itself for his pent-up emotions to find an outlet. He meets a child about nine years old in the street who has lost some money. He is attracted by her story, takes her to her home, learns her tale is true; he pities her and her mother, and provides not only a schooling for the child but better living quarters for both her and her mother.

The war comes. His employer tells him that he is not expected to go since he is 35. He doesn't want to go because he is afraid. He hopes that his wife will tell him not to go but having to make a patriotic speech to his employees urging *them* to go to war, he realizes that the logical thing for him to do is also to go. On his return home he announces his intention to enlist. She agrees that that would be the right thing for him to do. He senses in his employer a relief in his decision which strengthens him. He enlists.

After three years of fighting he has made firm friends with a physician by the name of Clayton, who, realizing how much of himself Oswald has given to the boys "over there," urges him to use the privilege granted him by dint of his illness to return to England. Oswald however refuses and though feverish, that very night leads a charge.

After his discharge from the army he comes home, resumes his position with his firm finding that in the meantime his investments have turned out well and that he has become a very wealthy man.

Facing the alternative of heading a combine that would bring him untold wealth or giving himself to philanthropic work, he again, aware of the fact that his friends would expect him to do the latter, sets aside the opportunity to make more millions. His home becomes recognized as the rendezvous of the elite. At this time while he has reached the height of his reputation, he meets a woman with whom he really falls in love and he is now tempted to part with his wife, break up his home and for the first time in his life to follow the promptings of his own desires regardless of the consequences. But the habit of doing the right thing for so many years has now become so much a part of himself that, through no outside urging, he overcomes the temptation.

The book might have ended here but another incident proves the value of his hitherto acquired habits. He sees a child in danger of being run over by a truck. He jumps to the rescue instinctively. In saving the child he himself is injured almost fatally. All give up hope for his recovery. Being exceedingly tired of all the struggles with himself, he feels that it would be the right thing for him to die. But his habit of overcoming the tendency to weaken asserts itself and strengthens his will to live. On this hopeful note, the book closes.

Throughout his career, Oswald continually kept looking into his soul. He was given constantly to introspection and self-analysis. His admiration for people who possessed courage and charm and innate dignity of carriage profoundly impressed him; his sense of pity and compassion led him ever to acts of self-abnegation; and his desire for approbation which meant his fear of falling below the standard of that which he thought people expected of him, all combined to make of him a new being. And society gained a good man, Mr. Oswald Raikes. By giving him praise readily, by accepting him at face value, by having confidence in him, and calling him a good fellow, he was strengthened and enheartened to live up to that creative assumption of his really being an admirable personality.

Our remarks this evening would be pointless if we did not dwell a few minutes longer on the inevitable implication of what we've been saying. Applying it all to the Jewish people we can see that the two names by which the Jewish people is known in the Bible are Jacob and Israel. Jacob represents the attitude of knowing the Jewish people to be no better than the rest of the nations, Jacob is the Jewish people as it really is; while Israel represents the attitude of assuming the Jewish people to be of a superior type morally, Israel is the Jewish people as it ought to be. This is the meaning of the term עם סגולה—CHOSEN PEOPLE. I am not so chauvinistic as to think that the Jewish people were in the main much better than other people. The term Chosen People represents the picture which is in the mind of the world of what the Jewish people ought to be. The story we have just heard in detail gives us a symbolic picture of the struggles the Jewish people had to go through—struggles against all the powers of evil that beset it, inner forces even more than outer powers. Many a time and oft did the Jewish people want to break away from the course of conduct it had outlined for itself, times innumerable did the cry go out:

נהיה כגוים כמשפחות הארצות לשרת עץ ואבן

[We will be like the nations, like the families of the lands worshipping wood and stone—Ezekiel 20:32].

But it was always recalled by the voice saying:

רק אתכם ידעתי מכל משפחות האדמה, על כן אפקד עליכם אֶת כל עוׁנתיכם

[You alone have I singled out of all the families of the earth—that is why I call you to account for all of your iniquities—Amos 3:2].

How then did Israel, the nation, aspire to live up to its name? By setting up the following standard:

שלשה סימנים יש באומה ישראל: רחמנים ביישנים גומלי חסדים

[There are three qualities found in [the people of] the nation of Israel: [They are] merciful, shamefaced and desire to be of service—*Talmud Yevamot* 79a].

As long as we dare call ourselves ISRAEL and the CHOSEN PEOPLE we are in a similar position with respect to the nations of the world as was Oswald of our story. Just as he acquires the habit of doing the right thing because it is expected of him, so also will we have to do the right thing because the world expects us to live up to a higher standard than that of the other nations. It's a difficult thing to do; many times are we tempted to drop it all in favor of נהיה כגוים [we will be like the nations]. This struggle is most trying and yet it's the most worthwhile thing we possess. As in the case of Oswald when he falls in love with his wife's friend; think what a disillusionment it would be if the Jewish people were now to yield to strange loves after all these weary years of striving after an ideal. Think what a tragedy it would be if, after so many thousands of years of struggle striving to become an Israel and an עם סגולה [chosen people] and withstanding the temptations of nations, races and creeds, we should fall before the temptation placed before us here in America—the temptation of prosperity which would take us away from our Jewishness.

But then I don't think we really could do this—the sense of *noblesse oblige* would prevent us, especially as with us Jews the *"noblesse"* is not as it is generally understood, a *"noblesse"* of birth, but rather the *"noblesse"* of reputation. We WOULD be loyal to the royal within ourselves; finding our greatest self-realization in the struggle with self. Aren't you of the same opinion?

The name Israel is conferred upon Jacob in recognition of the fact that he came out victorious from his struggles with gods and men. In the two-fold designation of the Jewish people as JACOB-ISRAEL the Bible writers seem to have sensed the truth that the Jewish people possess a dual character or dual personality. Jacob is reminiscent of being the supplanter, Israel suggests the prince of God. The history of the Jewish people is the history of a dual personality. The higher and better personality gradually grows stronger through the striving for the approval of God and man. JACOB represents that which the Jewish people regards itself as actually being; ISRAEL that which the Jewish people would like to become.

The Talmud version of Jacob's dream when he fled from his father's home is as follows etc etc etc etc etc etc etc etc.[170]

What is the process by which Jacob became Israel? The answer is, let the Jewish people continue to play the part of Israel. Let it try to do all that is expected of it as the chosen people however unnatural and difficult such a part may be to play. In time that part will become not only second nature but inherent and only nature. In other words, by LIVING AS IF WE ACTUALLY WERE THE CHOSEN PEOPLE, we will actually become the Chosen People of God.[171]

---

[170] Presumably Signer had a specific example to impart here which he did not write down.

[171] At this point in the sermon, Signer added a much more concise summary of the book *The Man Who Pretended*. It's unclear which version he actually used when preaching. The editor has decided to omit this repetitious section and end the sermon before the additional section.

response from
Shalom Flank

Dear Rabbi Signer,

    Your *drash* [sermon] for *parshat Va-Yishlach* (5690) was a pleasure to read. I admire your ability to craft a well-turned phrase and draw in the listener. And though you knew no other approach, I felt I understood more of your thinking by seeing your revisions, inserts, and reworking of the pages that you typed by hand and revised with a pen (yes, those techniques and technologies are close to extinct today).

    Perhaps it's merely a testament to your persuasiveness, but I found nothing controversial or objectionable in your main thesis. We believe nowadays in positive reinforcement, and especially for children, almost endless praise. Your astute psychological observation that living up to an internalized ideal can shape behavior beyond one's base reactions or desires has been reduced to a crass bumper sticker (another innovation you wouldn't have known at the time): "Fake it till you make it." Or as an oft-read modern psychologist phrases it: "I frequently get asked, 'How can I develop my strengths?' I respond, 'Pretend that you have them. Act *as if* you are kind, or forgiving, or curious.'" Interestingly, she cites Alfred Adler's "acting as if" role-play method as her foundation—which he was developing at the same time as you were giving that sermon (see *The Practice and Theory of Individual Psychology*, 1925). I wonder, were these ideas simply in the air at the time, or did you have Adler specifically in mind?

    Yet I found myself wondering why your presentation of this sound and interesting idea wasn't, well, very Jewish. Where's the discussion of the conflict between our יֵצֶר הָרָע and our יֵצֶר טוֹב, our competing impulses for evil or good (or as some portray, within our one-and-only-*Yetzer*[172])? Where's the reminder from Avot 1:6, צָרִיךְ הָאָדָם לָדוּן אֶת כָּל אָדָם לְכַף זְכוּת, that we need to be as generous as we can in our assumptions about the motivations of others? Or, as *Rebbe* Nachman teaches, to take the same forgiving approach with ourselves? What about the Jewish version of a consequentialist framework to help us understand why the correct *actions* may matter more than the correct *intentions*, if what follows is מִדָּה כְּנֶגֶד מִדָּה [measure for measure]? It's not that your text is devoid of either Jewish concepts or Hebrew itself.

    But in our day, the *Rav* [Rabbi] giving your *drash* (note: at least in the communities I'm part of, we don't call them sermons anymore) would have sprinkled

---

[172] https://www.academia.edu/243482/Two_Rabbinic_Inclinations_Rethinking_a_Scholarly_Dogma.

in far more Hebrew phrases. Though careful to always translate them, they would signal both his or her (yes, her) grounding in the traditional sources, and trust in the *kahal* [congregation] to understand and to prefer such references. I think it's not just a matter of style, but actually reflects part of your original message. Let me explain.

Even more striking is that today's דרשן [preacher] would *never* have devoted so much time to a purely secular book as *The Man Who Pretended* (or what might have been today's egalitarian version of the title, *The* One *Who Pretended*). Perhaps because in this generation, we have no need of either pretension or reassurance that we are Americans and fully invested in contemporary society. It is rather our Jewish identity that needs shoring up. If a common idea can be expressed with a Hebrew phrase that will be recognized, then it's preferable to the English equivalent. If an idea can be sourced to either today's latest thread on the X platform (formerly known as Twitter) or to a passage in the *Gemara*, then by all means, let's hear it from חז"ל [our sages of blessed memory]. In other words, in many parts of today's Jewish communities, we go out of our way to present ourselves as that which we wish to be, even though some of us may feel like we're "faking it," in hopes that it will ultimately come true.

You believed that the greatest temptation (the parallel to Oswald's attraction to someone other than his spouse) was America's prosperity that would "take us away from our Jewishness." Despite similar concerns being part of the grant proposals and funding justifications for essentially every Jewish organization in the century since you wrote that, it has assuredly happened, though I think not so much as the series of ethical compromises that you feared, where individuals consciously gave up part of their Jewish identity in return for social acceptance or business success.

That was certainly part of the first generation's American history. My grandmother arrived in America as a *frum yid* [religious Jew], so committed to keeping *shabbos* that she was fired from job after job, until, desperate and hungry, she concluded that no God could possibly demand such onerous loyalty. (Though she was never one to make ethical compromises—so she became a committed atheist and communist, and never set foot in a *shul* again for more than 50 years, until her oldest granddaughter's *bat mitzvah*—but that's another story.)

No, today's American Jews are simply American by birthright. The vast majority grew up immersed in the secular culture, despite varying degrees of awareness of being different, whether from simple knowledge of family history or from always having to miss the Saturday soccer games. It's not a question if we would be firm enough in our ethics to remain "loyal to the royal within ourselves" (quite a turn of phrase). It's a question of whether we recognize who we are as Jews, and maintain what can feel like a tenuous, perhaps superfluous, and certainly optional connection. In a phrase that would take too long to explain, we know we can "pass," and have to make a conscious choice *not* to.

The question of our acceptance of the status of a Chosen People has changed a lot since your time. As I've said, assimilation in America is basically a *fait accompli*. Chosenness itself is a bit of a taboo, at least among even vaguely progressive communities. As you yourself noted, we don't want to be so chauvinistic as to admit, or to fall into the habits of thinking, that we are somehow inherently superior to other groups. But in terms of the standards that we hold ourselves to, I think the biggest change is one that might have been impossible to foresee in the 1920s: Should the nation of Israel, the Jewish State (yes, there is one now!), be criticized when it does what so many other nations do? Even when those actions fall far short of that sense of *noblesse oblige* that you thought is innate to the Jewish people (a phrase we wouldn't use as a compliment today). At the national level, is the goal to present a façade of being our best selves, *knowing we'll fall short*, in the hopes of at least coming closer than we otherwise would have? Or does that simply invite criticism and opposition from the other nations, whose viciousness when directed against Jews in particular has perhaps declined less than one would have predicted a century ago. As the *pasuk* [biblical verse] following the one you recited from Ezekiel (20:32) tells us, we seem to have no choice but to be on the receiving end of those heightened yet unmet expectations:

בְּיָד חֲזָקָה וּבִזְרוֹעַ נְטוּיָה וּבְחֵמָה שְׁפוּכָה אֶמְלוֹךְ עֲלֵיכֶם—

> As I live—declares the Lord God—I will reign over you with a strong hand, and with an outstretched arm and with overflowing fury (Ezekiel 20:33).

Finally, to return to the core of your ethical message, it encouraged me to reflect on a recent personal experience. We had the great pleasure of acting *in loco parentis* for a dear friend who wanted to stay with us for a semester of pandemic-enforced remote college. Those months brought the welcome challenge of consistently being our best selves, because someone else was watching (and learning). *The Man Who Pretended* is full of that sense that "somebody's watching"—a common motivation, whether it's an impressionable family member, the angel-on-the-shoulder from *Shabbat* 119b[173], one's superego, or *ha-Shem*, before whom there is no forgetting, כִּי אֵין שִׁכְחָה לִפְנֵי כִסֵּא כְבוֹדֶךָ ("There is no forgetting before Your throne of glory"—High Holiday liturgy). Our psychology seems to respond by stepping up, making that extra effort, even when we can only do it in the guise of *The Man Who Pretended*.

I actually ordered online (don't ask) a copy of the novel. What was hot off the presses in your day is now rather obscure, so I was able to obtain a nearly century-old first edition for the cost of a sandwich. Maxwell's novel (which I admit I haven't quite finished at the time of this writing) differs from the impression I'd gotten from your *drash*, particularly in the attitude of the pretender. The hero/anti-hero of the novel pretends to be good, and thus turns out to be good. That's all well and good. But alas, Oswald is consumed with such self-loathing in the process! He finds nothing positive about his pretending. For to his understanding, it betrays not only his core impulse to want to do something other than the highest, most ethical course of action, but it also betrays him as having the "profoundest caverns of baseness and duplicity," filling him with the "horror of his own pretenses and contempt for himself" (pp. 39-40).

Yet your sermon makes little mention of this trait. Perhaps because Oswald evolves in the course of the novel, but also because your goal, I believe, was to offer Rabbinic approbation for acting "as if." That the performance of *mitzvot* [commandments], even if the *kavannah* [intention] may be sometimes...often...perhaps even *always* lacking, is nonetheless a worthwhile endeavor. That if שְׂכַר מִצְוָה, מִצְוָה (The reward for performing a commandment is another commandment—*Pirke Avot* 4:2) then the ethically ideal journey of a thousand steps might begin with a bit of pretending. Not a bad message, in your day as in ours.

Shalom Flank, Ph.D., first wandered into Havurat Shalom in Somerville, Massachusetts in 1987 while starting grad school at MIT. He has since become a frum, feminist, nigun-loving yid who makes aliyah to Somerville for yontiff. He has also become the nation's first "Microgrid Architect," pioneering new ways to incorporate local and renewable energy resources into neighborhood-scale community energy infrastructure, and an adjunct professor at Georgetown University teaching urban planners about sustainability and low-carbon cities.

---

[173] Rabbi Yosei bar Yehuda says: Two ministering angels accompany a person on Shabbat evening from the synagogue to his home, one good, and one evil. And when he reaches his home and finds a lamp burning and a table set and his bed made, the good angel says; May it be Your will that it shall be like this for another Shabbat . . .

Solomon Ibn Gabirol

Delivered in Manhattan Beach, New York at Temple Beth El,
November 16, 1928, for *Parshat Tol'dot*

When we think of the Jewish religion we immediately associate with that term laws, statutes, and judgments. Our Torah is given over to a large extent to these legalistic portions; and custom decrees that these laws be dwelt upon in the Synagogue and classroom, although they are seldom observed and so many of them are obsolete. In this manner have we come to identify a religious Jew with a bowed and pious man, with greying hair and beard, humbly obedient to and scrupulously observing the [Jewish laws].

This is directly due to the influence of the Middle Ages and Eastern Europe upon our thought processes. And without in the least practicing what has been held up as the ideal, we accept that ideal of the civilization of yesterday. Judged from this standard—which we call Orthodoxy—it is no wonder that the proverbial 99.44/100% of Jews are un-Jewish and non-Jewish.

How different our attitude towards Judaism would be—how much more welcome Judaism would be to us if we could adopt another attitude of mind with respect to it. Having faith won't make us real Jews; trying to rationalize about Judaism won't accomplish it either. Judaism will come to mean something worthwhile to us only if we can have the poetic experiences about it.

After all, to some degree we are all poets. Poetry need not necessarily reveal itself to us through versification and rhyme and meter. When we are dazed by the glorious coloring of a sunset—when we are awe-stricken by the rumbling of the thunder—when we are refreshed by the perfume of the woods—when we stand spell-bound by the majestic grandeur of a towering snow-capped mountain—when we thrill at a stirring piece of music—or are carried away on the wings of song—then we enter the poetic mood.

Now the degree to which we can have the poetic experiences about Judaism and the practice of its ceremonies and customs—the extent to which our spirits can be attuned, for example, to the soothing message of the Sabbath rest—to that extent are we really Jewish. In other words, Judaism to be lived at its best, must be lived through the senses. I will come back to this theme again, for in it is bound up my philosophy of Judaism—a philosophy which I would like you to have as well—since that will give you the best reason and justification for remaining Jews and living as Jews.

That is why I never like to refer to the Jewish religion as such but rather to Judaism—for Judaism is more than a *Shulchan 'Aruch*—a code of laws. I dare to assert that Judaism contains more of poetry and philosophy—more of emotion and thought than of laws. And to be a Jew means to feel, to be thrilled and moved by the poetry and majesty and grandeur of the Jewish system of life.

Looked at in this way, we can realize how there should have arisen great poets, sweet singers whose souls were touched by the symbols of Judaism, by its outlook on life, by its ceremonials. Such a singer King David of old was reputed to have been. It is not to be wondered then that legends could spring full-grown out of nothingness about him, his Muse and his harp. David, says one legend, had a harp which hung at night outside of his window. When the faint morning breath of the wind played a tune on it, David would arise and sing praises to God, trying with his vision to penetrate the mysteries of life and love, of struggle and existence.

Another legend quaintly tells us that the Angel of Death could not separate David's soul from his body at the appointed time because his breath was giving voice to song and so the angel was forced to divert his mind and thereby cause him to stop poetizing and rhapsodizing. Only then could he take the King's life.

Looking for the poetic feeling of our ancestors in the past we see clearly that the Bible above all things is for us a record of these aesthetic experiences. It is a book of poetry. There are songs of victory—the songs of Moses and Deborah. There are lamentations and dirges—the songs of David for Absalom and Saul, the songs of Jeremiah and Job. There are lyric masterpieces such as the 23rd Psalm. And is not the Song of Songs the greatest love song of all literature? For that matter, even the wisdom literature and prophecies come under this heading of aesthetic experiences—for although they may have a particular and definite or local reference, they nevertheless possess a universal significance. So all occasions of life—joyous as well as sorrowful—have found expression in poetry and song.

It is greatly to be deplored that we Jews are laboring under the erroneous impression that poetry ceased with the Bible. If we thought otherwise we would certainly know more about the poets of the past and the singers of the present. Even mention of their names calls forth no answering spark of recognition. To how many of us are such figures as Jehudah Halevi, Samuel Hanagid, the Ibn Ezras, the Kalonymides more than names? How many of us are aware that Tchernichovsky—reckoned by many as the greatest living Hebrew poet—greater than Bialik—is at present a visitor to this country and this city?

Nonetheless it is true that at all times poets arose among Jews. Times of stress and times of exultation and exaltation impelled the sensitive souls to self-expression. Our liturgy, our prayers have been enriched by poetic selections which, in beauty and majesty of thought, as well as in sublime mind-pictures few productions of the religious poetry of the world can compare. It is very unfortunate indeed that so many of these poetic selections have been in the past omitted from our books of worship; It is that I would like to see remedied, and their inclusion into our prayer-book which I would urge upon you, my friends.

Such songs—by developing and calling forth in the Jews the poetic mood—ennobled the Jewish soul. They would move ordinary men and women to play the part of heroes; they inspired them with courage to live and die for the things they held most precious.

Probably the greatest of all Hebrew poets was Solomon Ibn Gabirol. He was not only a great poet, but also a great philosopher. He saw further than the average poet and felt deeper than the ordinary philosopher.

To obtain an adequately complete view of the life of this great Jewish poet-philosopher we must devote more time than can be given to it now. But to gain a glimpse of his life we must for the moment step out of the present and, leaping over centuries and bounding over continents, transfer ourselves to one of those delightful towns of Spain 900 years ago. We must try to visualize this man of the eleventh century, as he lived his daily life, as he feasted and fasted, as he communed with his God or chatted with his neighbor, as he greeted his friends or raged against his enemies; as he pored over his books or roamed in the field, as he suffered at times and at other times bubbled over with joy. To know him more intimately we should have to enter his private study and, looking over his shoulder, see how he wrote and polished what he wrote.

Solomon Ibn Gabirol was born in Malaga in the South of Spain in 1021. His father was a scholar and a man of considerable repute. He was left an orphan early in life—as we read his complaint [in one of his poems]:

> Grieved without mother or father, inexperienced, lowly and poor I am alone without a brother and without friends, save my own thoughts.

Despite these disadvantages, his literary activity began at a remarkably early age and, with his phenomenal gifts, he easily acquired all the learning of the age in the city of his birth which was then noted as an important center of culture for Jewish scholars, poets and scientists, as well as for its wines. He loved wisdom as he loved nothing else:

> How can I forsake wisdom,
> And the spirit of God which has made a covenant between me
>   and her
> Or how can she forsake me when she is to me like a mother and
>   I to her as a child of old age?

Gabirol was conscious of his poetic powers from the very beginning of his career. This youth of 16 proclaimed himself superior to anyone of his generation:

> I am the master singer and song is my slave
> Though I am but 16 I have the wisdom of a man of 80.

This is not vain boasting. It is rather the self-expression of exuberant youth. And we, who are removed from him by 900 years and know the true merit of his works, feel that he did not overestimate himself. He was indeed one of the greatest poets of his day and one of the few great poets of all time. But his contemporaries evidently did not relish his claim to superiority. They resented his bland claims and were incensed at his seeming egotism. So much so that they in turn aroused Gabirol's anger. He was unable to control his temper, and cries out:

> I am filled with wrath when I behold fools parading as wise men
> They deem their song superior to mine whereas they do not
>   even understand it...
> Tiny little ants that they are, they venture to compare them-
>   selves with me.

He numbered among his friends and admirers the most exalted personages of his time. He produced literary monuments that have withstood the current of these many centuries and will undoubtedly remain on their high pedestal for ages to come. Though he died at the early age of 47 he produced important works in grammar, then a new science, in philosophy and ethics and in poetry.

Gabirol certainly knew the gentle art of making enemies, and they managed to get the better of him. They succeeded in so embittering his life that he felt compelled to leave his native city.

Gabirol devoted all his energies to his literary pursuits. He had no one dependent on him for he never married. Nay, he even boasts that he never loved: "Behold I have spent my life in search after truth, while others have wasted their substance on love." His sole ambition was to study and enjoy the friendship of great men. And he lived to realize his ambition.

His poems are simple in their grandeur and all-embracing. There is both exquisite beauty of expression and great depth of thought. There is that in his poems which makes a permanent appeal to the emotions, passions and aspirations of mankind. He touches the springs of human nature, human suffering and human exultation. His poetry interprets life for us, consoles us, sustains us, and what more need we ask of it?

Sometimes he touches our heartstrings and plays upon them the melody of eternal hope. Sometimes he lays bare the wounded heart of Israel and lets the sacred fountain of consolation play upon it in a stream of healing waters that soothe and sustain. Sometimes the agony of his people stabs his soul so deep that he raises a piercing cry to heaven and we feel that in him we have a pleader whose voice must be heard. He brings us nearer to God and we feel that we have a Father in Heaven. Ecstasy #12; At the Dawn #1[174]

---

[174] Signer is referring to two poems from *Selected Religious Poems of Solomon ibn Gabirol*, Jewish Publication Society of America, 1924, 1952, paperback in 1974. He has paraphrased extensively from the introduction to this book in his description of Gabirol's life and temperament. The poems were translated by Israel Zangwill (1864-1926).

Ecstasy, poem #12, on page 15 (written as a prelude to the *Nishmat* prayer from the morning service):
My thoughts astounded asked me why
Toward the whirling wheels on high
In ecstasy I rush and fly.
The living God is my desire
It carries me on wings of fire
Body and soul to Him I aspire.
God is at once my joy and fate,
This yearning me he did create
At thought of Him I palpitate.
Shall song with all its loveliness
Submerge my soul with happiness
Before the God of Gods it bless?

At the Dawn, poem #1 on page 2 (written as a petition to God)

   At the dawn I seek Thee
Rock and refuge tried
   In due service speak Thee
Morn and eventide
'Neath Thy greatness shrinking
   Stand I sore afraid.
All my secret thinking
   Bare before Thee laid

All the arts as we know now began with religion and religious expression. To be a religious man one should therefore try to appreciate music, painting, poetry. In the Golden Age of Spain, about the year 1100, Jews took active part in all walks of life and the poets of the age sang not only of God but also of wine, women and song. A poet like Gabirol painted the sunset and the night spreading her wings over the tired day with as much vividness and beauty as he cried over his people's wounds. He could even come down to earth sufficiently long enough to curse his host in verse, for giving him water, not wine, when the poet was thirsty:

> May the man, his son or daughter
> Be forever doomed to water.

We today can appreciate what an awful curse this is.[175]

If you will become familiar with Gabirol the familiarity will not breed contempt but enhance delight. You will love him with the love that moves the heavens and all the stars. His poems are a monument of glory to Israel and his lyrics may indeed become a sanctuary to which the weary at heart will turn for consolation, the troubled in mind for guidance; and all who love the beautiful, for the participation of his songs, for doesn't the poet say: "A thing of beauty is a joy forever."

Little to Thy glory
  Heart and tongue can do.
Small remains the story,
  Add we spirit too.
Yet since man's praise ringing
  May seem good to Thee
I will praise Thee singing
  While Thy breath's in me.

[175] Signer is referring to Prohibition, which lasted from 1920-1933.

response from
Debby Arzt-Mor

Dear Rabbi Signer,

I write in conversation with you, responding to some of your thoughts and musings. What drew me to this particular sermon of yours was what I read as your opening assertion that a Jewish life can be lived in varied rich and authentic ways, while not restricted to the confines of Orthodoxy. I resonate strongly with the way in which you write about spiritual experience, or the poetic experience, as you call it. It seems to me that you are inviting us to go beyond the tenets of Jewish practice, to make room to experience the divine, through our senses, an invitation which I happily accept. My deepest spiritual moments have been in settings of grandeur, in moments of silence or meditation, or in song-filled connection with community.

For you, poetry is one of the ultimate expressions of spiritual experience, and you remind us of the biblical poets. I must admit that I am not a poetry buff. I find that so much of modern poetry goes above my head and does not hold my attention for long. In order for any poetry, biblical or modern, to resonate with me it must speak straight to my heart. I, too, love the Song of Songs, and in fact, many of my favorite songs, associated with the land of Israel, draw from its passages. I wonder what poetry of the early 20th century spoke to you? Did you read Rabbi Abraham Joshua Heschel's poetry, which he wrote as a young man?

I grew up in the modern state of Israel, which came into existence after your passing. You would be gratified to know that streets, neighborhoods, institutions and schools throughout the state are named after the Hebrew poets that you mentioned. Tchernichovsky, Yehudah Halevi, Shmuel Hanagid, are all names known to Israelis of all ages, and students in Israeli schools study their writing to this day. In fact, in modern-day Israel, we have seen a resurgence of the *piyut* (devotional song), with a plethora of *Paitanim* (singers of *piyutim*), bringing to life the work of many *mizrachi* [of southern European, African or Asian origin] poets, who were not as visible in the Israeli public sphere in the first 60 years of its existence.

In your sermon, you express your dismay with the way in which poetry has been omitted in the past from our prayer books. I think you would have been gratified to open some of the *siddurim* [prayerbooks] that have been published in recent years, providing, alongside the *Keva*, or set prayers, a richness of poetry and alternative readings. These creative approaches, alongside the prayers that I grew up with, have spoken to my heart, and have often helped me find deeper meaning in the ancient prayers.

It is interesting that in your introduction to Solomon Ibn Gabirol, you state that in order to really appreciate his writing, we would have to visualize him in the day-to-day of his life, in Spain during the eleventh century. While I am drawn to the biographies of famous men and women, I feel that truly great poetry takes on a life of its own, defined by those who read it and resonate with it. Isn't that the greatness of artistic expression? When asked about the meaning, or the reason for their art, it seems common for the poet or artist to say that that is not of importance; rather, the viewer's or reader's interpretation or experience is what matters most.

In the examples you gave of Ibn Gabirol's writings, I am most drawn to his timeless utterances that give expression to his love of wisdom and song. I am drawn most to that aspect of his work which transcends the day-to-day occurrences of his life, and speaks to the mysteries of spiritual experience.

I share with you one such example:

> I Look for You Early
> by Solomon ibn Gabirol
> English version by Peter Cole
> Original Language Hebrew
>
> I look for you early,
> my rock and my refuge,
>   offering you worship
>   morning and night;
> before your vastness
> I come confused
>   and afraid for you see
>   the thoughts of my heart.
> What could the heart
> and tongue compose,
>   or spirit's strength
>   within me to suit you?
> But song soothes you
> and so I'll give praise
>   to your being as long
>   as your breath-in-me moves.

DEbby Arzt-Mor

(From Selected Poems of Solomon Ibn Gabirol, translator Peter Cole, Princeton University Press, 2000)

Thank you for the opportunity to be in conversation with you, to share my own thoughts, and to be reminded of how the words of poets, from ancient to modern times, offer a path to personal spiritual experience.

The daughter of Olim [Jews returning to Israel], Debby Arzt-Mor grew up in Israel and moved to San Francisco in her mid-twenties. Debby has lived in San Francisco for many years, where she and her husband Boaz have raised two (now adult) children, Tal and Edan.

Debby is Director of Jewish Learning at The Brandeis School of San Francisco, a K-8 school reflecting the diversity and dynamism of the Bay Area Jewish community. As a member of Brandeis' senior leadership team, Debby partners with faculty and staff in guiding Jewish and Hebrew programming and curriculum throughout the school. Debby is a graduate of The Davidson School's Day School Leadership Training Institute, and of the Melton Senior Educators program at The Hebrew University. Debby holds a BA in psychology and Jewish philosophy (University of Haifa), and a master's in nonprofit administration (University of SF).

Debby travels regularly between her two homes (SF and Jerusalem), and loves spending time with her parents, Roz and Ray Arzt, in her childhood home.

Joy, Goodness and Caring

Happiness

Location and date unknown, delivered for *Parshat Vayeshev*

1. This statement is typical of the mental attitude of the Jew in the past.

2. What was it? The assumption that no one had a claim to happiness in this world. This assumption was set up against the natural selfishness of the human being. Anything which seemed to play into the hands of selfishness was suspected and illegitimate. The abuse of this was to make people content with their lot. It was the basis not only of religious ideas and practices but also of economic and political life. For example, [it was not to be expected] that his country should add to his measure of happiness—his business was to serve his king. The whole economic order as well was based on this assumption. The worker had no right to expect a full dinner pail. The normal thing for him was to go hungry because of the deficit of good existing in the world.

Enjoyment as such—pleasure—was frowned upon. For instance, it was necessary to eat without enjoyment, to tend the family without permitting oneself to experience sense of delight, even satisfaction of our wants was regarded as wrong. Living through normal human experiences was sinful and therefore to be avoided on pain of losing one's portion in the world to come.

This conception obtained among all peoples, Jews and Gentiles as well. Our mistaken idea as to Greek belief. For example, Epicurus[176] departed from current Greek conception. Protestants likewise take over this conception of life, for example, Calvinism, Puritans. It is still going strong among conscientious Catholics. Among the later generations are still found a great many men and women with this morbid state of mind. One mustn't laugh too heartily.

Therefore we have to:

1. Dispel the illusion that religion today is committed to this assumption.
2. Show that even in the Dark Ages the right to happiness was not altogether denied. Nazir to bring a sin-offering because he refused to enjoy wine.[177]

---

[176] Epicurus (340-270 BCE) was a Greek philosopher who considered that life should ideally be lived with happiness, tranquility and absence of pain and fear.

[177] A *"nazir"* or *"nazarite"* was a person who took a vow to abstain from cutting the hair and from consuming any grape products. At the end of the vow period, they were instructed to bring a sin offering, implying that making and keeping the vow, and denying oneself the pleasure of grapes or wine, included an element of sin.

3. To discover the method of spiritualizing and socializing the right to happiness.

In other words, not only to prevent the right to happiness from degenerating to the right to selfishness, unconsidered self-gratification but also to find a way of making an enhancement of general happiness the accepted standard of human conduct. Economic, political and religious institutions must be created for this purpose. At the present time we lack the social machinery that would enable this assumption to be practiced with the danger of individualism running riot. The problem of Judaism then, is to stimulate thought and interest in the formulation of ethical and spiritual life on the basis of this assumption. Example, problem of Companionate Marriage.[178] Rabbis have no standard by which to judge. We are at a loss concerning which is right and wrong because we have not as yet recognized this principle in Jewish life, nor have we evolved the machinery which we might apply to the home. What is proper recreation? Distrust of wealth. Judaism will have to face these problems and will have to lay down principles of what is right and wrong and will have to reckon with this assumption.

4. Although we have not the machinery today, we are yet in a position to lay down one or two principles which should govern our daily life.

a. Negative Principle—"We dare not interfere with the happiness of others." By that we mean more than was meant in the past. Today we feel that we dare not dictate to others what they should consider as happiness. We now realize that a person has a right to his own idea of happiness. Not only the right to what *we* consider as happiness for him.

b. Secondly, but positively, the principle that we should so enlarge the scope of our interest and sympathies that the happiness and achievement of others will of itself come to be our happiness. This is realized to some extent in the relationship to one's own immediate family. At times, we have this experience applied to our country and our people. Example, Lindbergh[179]—His success is in a measure our success and our happiness.

---

[178] An early modern idea envisioning a marriage not governed by economics, patriarchy and family but by emphasis on the spousal relationship, including companionship, equality and mutual physical gratification. American judge and social reformer Ben B. Lindsey (1869-1943) wrote a book, *Companionate Marriage*, in 1927, which is where Signer may have obtained his information.

[179] Charles A. Lindbergh (1902-1974) initially became prominent in May 1927 after making the first nonstop flight from New York City to Paris. He was also known for the horrific kidnapping and murder of his infant son in March 1932. Based on this information, it's likely that Signer delivered this sermon in Manhattan Beach, New York between late 1927 and 1931.

5. The surest test of our having rendered ethical the goal of happiness will be when we shall find it feasible to speak not only of the right of being happy, but of the duty of being happy; when instead of urging goodness as a means to happiness, the time will come when we will be able to appeal to people by saying to them [that] when they will be happy they will be good. Even as we can already now appeal to people to promote their physical health as an appeal to goodness. Health is now recognized as a duty and we do not urge it in the name of selfishness but in the name of benefitting the social good.

In this connection it is interesting to note the real meaning of the word שלום ["shalom," usually translated as "peace"]: שלום שלום לרחוק ולקרוב אמר ה׳ ורפאתיו [It shall be well, well with the far and the near—said the Lord—and I will heal them Isaiah 57:19].[180]

---

[180] Signer equates "peace" ("Shalom") with happiness and uses the verse as proof that experiencing "peace" leads to healing, and, in addition, is a state that God wishes us to attain.

response from
Aliza Arzt

Dear Grandfather,

I never knew you, as I was named for you nearly three years after your death. Your Hebrew name was יצחק, "*yitzchak*"—Laughter, and my name is עליזה, "*aliza*"—Joy. For that reason alone it's fitting that I should be responding to your sermon about happiness. This sermon, unlike most of the others I've read, is more difficult to process since it consists of handwritten notes followed by a more fleshed out typed version which still does not achieve the "finished product" status of your other sermons. In a way, it helps me to know you better as I join you midstream in the sermon development process instead of being the recipient of a polished work.

This is one of the few sermons that doesn't include the date on which it was preached. I suspect that it was written in the late 1920s since you refer briefly to "companionate marriage" (the concept of marriage based on equality and shared goals as opposed to property, patriarchy and reproduction), which was actively controversial in 1927-28. At that time, you would have been married, contemplating fatherhood (my mother, your first child, was born in early 1929) and new to your position as Rabbi of Temple Beth El in Manhattan Beach, New York.

I approached this sermon with some trepidation for other reasons besides its incomplete nature. Despite the stirring words of the Declaration of Independence (". . . life, liberty and the pursuit of happiness"—I'm surprised you didn't allude to this in your sermon), I consider happiness to be somewhat insipid. What's the point of just being "happy"? What's meaningful about being happy? How could that be enough to expect given the needs and complexities of our world?

I need not have worried. You also seem to sense implicitly that "happiness" by itself isn't worth much. You were much more interested in viewing happiness as a social construct, and as a core component of living an "ethical and spiritual life." You go further, reminding us that the pursuit of happiness can lead to selfishness, which is a real danger, you say, given the individualistic nature of the society of your times. I wonder how you would have reacted to the politicization of "individual rights" versus the obligation to act on behalf of the public good, which is so prevalent in our day.

In keeping with the unpolished version of this sermon, it's clear that you had only begun to consider how Judaism could approach the concept of "happiness" in a systematic, meaningful way. You end the sermon somewhat abruptly with an allusion to the connection between what you'd said about happiness and the word *Shalom*, peace. You say, "In this connection it is interesting to note the real meaning of the word *'shalom'*," after which you conclude with a quote from Isaiah 57:19: "It will be well, well ("shalom shalom") with the far and the near—said God—and I will heal them." What did you mean by that? Did you say more when you actually delivered the sermon? We'll obviously never know and I won't speculate.

I will, however, conclude with the result of my own research into a common biblical word for happiness: אשרי (*ashrei*). Most of us are familiar with the word from its appearance as a psalmic (84:5 and 144:15) prelude to Psalm 145, which we recite frequently in our liturgy. It's translated by the New JPS: "Happy are those who dwell in Your house; they forever praise you. Happy are the people who have it so; happy the people whose God is the Lord." Looking at the occurrence of this root (אשר—aleph-shin-resh) elsewhere in Psalms, I discovered that it actually means "step" or "leg:" "As for me, my feet had almost strayed, my steps (אשורי - *ashurai*) were nearly led off course" (Ps. 73:2); "God lifted me out of the miry pit, the slimy clay, and set my feet on a rock, steadied my legs (אשורי - *ashurai*)" (Ps. 40:3). In other words, when we are in danger of slipping from our path, God steadies us. The same idea, using the same word, is expressed more abstractly in Proverbs: "Give up simpleness and live; walk (ואשרו - *v'ishru*) in the way of understanding" (Prov. 9:6). "Happiness" occurs when we are assisted by God to avoid "pitfalls" and to set ourselves on the right path. You and I, separated by time and mortality, connected by family, are certainly walking that path together.

Aliza Arzt has been a member of Havurat Shalom in Somerville, Massachusetts for many years. She considers herself to be a Hebraist and Bible investigator by avocation, and has studied both these subjects as well as linguistics at the University of Pennsylvania and the Jewish Theological Seminary. She works professionally as a health care provider but has reduced her hours in order to focus on her other passions: revising the liturgy, reptile keeping, ceramics and combatting food insecurity in her city.

Don't Lose Your Nerve

Delivered in Manhattan Beach, New York at Temple Beth El, September 23, 1949, for *Rosh Hashonah* [Jewish New Year]

In the physical world the seismograph records the tremors and quakes of the earth. In the world of ideas, this function is performed by literature. When we read this intellectual seismograph we become aware of the extent of the tremors which pervade our world. Our own age abounds in philosophies of despair. The odor of corruption fills contemporary literature. Violence, lust, brutality have crept into the very ink with which so many novels are written, and the most clearly defined outline of the shape of things to come is George Orwell's terrifying "1984." Existentialism is the latest nihilistic version of philosophy pleading for a courageous despair in the face of a purposeless existence. Books like "How to Stop Worrying and Start Living,"[181] "Peace of Mind,"[182] "Peace of Soul,"[183] "A Guide to Confident Living"[184] are the spiritual aspirins of our day. To sum it all up, we are characters in search of meaning, creatures seeking some sure stance.

In contrast to the demoralizing reading provided by "1984," Judaism offers such reading as Psalm 27 which is also the expression of a person living in a world of turmoil much the same as ours. But unlike his latter day brethren, the psalmist reacts differently:

> When evil men assail me with their slanders
> 'Tis they, my enemies and foes who stumble to their fall,
> Even though an army were arrayed against me, my heart would
>   not be afraid.
> Though war were waged against me, still would I be confident,
> Leave me not to the fury of my foes,
> for false witnesses have started up against me,
> breathing injury to me.
> I do believe I shall yet see the Eternal good to me, in the land
>   of the living.
> Wait for the Lord; Be strong my soul; be brave.
> Yes, wait for the Lord.

---

[181] Written by Dale Carnegie in 1948.
[182] Written by Joshua L. Liebman in 1946.
[183] Most likely the book written by Fulton J. Sheen in 1946.
[184] Written by Norman Vincent Peale in 1913.

It is this promise of confident living, *here and now*, that Judaism offers us. It finds clear expression in our Service on Rosh Hashonah. It is a three-point program, carefully worked out for us. It is ours for the taking. It is even carefully labelled and well outlined in our Musaf [Additional] Service, so that none who wishes finds it beyond his capability to acquire or his capacity to remember.[185]

I.
JUDAISM TEACHES THAT LIFE MUST BE INTEGRATED.

With this concept the history of the Jew begins. Abraham, the first Jew in recorded history, had his life's purpose summed up for him by God: "Walk thou before me and be whole-hearted" (Gen. 17:1). This concept is at the bottom of Jewish legislation. "Wholehearted shalt thou be with the Lord thy God." (Deut. 18:13).

Life must not be fragmented. It must be seen whole, each part in proper relation to every other part of it. There must be *one* all-pervading purpose. There must be no wavering in our determination to achieve such integration of life.

This one all-embracing aim in Judaism is *to live in companionship with the highest*. Everything a Jew does must be done "for God's sake," *L'ma'an Hashem*. Every gesture, every act, every thought must be dedicated to help achieve our companionship with the highest. A Jew is made conscious of it by his repeated references to God as the creator of the universe. Not only when a Jew performs such an important act as consecrating his marriage does he begin by saying: "Praised be Thou, O Lord, ruler of the universe," but traditionally he uses the identical phrase when he takes a drink of water.

It is this ever-conscious purpose of an integrated life lived in companionship with the highest that gives every individual a sense of incalculable worth. Any one of us may feel, as we all do at times, that he is a cipher, a nothing, a Zero. By putting the *one* God in front of man, our Mr. Zero obtains large significance, and the addition of more zeros after this one, more people like him, gives added strength to each.

This is the meaning of our repeated insistence that God is sovereign. In His royal household, which is the entire world, every man is an *"eved Adonai"* [literally

---

[185] Signer is alluding to the three themes of the "silent prayer" in the New Year Additional Service (*Musaf*). Each theme consists of ten biblical quotes, after which, when the prayer is repeated by the service leader, the *Shofar* (ram's horn) is blown: *Malchuyot*—Sovereignty, *Zichronot*—Remembrance, *Shofarot*—Ram's horn blasts.

a "servant of God"], a minister with royal dignity, and with rank commensurate with such status. It raises man to the highest level.

II.
JUDAISM TEACHES THAT THE INDIVIDUAL MUST LIVE IN TERMS OF HISTORIC PERSPECTIVE.

Moses begins his final exhortation to his people with the plea to "remember the days of old, review the years, age after age" (Deut. 32.7). While the Jews, like the ancient Greeks, saw evidences of God in nature, it was the Jews alone who discerned his most meaningful manifestation in history, the record of human events. In this, our ancestors added a new dimension to human thinking. In so doing, they dedicated themselves to a purpose that is anchored in time long before we arrived here, and will continue long after we leave. Such historic outlook upon the world gave each Jew a sense of his place in the march of time, and emancipated him from the inevitable apathy and cynicism which seizes us when faced with temporary setbacks. Such a view of life raised the Jew above the inevitable trivialities that beset us. A purpose as large as this, coextensive with space and time—the Universe and history—can continue to give each Jew a very important place in the world.

It certainly is not easy to achieve universal peace and justice in the world, but we can only carry on when we recognize its importance in human history, which makes us feel that we have a rendezvous with destiny. It lends importance and dignity to our lives when we link it with the past and the future. It gives us greater sure-footedness as we stretch out our hands to be grasped by the past and the future. We are less likely to be blown over by the gales of the present. When faced with despondency, this sense of history recalls to us what we are here for. This is what we read in our Service today:

> Thou rememberest what was wrought from eternity and art mindful of all that hath been formed from of old ... Thou, who lookest and seest to the end of all generations ... They that seek Thee shall never stumble.

This sense of historic perspective reaching out from the distant past to the far-off future is expressed climactically in this sentence from our Rosh Hashonah prayers: "I will remember my covenant with thee in the days of thy youth, and I will establish unto thee an everlasting covenant."

III.
JUDAISM TEACHES THAT NOTHING THAT OUGHT TO BE IS IMPOSSIBLE OF ACHIEVEMENT.

The world has long cherished the hope of fulfillment of Micah's vision when:

> He (God) will decide the disputes of many races,
> And arbitrate between strong foreign powers,
> till swords are beaten into ploughshares,
> and spears into pruning-hooks;
> No nation draws the sword against another,
> No longer shall men learn to fight,
> but each live underneath his vine
> and underneath his fig-tree
> in terror of no one.
> All nations may live loyal each to his own god,
> but we will be ever loyal to our God.
> (Micah 4:2-5)

Eventually, this will have to come about, if we are to exist at all. The obstacles in the path of achieving this goal may seem insurmountable, but none doubts that without its realization man will be hurled back, quickly, into a primeval stage, what with man's increasing capacity to hurt and destroy.

This idea, that nothing that ought to be is impossible of achievement, has been doubly validated in our own day. In the life of Israel, the establishment of an independent state on the shores of the Mediterranean, in the face of every conceivable obstacle—political, geographic, economic—and in the face of international conspiracy against it by religious and political groups, is living testimony to the historic teaching of our people that nothing that ought to be is impossible of achievement. For all mankind, this same truth has been equally validated in the acceptance by 60 nations[186] of the revolutionary concept of world peace.

How little do we realize that the belief in its practicability is so recent. It was Woodrow Wilson who but yesterday successfully helped bring into being the League of Nations. If we are discouraged by its lack of achievement or that of its successor, the United Nations, and if we become impatient with the lack of Four

---

[186] "In total, 63 states became members of the League of Nations (with at most 60 at the same time), which represents a great majority of the states existing at that time." https://www.ungeneva.org/en/about/league-of-nations/overview.

Freedoms,[187] Mr. Roosevelt's rewording of Micah's vision, it is only because we measure the slow progress of these great ideas by the yardstick of our own lives. But when we can project our minds and measure our hours in the light of the centuries, we are much encouraged. Today, 60 nations may give only lip service to universal peace, but none dare break the spell by an overt act.

This is why we Jews never have nor can we now surrender the idea of the Messianic era, when universal peace, brotherhood and justice shall reign supreme. These are the things that ought to be, and inevitably they must come about, because justice and peace are a part of God's plan of orderliness in the universe. These ideals will come about much faster if we believe in them strongly enough and act on our beliefs firmly enough. The shofar is blown today to remind us to bestir ourselves on behalf of these universal truths, that they *can* come to pass if we will them sufficiently.

These, then, are the three teachings of Judaism contained in our Musaf Service under the three headings which speak of the Sovereignty of God, the sense of historic memories, the blowing of the Shofar. We are reminded that while the length of our lives is in God's hands, the quality of our lives is in our own hands.

> Here and now I call heaven and earth
> to witness against you that I have put
> life and death before you, the blessing
> and the curse: choose life, then, that you
> and your children may live. (Deut. 30:19)

Professor Horace Kallen, in reviewing Professor Wolfson's book on Philo in the recent *Menorah Journal*,[188] points out that at the time of the breakup of the Graeco-Roman world, men lost their nerve. They had nothing to live for. It was Judaism, he points out, with its positive, persistent program for meaningful living that salvaged civilization at that time. This same Judaism should help us regain our nerve once again in a world that is as jittery and shaken today as it was 1,900 years

---

[187] President Franklin D. Roosevelt spoke of "four freedoms"—the freedom of speech, the freedom of worship, the freedom from want, and the freedom from fear, to explain what America was fighting for as it entered World War II.

[188] Horace Kallen (1882-1974) was a professor of Philosophy and taught at a number of colleges during his career, including Princeton, Harvard, University of Wisconsin and The New School. Kallen was one of the founders and editors of the *Menorah Journal* (1915-1962). *Philo: Foundations of Religious Philosophy in Judaism, Christianity and Islam*, Harvard University Press (1947) was written by Harry Austryn Wolfson (1887-1974), who was the first chairman of a Judaic Studies program in the U.S. at Harvard.

ago. Several centuries before the catastrophic breakup of the Graeco-Roman world there was another crisis in world history for the Jews. It came in the wake of the breakup of the mighty Babylonian empire. It was then that Nehemiah called upon his fellow Jews not to lose their nerve. He assembled them, as we are assembled now, read the Torah to them, explaining its teachings and inspiring them with it very much as we are now doing, and sent them home, as we send you home today with the same benediction:

> Come, eat the dainty pieces and drink sweet wine, and send a portion to him who has nothing ready, for this is a day sacred to our Lord. Do not be downcast, for to rejoice in God is your strength. (Nehemiah 8:10)

response from
Adam Arzt

Dear Grandfather,

In your sermon, given on Rosh Hashanah 5710 (1949), you discuss a feeling of generalized despair that seemed to be pervasive, borne out in the literature of your time, citing George Orwell's *1984* (published that year) as an apropos example. You go on to say that in contrast to this pessimistic view, Judaism offers a more confident view of life, and this optimism is mapped out in the three highlighted sections of the Rosh Hashanah Musaf service, through consistently reminding ourselves of God's sovereignty and aligning ourselves with God (*Malchuyot*), recognizing the important role that historic perspective plays in uplifting people from cynicism (*Zichronot*) and reinforcing the notion that we can achieve what may seem to be impossible, and the importance of continually striving to do so (*Shofarot*).

In the last part of the sermon, you suggest that it was Judaism, with its positive approach to a meaningful life, that salvaged civilization at the time of the fall of the Greco-Roman world and that perhaps Judaism could play the same role in your time where the world seemed as jittery as it did 1,900 years before.

In the present day we face challenges that were unimaginable in your time. We live in an era where we cannot even agree on what the facts are, let alone what they mean. The ease and speed at which misinformation is disseminated as well as the feeling of justification in attacking those whose views differ from whatever position is taken, paired with the effects of a worldwide pandemic, ongoing climate issues and the global effects of military conflicts beyond the actual battle site make it even more tempting today to take a very pessimistic view of our future.

I think the principles you propose in your sermon can and should be applied today. Aligning ourselves with the sovereignty of God, and continuously reminding ourselves of that link, allows us as Jews to set an example of how to treat each of our fellow humans better, in a time that suggests there is less reason or desire to do so. Being aware of our past and cognizant of our future reminds us that we do have a place in the overall history of the world and allows us to continue to strive to achieve universal peace and justice. Trumpeting the importance of continuing to strive for universal peace, brotherhood and justice helps us persevere even in times of great ideological and natural challenges that could lead us to feelings of hopelessness.

My dear Grandfather, just as in the time you delivered this sermon, your words have given us a roadmap of how we may respond to our own present-day struggles.

At its core, your sermon serves to provide us with hope under circumstances where it seems more elusive and suggests that Judaism can supply the inspiration to maintain hope for a positive outlook on the future when we are increasingly surrounded by pessimism and despair. It taps into the continued need for hope by Jews as a people. You also suggest that our faith and approach to hope can be a model for others in maintaining optimism on issues of a more global significance. Your words themselves provide us with hope, just like the words of Nehemiah with which you closed your sermon—"Do not be downcast, for to rejoice in God is your strength" (Nehemiah 8:10).

Adam Arzt is Isador Signer's grandson. He graduated from the University of Pennsylvania in 1982 with a B.A. and again in 1989 as a Doctor of Veterinary Medicine. Adam is currently a practicing veterinarian in Milford, Massachusetts, and is past president of the Massachusetts Veterinary Medical Association, receiving its Distinguished Service Award in 2012. Adam and his wife Nancy are accompanied by Homer, their devoted lab, and 3 rambunctious cats. Adam is also a collector of vintage animation art.

Double Talk
Or
Saying It Two Ways

Delivered in Manhattan Beach, New York at Temple Beth El,
December 12, 1938, for *Parshat Vayetze*

The Jewish version of the popular saying, "coming down to brass tacks" is 'ברחל בתך הקטנה' ["... for your younger daughter Rachel"].[189]

We appreciate the importance of being specific when our personal and individual interests are affected, but when the interests of a public character are at stake, we take refuge in vague generalities. We are very careful in drawing up contracts, recognizing the impossibility of conducting business unless we calculate every item of overhead and other expense. When we want to put up a building we do not content ourselves with the mere picture of the façade. We cannot conceive how any work on a building can be done without drawing up multifarious specifications. The same is true in all the arts and professions. The one field where we content ourselves with vagueness is that of matters spiritual and ethical. We imagine that the general principles of action ought to be effective. We express surprise that exhortations should seem to make so little an impression on human life. The Ten Commandments seem impotent. People kept on stealing, shedding blood, committing immorality despite the belief that the commands against them were spoken by GOD on Mt. Sinai. Christianity came along and selected from among the teachings of the Torah the command "And thou shalt love Thy neighbor as thyself." Yet the Church saw no inconsistency in hounding and condemning its victims to tortures of the most excruciating kind. When the Golden Rule seemed to fail, the representative philosopher of modern times, Kant, suggested the substitution of another rule, known as the categorical imperative.[190] That proved no more effective in leading men to do the right than the general principles of religion which it tried to supersede. Can there be a nobler doctrine than that of duty for duty's sake?

---

[189] Genesis 29:18. Jacob tells his uncle and future father-in-law Laban: "I will serve you seven years for your younger daughter Rachel." He specifies exactly what he will do and exactly which daughter he would like to marry.

[190] Immanuel Kant (1724-1804), German philosopher, stated in his book *Groundwork of the Metaphysic of Morals* "Act only according to that maxim whereby you can, at the same time, will that it should become a universal law," as translated by James Ellington (3rd ed.).

Yet this proved as dangerous as it is noble. It was seized and exploited by the philosophers of militarism. Nothing could be better adapted to their needs than the prevalence among the people of a sense of duty which asks no questions. Treitschke[191] identifies national honor with the CATEGORICAL IMPERATIVE. National honor is the sublime moral good which has something about it in the nature of unconditional sanctity, which thus compels the individual to sacrifice even himself to it. This is why the thought of war lifts up the soul. He is sure that God will see to it that war should always recur as a drastic medicine for the human race. War is the categorical imperative in uniform.

We are shocked when we learn that people who are identified as upholders of religion and morality turn out to be vicious and criminal.

If you wish a thing hard enough, you get it.

This may be called the magic conception of the power of moral and spiritual ideals. If this delusion were at least harmless we could afford to overlook it. But the fact is that it is due to the magical conception of the potency of abstract ideals that religion and morality have fallen on evil days, at the present time. The war undoubtedly wrought a tremendous change in man's attitude towards the sanctities of life. That attitude is for the most part negative and destructive. This effect may be traced to the campaign of propaganda which was managed with the technique employed in a gas attack. Never were such high principles of morality and religion appealed to. Never before were there such fervent protestations of the most exalted ideals.

Having been under the delusion that general principles of right and wrong ought to have a direct influence upon human conduct, the majority of thinking men have been shocked by what they term the hypocrisy of the war leaders. The disillusionment through which we are passing at the present time has generated a deep disgust for all sorts of principles and ideals. In current literature it is enough to call one "a man of principle" to characterize him as a worthless liar. Note, for instance, the disesteem in which the character of [Woodrow] Wilson is now held. Nothing is so irritating about him, to the modern critic, as his constant appeal to principle, his continual indulgence in the vocabulary of idealism, his too frequent references to truth, righteousness, service and faith. It is admitted that Wilson believed in them, that he was not an aspiring demagogue, that to him these principles meant something real and that was why he arrested the public attention. The weakness of Wilson in failing to live up to his ideals is considered proof positive of the illusory character of idealism as such.

---

[191] Heinrich von Treitschke (1834-1896), German historian, nationalist and member of the *Reichstag* whose militaristic and racist views were felt to be the forerunners of Nazism.

But this present-day contempt for idealism and spirituality would not have been the outcome of the war had men not been led to expect too much from the abstract principles of right and wrong. Despite the magic conception of idealism we must cultivate an *instrumental view*. A moral principle is nothing more than a point of view from which we are called upon to consider an act. We sometimes hear it said that the universal adoption of the Golden Rule, to regard the good of others as we would our own, would settle all industrial difficulties. Supposing that the principle were accepted in good faith by everybody, it would not tell everybody just what to do in all of the complexities of his relation to others. We are not certain what the good of others may be. How does it help us to decide matters to be told to regard the good of others as we would our own? Because I am fond of classical music it does not follow that I should thrust as much of it as possible upon my neighbor. Recently there died a man known as Golden Rule Nash.[192] Admired as he was by some, others designated him as a faker and limelighter.

> All educated and virtuous persons in the same country practically agree upon the rules of justice, benevolence and regard for life as long as they are taken in such a vague way that they mean anything in general or nothing in particular. Everyone is in favor of justice in the abstract; but existing political and economic discussions regarding tariff, sumptuary laws, monetary standards, trades unions, trusts the regulation of capital and labor, the regulation of ownership of public utilities, the nationalization of land and industry, show that large bodies of men—intelligent and equally well-disposed—are quite capable of finding that the principle of justice requires exactly opposite things.[193]

The problem of the moral life is not the problem of mastering general principles, of making pious resolutions, of mealy-mouthed platitudes, and indulging in unctuous rhetoric, but in applying them to the affairs of men and to the particular

---

[192] Arthur Nash (1870-1927) was an Ohio businessman and, intermittently, a preacher. On acquiring a clothing business and finding out that he had bought "a sweatshop" he decided to operate his business according to the Golden Rule. He announced to his workers that he considered them to be his equals and immediately tripled their wages and later provided other benefits such as a cafeteria on the premises. Although he didn't expect his business to last more than a few months, the business became exceedingly profitable and operated successfully until it was sold by his heirs two years after his death.

[193] Quote from *Ethics* by John Dewey (1859-1952) written with James Hayden Tufts, 1932.

circumstances in which we find ourselves. The details which are necessary are not those that take the form of what is known as CAUSISTRY in which the attempt is made to foresee all the different cases of action which may conceivably occur and provide in advance the exact rule for each case. What we need is to work out the machinery by which any ideal may be achieved. Maynard Keynes in his account of the Peace Conference[194] said of Wilson, "He had no plan, no scheme, no constructive ideas whatever for clothing with the flesh of life the commandments he thundered from the White House. He could have preached a sermon on any of them or have addressed a stately prayer to the Almighty for their fulfilment, but he could not frame their concrete application to the actual state of Europe." If mankind were to devote one percent of the energy which it devotes to the details of peace we would undoubtedly be nearer the attainment of world peace than we are at the present time. It is said of Napoleon that his strength lay in "thinking out" the plan of battle. If it were realized that the attainment of peace is a battle against innate prejudices and instincts, against economic stupidities, and a plan were laid accordingly, we might get somewhere.

The realization of this truth would revolutionize our educational methods. But even before we succeed in evolving the machinery necessary for the remaking of human nature let us realize that the spiritual aspect of human life does not consist in vague and unctuous generalities, but of a highly intricate and complex process involving the myriad details of the everyday business of living.

The reason the Pulpit is not treated seriously is because of the magic potency ascribed to it. Not until being a Jew will lead to the creation of the machinery to achieve the ideals with which Judaism has become identified will he contribute aught to the KINGDOM OF GOD. For the KINGDOM OF GOD is not a kingdom of ends, of goals, of ideals. It is a kingdom of consecrated means, of arduous details, of exacting specifications.

[The typed sermon is followed here by pages of handwritten notes. It is unclear whether this is material relating to the previous ideas of the sermon or whether the sermon continues in handwritten form].

---

[194] John Maynard Keynes (1883-1946), a notable economist. Early in his career, he represented the British government at the 1919 Paris Peace Conference, where the terms of the German World War I surrender were determined. Despite Woodrow Wilson's presentation of the "14 Points" at the time of the Armistice in November 1918, the more punitive "Treaty of Versailles" was adopted. Keynes spoke out strongly against this approach, accurately predicting that it would lead to serious economic and political repercussions in the world. He published his views in his 1919 book, *The Economics of the Peace*.

response from
Ezra Porter

Dear Great-Grandfather,

It's interesting how little can change in 85 years. You wrote this in 1938 but it could just as easily be delivered today. All types of disagreements today come down to one party accusing the other of dealing in "pious resolutions" and "mealy-mouthed platitudes" rather than offering specifics. Ground zero for this feeling is in politics, just as it seems to have been in 1938. It's a common complaint that every election cycle features the theater of a candidate with carefully laid plans followed by four years of the same. And, yes, the "disillusionment" you describe follows today as well.

In your sermon you suggest that the remedy is a renewed focus on details, "exacting specifications." "What we need is to work out the machinery by which any ideal may be achieved." There's a natural appeal to this point of view, I think, because of its hopefulness. If the problem is that we aren't yet practiced enough at enacting our ideals, our current failures can be easily explained away as temporary. We just need to do the hard work of fleshing out the reality of these ideals. There's also obvious truth to your point. Often, we use vagueness to avoid taking a stand and thereby avoid acting. Committing to a specific position opens us up to being held accountable.

However, when it comes to collective decisions, exacting specifications can be a double-edged sword. Just as vagueness, like you describe, can stand in the way of action, so can demands for specificity. We see this so often today. Real injustices committed by our institutions are met with factfinding commissions that only delay justice until the public has moved on. When confronted with literal existential threats our leaders ask, "How will we pay for this?" rather than "How can we afford not to?" In the hands of powerful people with an interest in maintaining the status quo, arduous detail and exacting specifications, along with vagueness, become tools to perpetuate injustice.

The opening passage of your sermon and the story behind it have a lot to say about the interaction of specificity and power. In Genesis, Laban asks Jacob how he should be paid for his work and Jacob is exacting: "With Rachel, your youngest daughter." The result after seven years of labor? Jacob didn't read the fine print. Custom dictates that eldest daughters must be married first, so he's stuck with the wrong sister. Jacob can be as exacting as he wishes but Laban has all the power. And endless specificity is really no match for power. Laban can always be more specific, drum up more local customs, change the rules of engagement—

because he has the power and status to prevail. It takes no less than two acts of divine intervention, displays of power, to allow Jacob to escape physically and financially intact.

The key insight I take from the story of Jacob and Laban is the importance of who decides what it means to be specific. You touch on this idea as well when you remark that all people "practically agree on the rules of justice … as long as they are taken in such a vague way that they mean anything in general or nothing in particular." The same can be said for specificity. We simply don't operate with an objective sense of what qualifies as specific. How could we? Specificity will always be subjective and context dependent. Any proposal or ideal can be judged to be lacking specificity if we choose the right standard. In isolation this may not seem so bad but in an unequal society it's a guarantee that the prevailing standard will reflect that inequality.

I've tried to offer a different side of the issues you raised in your sermon, not because I disagree with you, but because of how deep, intractable, and timeless these issues seem. In your writing I can feel you struggling with the same tension I've struggled with in responding. We're confronted with a world that seems deeply broken and everything in our upbringing and education tells us that we should be the ones to articulate the fix. You from your pulpit and me from behind my computer screen—we're the main characters. But are we Jacob or Laban?

Ezra Porter grew up in various Boston-area Jewish communities but identifies most strongly as a graduate of Gann Academy in Waltham, Massachusetts. He is a lifelong learner of philosophy, which he studied at the University of Rochester. There he also found a love of statistics which he went on to study at Villanova University. Ezra lives in Philadelphia where he works as a data scientist at the Children's Hospital of Philadelphia. In addition to these religious and intellectual communities, he is a product of the queer communities in which he's spent his adult life. He travels nationally to compete as a member of Philadelphia's LGBT flag football team.

The Song in the Night

Delivered in Manhattan Beach, New York at Temple Beth El, February 8, 1929, for *Parshat Mishpatim*

The song in the night is the song of songs. The night may be dark or silvery, filled with the red anger of a storm or with the elusive friendly grinding of unnumbered crickets; it may have cold terrors or comforting silences; it may [be] welcome—a release from the day, or it may be regretted as the end of the light; it may be a cloak or a shroud; it may hang over the desert like a temple dome lighted by a million candles or it may fill the sea with fearful forms that swirl upon the fogs. It may sting with its cold or stifle with its heat. The youngster greets it reproachfully with, "You stopped my game." The old man welcomes it with, "You opened my couch." In it babes are born and others die. It is the end of today; it is the beginning of tomorrow. It is inevitable. With the first gray pink of dawn it disappears and soon not a shadow of it remains, but from the moment of its passing it is returning. Nothing can postpone its coming. The sun sweeps up the sky with might enough to lift the ocean and to swing unnumbered worlds, but has no power to stay the night.

But the darkest night is not the night before which the sun retreats; the night which puts out the stars and covers the moon. The darkest night is the night of physical pain, of mental suffering, of spiritual torture.

Your body is broken and fever fills your veins. The nurse turns out all the lights, smooths your pillow and tiptoes softly away, leaving the door ajar. Then the anguish begins. Each hour is an age; each minute a century, and each second a day. The darkness has sinister faces, hideous forms and clutching hands. You cannot escape it. Close your eyes and still you see it; open them and it is still there. Job, the physically afflicted, hears Elihu's cry:

איה אלוה עֹשָׂי נותן זמרות בלילה

Where is God, where is God who gives songs in the night? (Job 35:10).[195]

There is the night of disaster. Some dear dream broken, or the coming of an overwhelming sorrow, or a great ambition thwarted, or an overturned fortune and the

---

[195] All bolded text in the sermon was typed in red in the original sermon.
  Elihu is another character in the book of Job, first introduced in Job 32:2, who responds to the comforting words of Job's three friends.

beginning of poverty. How black is the night when your disappointment closes over you. With all your strength to the extremity of your last resource you fight it off. You lift up your hands and cry out against it, but down, down it comes remorselessly like the all-enfolding overwhelming fogs of the River Hudson Valley. There are national disasters too that leave a people stunned and groping blindly—a destruction in Temple days, a Johnstown flood,[196] a Japanese earthquake,[197] a San Francisco fire,[198] a Mississippi inundation.[199] There has never been a physical night as dark as these.

And there is the night of doubt. Do you remember when the first doubt blew like a damp and chilling fog over your soul? If it has not come to you, I hope it never will. But some of us who know can remember. For the moment it seems to recede and may even vanish, but back it comes heavier and darker. Doubt of a friend, doubt of one's own integrity, doubt of every good, and doubt of even God. It is for this night of doubt that the lamp of faith must be turned up. Do you feel this fog approaching? Then fight it with all your might. The only real failure in life is the failure of the man who loses his way here. If you are ever lost in the night of doubt, you are lost, really lost.

There is the night of death. Licht, licht, mehr licht, ["light, light, more light"] cried the dying Schiller.[200] But no light came to flood the darkness of his passing.

And always sin, wrongdoing, injustice is night. Sin, so little a word, so stupendous a fact; so tiny when written, so appalling, so overwhelming when experienced. How sin stalks us in the night, leans heavily upon us, leers up at us in the gloom. Above all other noises and distractions, it screams in our ears and when nothing else would have disturbed our rest, it stings us into wakefulness and rouses us from sleep.

The song *in* the night is not the song *of* the night. Any song of the night would be as the night; a song of dark foreboding, of physical anguish, of doubt, of sin, and of death. Shakespeare has such a song:

> O comforting night, image of Hell
> Dire register and notary of shame
> Black stage for tragedies and murder fell

---

[196] A tragic flood that killed over 2,000 people in or near Johnstown, PA in May 1889.
[197] The great Kanto earthquake of 1923 which registered 7.9 on the Richter scale.
[198] A major fire in 1851 that destroyed ¾ of the city of San Francisco.
[199] Likely the Great Mississippi Flood of 1927.
[200] The dying utterance "mehr licht" is now attributed to Goethe, rather than to his friend Friedrich Schiller.

> Vast sin concealing! nurse of blame!
> Blind, muffled bawd! dark harbor for defame
> Grim cave of death! whispering conspirator
> Clove tongued treason and the ravisher.[201]

This is the song of the night. This you may associate with that stupendous folly of all follies, war. The song of the night is the ceaseless staccato and ripping of machine guns; the muffled roar of ammunition trucks; the churning of motors overhead; the dripping of the foul water in the springs beside the ruined formal gardens of Belgium; the whimpering of the delirious dying boy who keeps calling for his mother. This is the song *of* the night. But the song *in* the night: that is different.

> And the night shall be filled with music
> And the cares that infest the day
> Shall fold their tents like the Arabs
> And as silently steal away.[202]

The song *of* the night *mounts from the fog and gloom enshrouded earth to highest heaven and far beyond the reach* of man's most penetrating vision sings out its hope. It doesn't have the power to dispel the night. No—the night remains still the night with its rumors of fear and its promise of death, but the song *in* the night is the chariot of the soul and upon it we sweep to the face of the sun. The accident that lays us low in pain is more generous than at first appears, for it gives us time to hear the music soft and intimate we had not heard because of the thundering noises that filled our hurried days.

The song in the night may or may not originate in the night. Generally it does not. It comes more likely from behind the night, out of the music room of memory. In the night of grief we sing again the songs we learned in the day of gladness. These are the songs you cannot buy. These are the melodies which rich and poor

---

[201] Stanza from *The Rape of Lucrece* by William Shakespeare. The stanza is more exactly as follows:
'O comfort-killing Night, image of hell!
Dim register and notary of shame!
Black stage for tragedies and murders fell!
Vast sin-concealing chaos! nurse of blame!
Blind muffled bawd! dark harbour for defame!
Grim cave of death! whispering conspirator
With close-tongued treason and the ravisher!
[202] Last stanza of the poem *The Day is Done* by Henry Wadsworth Longfellow (1807-1882).

share alike. Israel sang the song with Moses as their choirmaster after the mighty Pharaoh and his pursuing host had been swallowed up in the sea, sang in the night of her risk and danger as it lifted toward another dawn,

אשירה לה' כי גאה גאה—I will sing unto the Lord for he hath triumphed gloriously (Ex. 15:1); זה אלי ואנוהו—This is my God, and I will enshrine Him (Ex. 15:2).

David, driven from his palace and banished from his capital, beset by enemies, bowed with age and broken by the treachery of his own children, reaches through the encircling gloom to the memories of God's unfailing past mercies and chants:

ואתה ה' מגן בעדי כבודי וּמֵרִים ראֹשִׁי.

But thou O Lord art a shield for me and the lifter up of mine head. (Psalms 3:4).

The song in the night is the song of courage and it brings relief. It is the song the Jews of York sang as they went to their self-inflicted death;[203] it's the song our ancestors sang as they were put to the sword by Provence and Mayence;[204] it's the song torn from bleeding lips under the rack in the torture-chambers of Aragon and Castile.[205] It is the song of ultimate triumph, triumph over the "all things" of life, triumph over sorrow, triumph over fear, triumph over pain; triumph over disaster; triumph over sin, injustice, wrongdoing and death. The song in the night has many settings and many words, but of all the words these are the most sublime:

בלע המות לנצח—Death will be swallowed up forever by the victory of everlasting life.[206]

What is your night? And in this congregation, for all I know, there may be every shade of darkness and every form of difficulty; we are a cross section of life. We are here with life's bitter and with life's sweet and in the bitter are to be found all

---

[203] Trapped in Clifford's Tower in York, England in 1190, many of the Jews committed suicide rather than be killed or forcibly converted to Christianity.
[204] Jews in Provence and Mayence (Mainz) were blamed for the Black Death and killed in 1348-9.
[205] Many Jews were killed under the authority of Ferrand Martinez, Archdeacon of Ecija, in Castile and Aragon and throughout the Iberian Peninsula in the late 14th century.
[206] Isaiah 25:8. The full text in English is "[God] will destroy death forever. My Lord God will wipe the tears away from all faces and will put an end to the reproach of His people. Over all the earth—for it is the Lord who has spoken."

the degrees and many of the details of the physical and spiritual troubles that are the lot of men and women. It is not for me to enumerate the particulars. Each one of us is more competent to particularize his own night. But what of the song? That is what I want to hear from your lips at all times. When you are tempted to cry out with Elihu איה אלוה עשׂי נותן זמירות בלילה "Where is God my Maker who giveth songs in the night? (Job 35:10)" I want to hear your answer: He is here. Closer to you than breath. He forms the very essence of your being.

And it is that costly tenderness, that tenderness of work and service and love for others and in their behalf that gives a song in the night.

response from
Leora Zeitlin

Dear Rabbi Signer,
    Let's talk about darkness. You begin your poetic and heartfelt sermon with, "The song in the night is the song of songs," and what follows is a nocturne, if you will, your own lyrical ruminations on torment, loss of faith, pain, and—song.
    But lest you be "in the dark" about who is writing you this letter, here are a few words of introduction.
    When I was my twenties and early thirties, around the age that you were when you wrote this sermon, I lived in Somerville, Massachusetts. I prayed and learned in the same Jewish community as Aliza, your granddaughter whom you never met and who is named for you. One year in the late 1980s, I had the opportunity to help make a video documentary about some elderly members of Temple B'nai Brith, a congregation that you yourself had briefly led some sixty years earlier. I may be wrong, but I think I recall seeing your picture on the wall, and only learning later that you were Aliza's grandfather. I see you standing in front of B'nai Brith's grand mahogany ark early in the 1920s and sharing your earliest sermons with its congregants.
    Now I am writing you across the decades, speaking to you from the living, while you have been gone for almost 70 years. Because you were born more than half a century before my birth, you are and always will be my elder. But the paradox is that I am now much older than you were when you died, and decades older than you were when you wrote this sermon.
    You were 29, in the first weeks after you became a father. I imagine you looking out your window on a wintry night and seeing the dark sky over the buildings. Your infant daughter is sleeping elsewhere in your home. Perhaps you are caught between the anxieties that often surface in those late hours, the "cold terrors" as you call them, and the resolve to make the world safe for your newborn daughter.
    Your insightful sermon speaks to both those impulses. It rests on two metaphorical pillars: "night" to represent suffering, and "song" to represent the hope and comfort that allays our suffering—brings out the daylight, as it were. These metaphors emerge from the plaintive cry of Elihu in the Book of Job, whom you quote early on: "Where is God, where is God who gives songs in the night?"
    How sensitive you were to human misery, to history, and to poetry. You clearly loved and knew poetry. In these few pages, we read lines by Shakespeare, Longfellow, and Schiller (though it was Goethe, not Friedrich Schiller, who cried, "licht,

mehr licht," on his deathbed), as well as poetic voices from Tanakh—Moses, David, and Elihu. And you clearly knew about suffering. You describe some of the anguishes people experience, from illness, to disappointment, to insomnia, to a series of other "nights:" The night of disaster. The night of doubt. The night of death. The night of sin and wrongdoing. The night of foreboding and of "that stupendous folly of all follies, war."

Seventy years later, we know so much more about all these, having witnessed unspeakable torments both from nature and human beings. When you wrote your sermon in 1929, the Jewish and national disasters you recall are the destruction of the Temple and the Inquisition, the Johnstown flood, a San Francisco fire. "There has never been a physical night as dark as these." Oh, Rabbi Signer, it is gut-wrenching to think of what was to come. But on an individual level, little has changed: we still suffer doubt, death, and injustice, conditions that transcend all time.

I do wonder why the pains of the world must be described as "nights," a metaphor you pick up from Elihu's cry. We suffer by day and night, at dusk and at dawn. Night, as you yourself describe in your magnificent opening paragraph, can be a time of "comforting silences," of "release from the day," as "the beginning of tomorrow." Indeed, when you wrote, "from the moment of its passing it is returning," I thought of the Ma'ariv [evening service] prayer, "rolling light away from darkness, and darkness from light." A time of blessing.

And "light," so often associated with learning, "enlightenment," and "The Enlightenment" can also blind us. Think of the people who feel they have found a truth, cling to it as a fixed and guiding "light," but cannot see beyond their certainty to a larger and more complex reality. They are blinded by the light. Ecclesiastes writes, "And the light is sweet, and it is pleasant for the eyes to behold the sun." So true. But the sun, the daytime, obliterates as well. When I was a child, my uncle took me on the roof of our building in Manhattan and taught me the constellations and the basics of astronomy. I learned that the night sky and stars take us infinitely back into history, make us confront our tiny place in the cosmos, and demand bigger questions than our bright sun can ask. Night can be a time of deeper thought than day; when the brilliant sun is absent, we behold the depths of the heavens.

But this is a minor quibble about metaphor. I get what you are saying, of course. Even though I love nighttime, I have also suffered insomnia since my earliest childhood, when "each hour is an age, each minute a century, and each second a day," full of hideous and fearsome thoughts.

When you write about all those nights, you evince deep understanding of what humans feel and endure. You've "been there," even as a young man, and even before the Holocaust, before Hiroshima and Nagasaki, before the other killing fields of the 20th century, and the global climate and human-led disasters of the 21st. Your heart is so open. And your wish is for a song, a song in the night—Elihu's words—that will bring comfort.

My professional life revolves around poetry and music, and so I naturally harken to the use of "song" as a metaphor for hope and solace. In Hebrew, the word *shir* covers both poetry and song. Your whole sermon is a kind of *shir*, a poetic elucidation of Elihu's question in the paradigmatic book about suffering and doubt, Job.

You describe the "song in the night" as the "chariot of the soul." In your words, it is a song from God, the notes of hope that lighten (in all senses of that word) our way. It is a song that strengthens us to overcome what has plagued us: fear, disaster, pain, sin, even death. For you, it is a song of eternal life.

I have heard that song, snatches of it anyway, while walking in the woods or on a desert hike, sometimes when we sing on Shabbat, sometimes in reconnecting with a beloved friend. That moment when suddenly one feels uplifted, suffused with a sense of possibility instead of impossibility. I can't say that it overcomes death for me, or achieves the triumphant vision you present. I learned long ago to be satisfied with smaller moments of reprieve and more subtle solaces, and to be suspicious of triumphalism. Would you have felt similarly later in your life, I wonder? When we are young, our visions are grander. Later, we may ask less from the world.

But your view of the song brings us to what may be the heart of your sermon: that we can only hear the song when we have experienced the night. They are predicated on one other. "The accident that lays us low in pain is more generous than at first appears," you write, "for it gives us time to hear the music soft and intimate we had not heard because of the thundering noises that filled our hurried days." Hurts and struggles and calamities deepen our understanding of life, and often strengthen our empathy and faith. You may be saying that no matter how difficult this moment is, don't give up.

Rabbi Signer, at the end of the sermon, you turn to your congregation and invite them to reflect on their own sorrows and to seek that tender song in the night for themselves. You want it to be God's song. I hear it as the song of this world, of this inscrutable, rare, sacred world with all its faults and all its promise (and our faults and promise). Maybe we mean the same thing. When we reach out to others, as you do in the final lines of the sermon, when we attend to each other, we bring a message: night will fall again, but try—try to listen closely for a song of hope in the shadows.

Leora Zeitlin is an editor, publisher, writer, and classical music radio host. She is the co-director of Zephyr Press, an award-winning literary press based in Boston that publishes contemporary poetry and prose in translation from Russia, eastern Europe, Asia and elsewhere, as well as innovative American literature (zephyrpress.org). Leora is also a music host at KRWG Public Media in Las Cruces, New Mexico, which broadcasts throughout southern New Mexico and into west Texas. She has hosted her own show, "Intermezzo," since 2000, and many of her award-winning interviews can be found at krwg.org. She is actively involved in a few Jewish communities.

Final Reflection — Lionel Moses

The Sermons of Rabbi Isador Signer: A Reflection

Among the many and variegated tasks and expectations of the congregational rabbi is that he or she deliver a "homily," better known as a sermon, at Shabbat and Festival services. The priority of the sermon in the panoply of responsibilities assigned to the rabbi has changed over the generations. A century ago, especially in large Reform, Reconstructionist and Conservative congregations, but even then, in large Orthodox congregations with a largely English-speaking and American-born membership, the Shabbat and Festival sermon was at the top of the rabbi's weekly priorities. Many began "working" on next week's sermon almost as soon as Shabbat was over and they finished reciting *Havdalah*, the prayer ritual that marks the distinction between Shabbat and the other six days of the week. My own Emeritus Rabbi, Maurice Cohen, z"l ("of blessed memory"), of Shaare Zion Congregation in Montreal, was known to spend upwards of 20 to 25 hours each week "crafting" the weekly lesson.

Certain things have changed over the past century. Rabbi Signer and Rabbi Cohen were "expected" to speak for as much as 40 minutes on a regular Shabbat, especially if there was a special occasion, such as a Bar/Bat Mitzvah and a larger than typical crowd could be expected. Today, rabbis are aware of the congregants' more limited attention span and speak for no more than 20 minutes and oftentimes no more than 12 or 13 minutes. (I am reminded of the oft-quoted quip of the late Rabbi Max Arzt, z"l, whose son, Rabbi David Arzt, z"l married Rabbi Signer's eldest daughter, Edya, z"l. Rabbi Arzt was known to "admonish" long-winded rabbis by telling them that if they had not struck oil in 15 minutes, they should "stop boring".)

But long or short, the weekly preparation of a sermon and, in a bygone era, when the so-called Late Friday evening service attracted as many congregants as the Shabbat morning service, even two distinctly different sermons, each sermon required significant forethought. What would the weekly sermon be about? Would the topic come from the front page of the *New York Times* or would it be a more parochial topic, such as Israel, antisemitism, Jewish education or Jewish poverty? How would the topic relate either to the weekly Torah portion or to a classical rabbinic text? Was there an anecdote that would make the theme of the sermon memorable, because people remember stories better than they remember abstract sentences? Would the sermon be a fully fleshed-out, written text or would it be an outline, giving the rabbi more opportunity to extemporize? These preliminary questions then, as now, required the rabbi to research the weekly Torah portion, its classical commentaries and its more contemporary interpretations, and find a pithy quotation which could either introduce the sermon or serve as a "proof-text" to validate the rabbi's thesis at a later point in the sermon.

For a sermon to be impactful, it needs to do two or three things. First, the sermon ought to teach a Jewish text or Jewish idea. Ideally, the text should be one that at least some congregants recognize, but in all cases, the text needs to be explained and interpreted, so that it introduces or explicates the theme of the sermon. Secondly, the sermon needs to address an issue of concern. Sometimes, the issue will be parochial; at other times, it will be universal. Civil rights are a universal issue, but they are ones with definite Jewish ramifications and responsibilities. And thirdly, the sermon ought to be practical. The sermon ought to motivate congregants to put the words of the sermon into action and provide practical examples on how to do so. And all in fifteen minutes or less.

Not every sermon hits a "home run." Some are clunkers. Nor do most sermons have universal staying power. They were meant for the occasion, not for posterity. Sermons delivered by newly-minted rabbis only occasionally have the style and structure of a more seasoned colleague. This is evident in the sermon selections by Rabbi Signer. The change in style and substance of sermons that he delivered when he was in his mid-thirties show a maturing in both organizational skill and writing style over those he delivered when he was 23 or 24 years old, and so it should be expected. His maturing wisdom manifested itself when he clearly changed opinions he held in earlier sermons with opinions which were more current just a few years later. While his intellectual debt to Rabbi Mordechai Kaplan, *z"l* was evident throughout his rabbinate, Rabbi Signer's later sermons showed how he went beyond the thinking and writings of his teacher and mentor and carved an independent path as a successful *Darshan* ("sermon-giver") for over 20 years at his congregation, Beth El in Manhattan Beach, until his untimely death in 1953.

May Rabbi Signer's Torah continue to teach future generations through the publication of this collection of his *Divrei Torah*. Over the past century, the style of sermons has changed, the solutions to social, familial and religious issues may have changed, but the same issues remain and, in each generation, leaders, like Rabbi Signer, *z"l*, move the needle forward a little bit at a time, thereby enhancing Torah and making its words applicable to addressing the vital issues of the day and of all times.

Rabbi Lionel Moses is the Rabbi Emeritus of Shaare Zion Beth El Congregation in Montreal, a community he served full-time for 23 years. He has served on the Committee of Jewish Law and Standards of the Rabbinical Assembly, the Executive Council of the Rabbinical Assembly, and chaired The Joint Placement Commission of the Rabbinical Assembly and the United Synagogue of Conservative Judaism. He has been a member of the National Beit Din of the Conservative Movement since 1990 and currently serves as its Av Beit Din (Chair).

Rabbi Moses is the past president of the Montreal Board of Rabbis and is a Senior Fellow of the Shalom Hartman Institute in Jerusalem, where he has been studying since 2010. He is married to Dr. Joyce Rappaport, the Executive Editor of the 10-volume Posen Library of Jewish Culture and Civilization. *They are the parents of three sons, all involved in their Jewish communities and the broader Jewish World.*

Acknowledgments

All books begin with an idea and a writer. This is rarely enough to guarantee that an actual book will result. I have learned during the past four years that "it takes a village" applies to other situations besides child-rearing and I'm grateful to everyone who assisted and influenced me directly or indirectly. I'm primarily grateful to my husband, Meredith Porter, who opened my eyes to the idea that led to the development of these conversations with my grandfather. Twenty years ago, after my mother's death, we discovered that she had kept my grandfather's original typed sermons. Meredith painstakingly scanned the sermons, annotated them to explain the idiosyncratic abbreviations that had been used, and sent them out to family members each week in conjunction with the Torah reading for that week. Some of the sermons were mundane, but many were quite moving in the writing style and the thoughts expressed.

The twenty-four people who agreed to read several sermons, choosing one with which to engage, and who came through consistently by responding to my emails for meeting deadlines, supplying biographies and signing releases have considerably bolstered my belief that a willing group can make room in their busy lives to provide the world with thoughtful ideas and engagement. Their sincere efforts to "communicate" with my grandfather and by doing so to weave their ideas of what's important with his, helped me to see Isador Signer as a complex, thoughtful human being.

This has been my first foray into the world of publishing. I want to thank Larry Yudelson of Ben Yehuda press and the Ben Yehuda publishing staff for shepherding me through this process and teaching me what I needed to know about publishing. I particularly would like to thank editor Laura Logan for putting the final polish on the words of us all.

Recent books from *Ben Yehuda Press*

Judaism Disrupted: A Spiritual Manifesto for the 21st Century by Rabbi Michael Strassfeld. "I can't remember the last time I felt pulled to underline a book constantly as I was reading it, but *Judaism Disrupted* is exactly that intellectual, spiritual and personal adventure. You will find yourself nodding, wrestling, and hoping to hold on to so many of its ideas and challenges. Rabbi Strassfeld reframes a Torah that demands breakage, reimagination, and ownership." —Abigail Pogrebin, author, *My Jewish Year: 18 Holidays, One Wondering Jew*

The Way of Torah and the Path of Dharma: Intersections between Judaism and the Religions of India by Rabbi Daniel Polish. "A whirlwind religious tourist visit to the diversity of Indian religions: Sikh, Jain, Buddhist, and Hindu, led by an experienced congregational rabbi with much experience in interfaith and in teaching world religions." —Rabbi Alan Brill, author of *Rabbi on the Ganges: A Jewish Hindu-Encounter*.

Liberating Your Passover Seder: An Anthology Beyond The Freedom Seder. Edited by Rabbi Arthur O. Waskow and Rabbi Phyllis O. Berman. This volume tells the history of the Freedom Seder and retells the origin of subsequent new haggadahs, including those focusing on Jewish-Palestinian reconciliation, environmental concerns, feminist and LGBT struggles, and the Covid-19 pandemic of 2020.

Duets on Psalms: Drawing New Meaning from Ancient Words by Rabbis Elie Spitz & Jack Riemer. "Two of Judaism's most inspirational teachers, offer a lifetime of insights on the Bible's most inspired book." — Rabbi Joseph Telushkin, author of *Jewish Literacy*. "This illuminating work is a literary journey filled with faith, wisdom, hope, healing, meaning and inspiration." —Rabbi Naomi Levy, author of *Einstein and the Rabbi*.

Weaving Prayer: An Analytical and Spiritual Commentary on the Jewish Prayer Book by Rabbi Jeffrey Hoffman. "This engaging and erudite volume transforms the prayer experience. Not only is it of considerable intellectual interest to learn the history of prayers—how, when, and why they were composed—but this new knowledge will significantly help a person pray with intention (*kavanah*). I plan to keep this volume right next to my siddur." —Rabbi Judith Hauptman, author of *Rereading the Rabbis: A Woman's Voice*.

Renew Our Hearts: A Siddur for Shabbat Day edited by Rabbi Rachel Barenblat. From the creator of *The Velveteen Rabbi's Haggadah*, a new siddur for the day of Shabbat. *Renew Our Hearts* balances tradition with innovation, featuring liturgy for morning (*Shacharit* and a renewing approach to *Musaf*), the afternoon (*Mincha*), and evening (*Ma'ariv* and *Havdalah*), along with curated works of poetry, art and new liturgies from across the breadth of Jewish spiritual life. Every word of Hebrew is paired with transliteration and with clear, pray-able English translation.

Forty Arguments for the Sake of Heaven: Why the Most Vital Controversies in Jewish Intellectual History Still Matter by Rabbi Shmuly Yanklowitz. Hillel vs. Shammai, Ayn Rand vs. Karl Marx, Tamar Ross vs. Judith Plaskow... but also Abraham vs. God, and God vs. the angels! Movements debate each other: Reform versus Orthodoxy, one- two- and zero-state solutions to the Israeli-Palestinian conflict, gun rights versus gun control in the United States. Rabbi Yanklowitz presents difficult and often heated disagreements with fairness and empathy, helping us consider our own truths in a pluralistic Jewish landscape.

Recent books from *Ben Yehuda Press*

Reaching for Comfort: What I Saw, What I Learned, and How I Blew it Training as a Pastoral Counselor by Sherri Mandell. In 2004, Sherri Mandell won the National Jewish Book award for *The Blessing of the Broken Heart*, which told of her grief and initial mourning after her 13-year-old son Koby was brutally murdered. Years later, with her pain still undiminished, Sherri trains to help others as a pioneering pastoral counselor in Israeli hospitals. "What a blessing to witness Mandell's and her patients' resilience!" —Rabbi Dayle Friedman, editor, *Jewish Pastoral Care: A Practical Guide from Traditional and Contemporary Sources.*

Heroes with Chutzpah: 101 True Tales of Jewish Trailblazers, Changemakers & Rebels by Rabbi Deborah Bodin Cohen and Rabbi Kerry Olitzky. Readers ages 8 to 14 will meet Jewish changemakers from the recent past and present, who challenged the status quo in the arts, sciences, social justice, sports and politics, from David Ben-Gurion and Jonas Salk to Sarah Silverman and Douglas Emhoff. "Simply stunning. You would want this book on your coffee table, though the stories will take the express lane to your soul." —Rabbi Jeff Salkin.

Just Jewish: How to Engage Millennials and Build a Vibrant Jewish Future by Rabbi Dan Horwitz. Drawing on his experience launching The Well, an inclusive Jewish community for young adults in Metro Detroit, Rabbi Horwitz shares proven techniques ready to be adopted by the Jewish world's myriad organizations, touching on everything from branding to fundraising to programmatic approaches to relationship development, and more. "This book will shape the conversation as to how we think about the Jewish future." —Rabbi Elliot Cosgrove, editor, *Jewish Theology in Our Time.*

Put Your Money Where Your Soul Is: Jewish Wisdom to Transform Your Investments for Good by Rabbi Jacob Siegel. "An intellectual delight. It offers a cornucopia of good ideas, institutions, and advisers. These can ease the transition for institutions and individuals from pure profit nature investing to deploying one's capital to repair the world, lift up the poor, and aid the needy and vulnerable. The sources alone—ranging from the Bible, Talmud, and codes to contemporary economics and sophisticated financial reporting—are worth the price of admission." —Rabbi Irving "Yitz" Greenberg.

Why Israel (and its Future) Matters: Letters of a Liberal Rabbi to the Next Generation by Rabbi John Rosove. Presented in the form of a series of letters to his children, Rabbi Rosove makes the case for Israel — and for liberal American Jewish engagement with the Jewish state. "A must-read!" —Isaac Herzog, President of Israel. "This thoughtful and passionate book reminds us that commitment to Israel and to social justice are essential components of a healthy Jewish identity." —Yossi Klein Halevi, author, *Letters to My Palestinian Neighbor.*

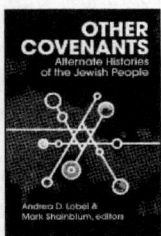

Other Covenants: Alternate Histories of the Jewish People by Rabbi Andrea D. Lobel & Mark Shainblum. In *Other Covenants*, you'll meet Israeli astronauts trying to save a doomed space shuttle, a Jewish community's faith challenged by the unstoppable return of their own undead, a Jewish science fiction writer in a world of Zeppelins and magic, an adult Anne Frank, an entire genre of Jewish martial arts movies, a Nazi dystopia where Judaism refuses to die, and many more. Nominated for two Sidewise Awards for Alternate History.

Reflections on the weekly Torah portion from *Ben Yehuda Press*

An Angel Called Truth and Other Tales from the Torah by Rabbi Jeremy Gordon and Emma Parlons. Funny, engaging micro-tales for each of the portions of the Torah and one for each of the Jewish festivals as well. These tales are told from the perspective of young people who feature in the Biblical narrative, young people who feature in classic Rabbinic commentary on our Biblical narratives and young people just made up for this book.

Torah & Company: The weekly portion of Torah, accompanied by generous helpings of Mishnah and Gemara, served with discussion questions to spice up your Sabbath Table by Rabbi Judith Z. Abrams. Serve up a rich feast of spiritual discussion from an age-old recipe: One part Torah. Two parts classic Jewish texts. Add conversation. Stir... and enjoy! "A valuable guide for the Shabbat table of every Jew." —Rabbi Burton L. Visotzky, author *Reading the Book*.

Torah Journeys: The Inner Path to the Promised Land by Rabbi Shefa Gold. Rabbi Gold shows us how to find blessing, challenge and the opportunity for spiritual transformation in each portion of Torah. An inspiring guide to exploring the landscape of Scripture... and recognizing that landscape as the story of your life. "Deep study and contemplation went into the writing of this work. Reading her Torah teachings one becomes attuned to the voice of the Shekhinah, the feminine aspect of God which brings needed healing to our wounded world." —Rabbi Zalman Schachter-Shalomi.

American Torah Toons 2: Fifty-Four Illustrated Commentaries by Lawrence Bush. Deeply personal and provocative artworks responding to each weekly Torah portion. Each two-page spread includes a Torah passage, a paragraph of commentary from both traditional and modern Jewish sources, and a photo-collage that responds to the text with humor, ethical conscience, and both social and self awareness. "What a vexing, funny, offensive, insightful, infuriating, thought-provoking book." —Rabbi David Saperstein.

The Comic Torah: Reimagining the Very Good Book. Stand-up comic Aaron Freeman and artist Sharon Rosenzweig reimagine the Torah with provocative humor and irreverent reverence in this hilarious, gorgeous, off-beat graphic version of the Bible's first five books! Each weekly portion gets a two-page spread. Like the original, the Comic Torah is not always suitable for children.

we who desire: Poems and Torah riffs by Sue Swartz. From Genesis to Deuteronomy, from Bereshit to Zot Haberacha, from Eden to Gaza, from Eve to Emma Goldman, *we who desire* interweaves the mythic and the mundane as it follows the arc of the Torah with carefully chosen words, astute observations, and deep emotion. "Sue Swartz has used a brilliant, fortified, playful, serious, humanely furious moral imagination, and a poet's love of the music of language, to re-tell the saga of the Bible you thought you knew." —Alicia Ostriker, author, *For the Love of God: The Bible as an Open Book*.

Eternal Questions by Rabbi Josh Feigelson. These essays on the weekly Torah portion guide readers on a journey that weaves together Torah, Talmud, Hasidic masters, and a diverse array of writers, poets, musicians, and thinkers. Each essay includes questions for reflection and suggestions for practices to help turn study into more mindful, intentional living. "This is the wisdom that we always need—but maybe particularly now, more than ever, during these turbulent times." —Rabbi Danya Ruttenberg, author, *On Repentance and Repair*.

Jewish spirituality and thought from *Ben Yehuda Press*

The Essential Writings of Abraham Isaac Kook. Translated and edited by Rabbi Ben Zion Bokser. This volume of letters, aphorisms and excerpts from essays and other writings provide a wide-ranging perspective on the thought and writing of Rav Kook. With most selections running two or three pages, readers gain a gentle introduction to one of the great Jewish thinkers of the modern era.

Ahron's Heart: Essential Prayers, Teachings and Letters of Ahrele Roth, a Hasidic Reformer. Translated and edited by Rabbi Zalman Schachter-Shalomi and Rabbi Yair Hillel Goelman. For the first time, the writings of one of the 20th century's most important Hasidic thinkers are made available to a non-Hasidic English audience. Rabbi Ahron "Ahrele" Roth (1894-1944) has a great deal to say to sincere spiritual seekers far beyond his own community.

A Passionate Pacifist: Essential Writings of Aaron Samuel Tamares. Translated and edited by Rabbi Everett Gendler. Rabbi Aaron Samuel Tamares (1869-1931) addresses the timeless issues of ethics, morality, communal morale, and Judaism in relation to the world at large in these essays and sermons, written in Hebrew between 1904 and 1931. "For those who seek a Torah of compassion and pacifism, a Judaism not tied to 19th century political nationalism, and a vision of Jewish spirituality outside of political thinking this book will be essential." —Rabbi Dr. Alan Brill, author, *Thinking God: The Mysticism of Rabbi Zadok of Lublin*.

Return to the Place: The Magic, Meditation, and Mystery of Sefer Yetzirah by Rabbi Jill Hammer. A translation of and commentary to an ancient Jewish mystical text that transforms it into a contemporary guide for meditative practice. "A tour de force—at once scholarly, whimsical, deeply poetic, and eminently accessible." —Rabbi Tirzah Firestone, author of *The Receiving: Reclaiming Jewish Women's Wisdom*

Enlightenment by Trial and Error: Ten Years on the Slippery Slopes of Jewish Mysticism, Postmodern Buddhist Meditation, and Heretical Flexidox Spirituality by Rabbi Jay Michaelson. A unique record of the 21st-century spiritual search, from the perspective of someone who made plenty of mistakes along the way.

The Tao of Solomon: Finding Joy and Contentment in the Wisdom of Ecclesiastes by Rabbi Rami Shapiro. Rabbi Rami Shapiro unravels the golden philosophical threads of wisdom in the book of Ecclesiastes, reweaving the vibrant book of the Bible into a 21st century tapestry. Shapiro honors the roots of the ancient writing, explores the timeless truth that we are merely a drop in the endless river of time, and reveals a path to finding personal and spiritual fulfillment even as we embrace our impermanent place in the universe.

Embracing Auschwitz: Forging a Vibrant, Life-Affirming Judaism that Takes the Holocaust Seriously by Rabbi Joshua Hammerman. The Judaism of Sinai and the Judaism of Auschwitz are merging, resulting in new visions of Judaism that are only beginning to take shape. "Should be read by every Jew who cares about Judaism." —Rabbi Dr. Irving "Yitz" Greenberg.

www.ingramcontent.com/pod-product-compliance
Lightning Source LLC
Chambersburg PA
CBHW050550160426
43199CB00015B/2609